CLASSIC POLITICAL PHILOSOPHY FOR THE MODERN MAN

Andrew Lynn has a Ph.D. in Renaissance literature from Cambridge University. He has lectured in Western civilization in Beijing and now practises law with a particular interest in the field of international dispute resolution.

www.andrewlynn.com

D1617385

CLASSIC POLITICAL PHILOSOPHY FOR THE MODERN MAN

ANDREW LYNN

HOWGILL
HOUSE

Howgill House Books

www.howgillhousebooks.com

Copyright © Andrew Lynn 2019

ISBN 978-1-912360-20-8

CONTENTS

INTRODUCTION

This is a dangerous book: what is contained here has the potential to awaken you to new ways of thinking not only about your own political condition but also about the political condition of the civilization of which you are a part.

For sure, you can read it—exoterically, one might say—as an introduction to the greatest political philosophers of the Western tradition. In the course of twelve chapters, we cover the best part of two and a half millennia of political thinking, providing introductions to and extracts from the most profoundly influential works from ancient Greece and the Renaissance all the way through to the early twentieth century. The selection itself is largely canonical: we begin with the seminal *Republic* and *Politics* of Plato and Aristotle respectively, before moving on to introduce the acknowledged master of the dark arts of statecraft (Machiavelli), the great apologist for absolutism (Hobbes), the herald of enlightenment and contractarianism (Locke), the standard-bearer of revolutionary republicanism (Rousseau), the founder of modern conservatism (Burke), the architect of utilitarianism (Bentham), the anatomist of democracy (Tocqueville), the godfather of libertarianism (Bastiat), the spokesman of classical liberalism (John Stuart Mill), and the advocate of political pragmatism—and American president—Theodore Roosevelt. In the choice of authors and texts to present, every effort has been made to give you the most readable and enduringly relevant of the traditional classics in an orderly way; there's been no attempt different or edgy for the sake of being different or edgy, or for advancing any particular political agenda.

Classic Political Philosophy for the Modern Man accordingly presents an affirmative political culture and ethos that represents the Western tradition in its broadest scope. That tradition, viewed as a whole, can best be described as a restless search for superior modes of political organization and for a more productive view of man's role in the state. Under that broad description, we can reasonably assert of the tradition other tendencies. It is, in the first place, marked by a spirit of free inquiry: dogmas, assumptions, and social norms are subjected to the most intense questioning and the most vigorous scrutiny. It prioritizes rationality over either conventionalism or emotionality: even the most conservative (Burke) makes reasoned argument in favour of his traditionalism; and even the most emotional (Rousseau) bases his passionately held views on a carefully worked through investigation as to the fundamental nature of the state. And it conceives of the state as a potential source of self-realization for its citizens in order to explore how that can best be made to happen. Of course, you don't need to take my word for it: there is no better way to appreciate these—and other—features of this tradition than to read the words of the great philosophers themselves, and that is why they are provided here.

This book's uniqueness, however, lies not so much in providing an introduction to Western political philosophy, as in providing a way of understanding this tradition as a source of practical wisdom for the current era. The great Western thinkers really do, as a rule, approach the fundamental questions of political philosophy with great courage and curiosity, and with the minimum of inhibition or self-censorship—so much so that they retain the power to shock us out of our complacency and towards new insights even today. Universalism, democracy, human rights, toleration, socialism, equalism—full-blooded critical consideration of these Holiest of Holies has been, since around the end of the Second World War, outside the parameters of debate in establishment and mainstream circles, and to subject them to serious political inquiry has been taboo in all but the most free-thinking of contexts. This is wholly a manifestation of the prejudices of our own era: Plato and Aristotle, for example, both looked dimly on democracy; Locke, father of liberalism as he may be, thought that toleration had sharply defined limits; Burke and Bentham poured scorn on the notion of natural rights; Tocqueville anticipated the connection between equalism and tyranny; Bastiat exposed socialism as plunder; John Stuart Mill alerted us to the oppressiveness of social conformity and self-censorship; and Roosevelt urged upon us the need for a healthy national consciousness and a future for our people. Critical inquiry into these and related areas is not, as is sometimes thought, at the periphery of our tradition; it is at that tradition's very core. This, then, is the esoteric reading of this book: it connects what has always been present all along—hidden in plain sight, so to speak—in the thinking of our forebears.

Behind our contemporary reluctance to address these fundamental issues is what we can conveniently refer to as the 'complacency of the current era'. There is, of course, no shortage whatsoever of academic and other 'critical' commentary produced in relation to the very same canonical authors and texts that you find in this volume. For the most part, though, this commentary is critical only in the sense that it is the original works that are subjected to criticism; rare and more challenging indeed is it for the insights of the philosophers under inquiry to be used as a base for reconsidering the conventional political viewpoints and platitudes of our own era. It is a relatively simple, uncontroversial, and uninformative task, for example, to criticize Plato for his advocacy of a caste system based on eugenics or to review Aristotle's *Politics* in order to signal one's disapproval with his opinion on 'natural slaves'; it is likewise uncontentious and unilluminating to observe that the strict utilitarianism of Bentham and Mill risks providing justification for a 'tyranny of the majority'. Considerably more difficult, controversial, and informative, would be to take seriously Plato's conception of how democracy tends towards tyranny or Aristotle's view that the purpose of the state is not security or economic prosperity but cultivation of the excellence of its members; likewise to explore in good faith John Stuart Mill's arguments that state education is 'a mere contrivance for moulding people to be exactly like one another' and that overpopulating a country, by increasing the pressure of competition, constitutes 'a serious offence against all who live by the remuneration of their labour'.

It is the task of high-end thinkers to think the unthinkable, not in order to reach outlandish conclusions, but rather to ensure that the issues in question have been approached from all possible angles; this activity is supported by what has been called 'negative capability', or the capability of being in uncertainties without prematurely driving for a conclusion. The philosophical tradition that is represented, in part, by the thinkers and texts in this book can help us to do this, but only if we retain minds that remain at least provisionally open for the duration of the task. If we assume that the consensus of the current era is correct in all fundamental respects, and that to the extent the philosophers of the past are not in agreement with this consensus they must be either in error or simply morally defective in some way, we will never be able to do it.

Openness to diverse viewpoints matters because human beings are highly conventional animals. We know already, through social psychology if not otherwise, of the power of conformity and 'social proof': the experiments of Solomon Asch, for example, have shown that people are likely to conform to the choice of the majority, even if it is plainly wrong, and that they do so not only through a desire to fit in, but also because their very perceptions are skewed towards those of the group. Whole societies can be affected to the extent that their most perspicacious minds are unable to see what would be obvious to even a relative simpleton at another time in history. Alexis de Tocqueville, from the perspective of an eighteenth-century Frenchman, observed as much when commenting upon Aristotle and his contemporaries: 'The most profound and capacious minds of Rome and Greece,' he said, 'were never able to reach the idea, at once so general and so simple, of the common likeness of men, and of the common birthright of each to freedom: they strove to prove that slavery was in the order of nature, and that it would always exist.'[1] When the inbuilt human tendency to conform is exacerbated by the forces of compulsory state education, ambient propaganda, and monitoring and control of thought and speech, then you have a heady mix indeed.

Openness to diverse points of view also matters because we stand at a time in history when powerful and concerted forces are directed at the masses so as to restrict the parameters of debate and cut out or paralyze dissent. We are, as a result, witnessing an unprecedented coarsening and debasing of our public discourse. Saul Alinsky's *Rules for Radicals* (1971) now appears to be the playbook for partisans across the political spectrum: in place of reasoned debate, we have an unremitting stream of smears and *ad hominem* abuse, which when unsuccessful are followed up by attempts to deplatform adversaries or harm them in their personal lives or careers. This is healthy for no-one.

And openness to diverse points of view matters because those words and concepts that sound, superficially at least, so

1. Alexis de Tocqueville, *Democracy in America*, trans. Henry Reeve, 7th ed. (New York: Edward Walker, 1847), Part II, Chapter III, 15.

attractive—democracy, human rights, toleration, socialism, equality—can all be, and have all been, deployed in the cause of evil. Alexander Solzhenitsyn, the Nobel Prize-winning author who had personal experience of life under a murderous totalitarian regime, gave a speech not long after his expulsion from the Soviet Union in 1974.[2] The speech was a survey of that regime and a warning that the darkness it represented was still capable of infecting other societies—including the Western democracies. Solzhenitsyn explained first that the leaders of the revolution were not, in fact, workers, but émigré intellectuals, and that the real workers quickly learned *their* place once the revolution was complete. He noted that his audience may have been surprised by what he called the 'alliance between our Communist leaders and your capitalists'.[3] And at the end of the speech he added:

> I would like to call upon America to be more careful with its trust and prevent those wise persons who are attempting to establish even finer degrees of justice and even finer legal shades of equality—some because of their distorted outlook, others because of short-sightedness and still others out of self interest—from falsely using the struggle for peace and for social justice to lead you down a false road. Because they are trying to weaken you; they are trying to disarm your strong and magnificent country in the face of this fearful threat—one which has never been seen before in the history of the world.[4]

Here Solzhenitsyn expressly recognized that, just as in Russia, those who sought to overturn the traditional order in the West would do so under the auspices of peace and social justice. It is absurd to think that they would do anything other than that; absurd to think they would appear in their true colours and advertising their true intentions. In this context, the best resistance we can make is to think these ideas through precisely, critically, and profoundly; what we must not do is deploy the rhetoric of social justice merely as a form of virtue-signalling or—worse—a convenient tool to shut our interlocutors down.

The philosophers and their works discussed in this book call out to

2. Alexander Solzhenitsyn, *Warning to the West* (New York: Farrar, Straus and Giroux, 1976), 3-50.
3. Ibid, 11.
4. Ibid, 49-50.

us from another era. They could never have imagined that Western man would have adapted so comprehensively to the soft (and occasionally hard) despotism of the modern all-encompassing state that—while nominally respecting its subjects' human rights—deigns to monitor and regulate their most trivial of actions and speech while traducing their historic traditions and freely liberating them of their wealth. Let us not forget how much has changed: standing armies were hardly seen in Europe until the seventeenth century; the most significant modern taxes (such as income tax and estate tax) were unknown in the English-speaking world until the end of the eighteenth century; and it was only in the early nineteenth century that modern professional police forces were established in England and the United States. The right of citizens to bear arms—a right long understood by thinkers from Aristotle and Machiavelli to William Blackstone and Thomas Jefferson to be essential to a free people—is now, even where constitutionally protected as in the United States, an increasingly contentious matter, despite the obvious fact that a state with full and permanent monopoly on the use of force is a state that will be able to expand its power and reach with nothing very much to stand in its way. 'What country can preserve its liberties,' asked Founding Father Thomas Jefferson rhetorically, 'if their rulers are not warned from time to time that their people preserve the spirit of resistance?'[5]

Just as in the parable of the boiling frog who does not perceive the gradual increase in the temperature of the water and is boiled alive, so we have by steady increments lost much of our liberty without realizing it. The works in this book cannot give that back; what they can do is to raise our consciousness of the many alternative paths we could have taken—and perhaps, if we have nerve enough, still can take.

---

5. Thomas Jefferson to William Stephens Smith, 13 November 1787.

PLATO, REPUBLIC

INTRODUCTION

The first great attempt in Western thought to present a detailed account of the 'just state' is that provided by Plato in his *Republic*.

Modern man has a great deal to learn from Plato's approach. His influence on Western philosophy has been incomparable—to the extent that it has been said that the European philosophical tradition is a series of 'footnotes to Plato'. What is more important for our purposes, however, is that he offers, in the general thrust of his work if not in the details, a way out of the stifling uniformity of much of what passes for political thinking at our current moment in history.

Plato was born in 428-7 BC during the early years of the Peloponnesian War between Athens and Sparta and their respective allies. A student of Socrates, teacher of Aristotle, and founder of the Academy, Plato's life was a life of the mind. But he was also an aristocrat—the scion of a wealthy and politically active family—who observed at first hand the defeat of the Athenian democracy at the hands of Sparta and who had watched that same democracy put to death his tutor, Socrates, for impiety and corrupting of the Athenian youth. It is in this way that history taught the young philosopher that the Spartan-style polity had a great deal in its favour as against a democracy not only incompetent to defend the state but also high-handed, illiberal, censorious, and—ultimately—murderous.

The broad outlines of the *Republic* are well known. It is a Socratic dialogue about justice, the just state, and the just man. Plato's teacher, Socrates, and several of Socrates' interlocutors, including Plato's brothers Glaucon and Adeimantus, begin by considering the meaning of justice and whether the just man is happier than the unjust man. They then proceed to discuss the form that the ideal state (referred to as *kallipolis* or 'beautiful city') would take. With even greater practical significance, for the modern reader at least, they ultimately go on to expound upon not only the nature and characteristics of the main political regimes—including oligarchy, democracy, and tyranny—but also the kind of men such regimes tend to produce and the trajectories such regimes tend to follow.

What, then, is Plato's view of justice and the just state? The Greek term used by Plato, δίκη (*dike*), is broader than what we understand by the word 'justice', and has been rendered in English as 'all-in rightness'. The just man, on this formulation, is he who gains mastery over himself. He has the internal parts of himself under good management and control: he does not allow the different principles within himself to do work other than their own. Those inner principles are three: a rational element (*nous*), a spirited element (*thumos*), and a desiring element (*epithumia*). In a well-governed soul, the rational element is the ruling principle, and is allied with the spirited element, so that both of them can keep guard over the desiring element, which in chasing after false pleasures exposes a man to internal disruption and weakens him as against his external enemies. It is this inward state of harmony and proper self-management that the just man brings to the conduct of all the activities and affairs of his life, from attending to the wants of his body to engagements in business and politics. To produce justice is to put the parts of the soul in their natural relations of authority and subservience; to disturb this relationship is to produce injustice.

The just state is the just man writ large. Justice in this expanded political sense, then, embodies the understanding that everybody and everything has its appointed place and its appointed function: when the elements of the state are all in their proper place and doing the work that is proper for them to do, then we have justice. In the best states, as in the best souls, the rational element is in charge, and these are rule by the best or 'aristocracy'; next comes timocracy (i.e. rule by a Spartan-type warrior caste), in which the spirited element is chief; then comes oligarchy, or rule by the wealthy, in which the desiring element, insofar as desires are necessary desires, has sway; thereafter we have democracy, which arises when the poor seize the reigns of state; and finally tyranny, when order and discipline have wholly broken down both in men's souls and in the state. Within established states, justice takes the form of 'the having and doing what is a man's own, and belongs to him', and is established when each class attends to what belongs to it and does its own work, and when members of each occupation do likewise. It is injustice, giving rise to great harm to the state, says Plato, when all intermeddle in each other's proper sphere and none mind their own business—when a builder attempts a shoemaker's work, for example, or a shoemaker a builder's.

Plato's concept of justice brings us back to the 'rightness' of having each of us, as far as possible, occupying the role and engaged in the work that is best for us and that allows us to exercise our highest faculties in service of the community as a whole. It is still possible for us to be inspired by this underlying vision of the just state, more than two millennia after the fact, when the core philosophy is presented shorn of its anachronisms and inessentials.

The specific features of Plato's ideal state are more controversial. In the first place, it will be a caste-based society made up of three castes: guardians, soldiers, and common people. Caste and class-based societies are prone to the objection that the more 'privileged' castes or classes obtain an unfair and unjustified advantage which is often neither fair nor conducive to stable social relations. In Plato's ideal state, however, there is a difference: the ruling elite constituted by the guardian caste is to be subject to expectations and restrictions that compensate for, and counterbalance, the privilege of rule. The guardians are to constitute a sophisticated warrior elite trained in culture and athletics.[1] They are to live together in a camp, sharing small houses and simple food, and having no private property beyond what is strictly necessary. Their marriage arrangements are to be organized by the state: brides and bridegrooms will be brought together seemingly by lot, but in fact pursuant to eugenic principles, so that the best parents produce the most offspring, with children being taken away at birth so that none know their own parents. And they are to be subject to the very strictest instruction and censorship: young guardians, for example, are to be taught to consider slavery worse than death, and they are to be kept well away from literary and other works that discourage decorum and temperance. The essential point here is

1. While usually translated as 'music' and 'gymnastics', Plato intended to indicate activities of much broader scope.

9

that Plato's ruling elite will be required to be properly shaped up for its role and properly constrained in its ability to extract private benefits from public office. We are, of course, entitled to turn away from the quasi-communism and eugenic programme advocated in the *Republic*. But that is not a basis for rejecting the much more important double proposition that we are right to have expectations of excellence of those who rule over us, and that we are right to subject those persons to the very strictest of codes of conduct.

There is much in Plato's *Republic* that is idealistic, but the work also manifests an awareness of another point of view altogether in the enigmatic figure of Thrasymachus, one of Socrates' several interlocutors. Thrasymachus is the great naysayer of the work: whereas Socrates is adamant that the just state is an unalloyed good and the just man the happiest, Thrasymachus contends for a wholly different and more cynical understanding of the matter. For, insists Thrasymachus, every government, from the democratic to the tyrannical, lays down laws for its own advantage, and punishes those who depart from them as law-breakers and unjust men. The conclusion, he suggests, is clear: justice is what is advantageous to the established government. Plato gives us to understand that Thrasymachus is bested in argument by Socrates, but it is hard to be convinced of this, and as a matter of both historical record and contemporary politics the argument of Thrasymachus has to a very considerable degree been borne out. Ultimately, the points of view of Socrates and Thrasymachus are not necessarily incompatible: true justice may, in principle, take the form that Socrates (through Plato) suggests, while at the same time what is given the name of 'justice' in particular states at particular times has, as a matter of fact, generally been whatever has been to the advantage of the incumbent regime. If anyone has had the last laugh, though, it must be Thrasymachus, since Plato's politics are condemned nowadays precisely as a result of the fact that his elitism appears to be unjust from the point of view of the democratic states in which he is read.

Plato's relevance today is not only in his portrayal of the ideal republic but also in his holding up a mirror to allow us to reflect upon our own political situation. For Plato in the *Republic* tempers his idealism with a sober-minded understanding that even if an ideal aristocratic state could anywhere be found or established, like all living things it would be subject to change and decay, first into a 'timocracy', next into oligarchy, then into a democracy, and finally into tyranny. Plato's notion of 'democracy' does not, it must be said, coincide precisely with the modern representative or parliamentary democracies that take the name of democracy today, but the relation is close enough to be meaningful. Democracy, says Plato, has its own particular good—freedom—the insatiable desire for which brings about its own dissolution: anarchy finds its way into private houses, the young have no respect for the old and the old adopt the manners of the young, teachers fear and pander to their students, the non-citizen is put on an equal footing with the citizen, and in the end all chafe at authority, cease to care for the laws, and will tolerate no one above them. From this context emerges what Plato calls the class of 'spendthrifts' who mobilize the masses to squeeze the self-sufficient orderly class for a little 'honey', as Plato puts it, depriving those 'squeezable persons' of their estates and distributing them among the people, while making sure to reserve the larger part for themselves. From here arises the desire of revolution, and it is only a matter of time before a 'protector' of the people arises. And thus it is, foretells Plato, that tyranny takes root.

BOOK VIII

SOCRATES-GLAUCON

And so, Glaucon, we have arrived at the conclusion that in the perfect state wives and children are to be in common; and that all education and the pursuits of war and peace are also to be common, and the best philosophers and the bravest warriors are to be their kings?

That, replied Glaucon, has been acknowledged.

Yes, I said; and we have further acknowledged that the governors, when appointed themselves, will take their soldiers and place them in houses such as we were describing, which are common to all, and contain nothing private, or individual; and about their property, you remember what we agreed?

Yes, I remember that no one was to have any of the ordinary possessions of mankind; they were to be warrior athletes and guardians, receiving from the other citizens, in lieu of annual payment, only their maintenance, and they were to take care of themselves and of the whole state.

True, I said; and now that this division of our task is concluded, let us find the point at which we digressed, that we may return into the old path.

There is no difficulty in returning; you implied, then as now, that you had finished the description of the state: you said that such a state was good, and that the man was good who answered to it, although, as now appears, you had more excellent things to relate both of state and man. And you said further, that if this was the true form, then the others were false; and of the false forms, you said, as I remember, that there were four principal ones, and that their defects, and the defects of the individuals corresponding to them, were worth examining. When we had seen all the individuals, and finally agreed as to who was the best and who was the worst of them, we were to consider whether the best was not also the happiest, and the worst the most miserable. I asked you what were the four forms of government of which you spoke, and then Polemarchus and Adeimantus put in their word; and you began again, and have found your way to the point at which we have now arrived.

Your recollection, I said, is most exact.

Then, like a wrestler, he replied, you must put yourself again in the same position; and let me ask the same questions, and do you give me the same answer which you were about to give me then.

Yes, if I can, I will, I said.

I shall particularly wish to hear what were the four constitutions of which you were speaking.

That question, I said, is easily answered: the four governments of which I spoke, so far as they have distinct names, are, first, those of Crete and Sparta, which are generally applauded; what is termed oligarchy comes next; this is not equally approved, and is a form of government which teems with evils; thirdly, democracy, which naturally follows oligarchy, although very different; and lastly comes tyranny, great and famous, which differs from them all, and is the fourth and worst disorder of a state. I do not know, do you? of any other constitution which can be said to have a distinct character. There are lordships and principalities which are bought and sold, and some other intermediate forms of government. But these are nondescripts and may be found equally among Hellenes and among barbarians.

Yes, he replied, we certainly hear of many curious forms of government which exist among them.

Do you know, I said, that governments vary as the dispositions of men vary, and that there must be as many of the one as there are of the other? For we cannot suppose that states are made of 'oak and rock,' and not out of the human natures which are in them, and which in a figure turn the scale and draw other things after them?

Yes, he said, the states are as the men are; they grow out of human characters.

Then if the constitutions of states are five, the dispositions of individual minds will also be five?

Certainly.

SOCRATES-ADEIMANTUS

...Again, let us see how the democratical man grows out of the oligarchical: the following, as I suspect, is commonly the process.

What is the process?

When a young man who has been brought up as we were just now describing, in a vulgar and miserly way, has tasted drones' honey and has come to associate with fierce and crafty natures who are able to provide for him all sorts of refinements and varieties of pleasure—then, as you may imagine, the change will begin of the oligarchical principle within him into the democratical?

Inevitably.

And as in the city like was helping like, and the change was effected by an alliance from without assisting one division of the citizens, so too the young man is changed by a class of desires coming from without to assist the desires within him, that which is akin and alike again helping that which is akin and alike?

Certainly.

And if there be any ally which aids the oligarchical principle within him, whether the influence of a father or of kindred, advising or rebuking him, then there arises in his soul a faction and an opposite faction, and he goes to war with himself.

It must be so.

And there are times when the democratical principle gives way to the oligarchical, and some of his desires die, and others are banished; a spirit of reverence enters into the young man's soul and order is restored.

Yes, he said, that sometimes happens.

And then, again, after the old desires have been driven out, fresh ones spring up, which are akin to them, and because he, their father, does not know how to educate them, wax fierce and numerous.

Yes, he said, that is apt to be the way.

They draw him to his old associates, and holding secret intercourse with them, breed and multiply in him.

Very true.

At length they seize upon the citadel of the young man's soul, which they perceive to be void of all accomplishments and fair pursuits and true words, which make their abode in the minds of men who are dear to the gods, and are their best guardians and sentinels.

None better.

False and boastful conceits and phrases mount upwards and take their place.

They are certain to do so.

And so the young man returns into the country of the lotus-eaters, and takes up his dwelling there in the face of all men; and if any help be sent by his friends to the oligarchical part of him, the aforesaid vain conceits shut the gate of the king's fastness; and they will neither allow the embassy itself to enter, nor if private advisers offer the fatherly counsel of the aged will they listen to them or receive them. There is a battle and they gain the day, and then modesty, which they call silliness, is ignominiously thrust into exile by them, and temperance, which they nickname unmanliness, is trampled in the mire and cast forth; they persuade men that moderation and orderly expenditure are vulgarity and meanness, and so, by the help of a rabble of evil appetites, they drive them beyond the border.

Yes, with a will.

And when they have emptied and swept clean the soul of him who is now in their power and who is being initiated by them in great mysteries, the next thing is to bring back to their house insolence and anarchy and waste and impudence in bright array having garlands on their heads, and a great company with them, hymning their praises and calling them by sweet names; insolence they term breeding, and anarchy liberty, and waste magnificence, and impudence courage. And so the young man passes out of his original nature, which was trained in the school of necessity, into the freedom and libertinism of useless and unnecessary pleasures.

Yes, he said, the change in him is visible enough.

After this he lives on, spending his money and labour and time on unnecessary pleasures quite as much as on necessary ones; but if he be fortunate, and is not too much disordered in his wits, when years have elapsed, and the heyday of passion is over—supposing that he then re-admits into the city some part of the exiled virtues, and does not wholly give himself up to their successors—in that case he balances his pleasures and lives in a sort of equilibrium, putting the government of himself into the hands of the one which comes first and wins the turn; and when he has had enough of that, then into the hands of another; he despises none of them but encourages them all equally.

Very true, he said.

Neither does he receive or let pass into the fortress any true word of advice; if anyone says to him that some pleasures are the satisfactions of good and noble desires, and others of evil desires, and that he ought to use and honour some and chastise and master the others—whenever this is repeated to him he shakes his head and says that they are all alike, and that one is as good as another.

Yes, he said; that is the way with him.

Yes, I said, he lives from day to day indulging the appetite of the hour; and sometimes he is lapped in drink and strains of the flute; then he becomes a water-drinker, and tries to get thin; then he takes a turn at gymnastics; sometimes idling and neglecting everything, then once more living the life of a philosopher; often he is busy with politics, and starts to his feet and says and does whatever comes into his head; and, if he is emulous of anyone who is a warrior, off he is in that direction, or of men of business, once more in that. His life has neither law nor order; and this distracted existence he terms joy and bliss and freedom; and so he goes on.

Yes, he replied, he is all liberty and equality.

Yes, I said; his life is motley and manifold and an epitome of the lives of many—he answers to the state which we described as fair and spangled. And many a man and many a woman will take him for their pattern, and many a constitution and many an example of manners is contained in him.

Just so.

Let him then be set over against democracy; he may truly be called the democratic man.

Let that be his place, he said.

Last of all comes the most beautiful of all, man and state alike, tyranny and the tyrant; these we have now to consider.

Quite true, he said.

Say then, my friend, in what manner does tyranny arise? That it has a democratic origin is evident.

Clearly.

And does not tyranny spring from democracy in the same manner as democracy from oligarchy—I mean, after a sort?

How?

The good which oligarchy proposed to itself and the means by which it was maintained was excess of wealth—am I not right?

Yes.

And the insatiable desire of wealth and the neglect of all other things for the sake of money-getting was also the ruin of oligarchy?

True.

And democracy has her own good, of which the insatiable desire brings her to dissolution?

What good?

Freedom, I replied; which, as they tell you in a democracy, is the glory of the state—and that therefore in a democracy alone will the freeman of nature deign to dwell.

Yes; the saying is in everybody's mouth.

I was going to observe that the insatiable desire of this and the neglect of other things introduces the change in democracy, which occasions a demand for tyranny.

How so?

When a democracy which is thirsting for freedom has evil cupbearers presiding over the feast, and has drunk too deeply of the strong wine of freedom, then, unless her rulers are very amenable and give a plentiful draught, she calls them to account and punishes them, and says that they are cursed oligarchs.

Yes, he replied, a very common occurrence.

Yes, I said; and loyal citizens are insultingly termed by her slaves who hug their chains and men of naught; she would have subjects who are like rulers, and rulers who are like subjects: these are men after her own heart, whom she praises and honours both in private and public. Now, in such a state, can liberty have any limit?

Certainly not.

By degrees the anarchy finds a way into private houses, and ends by getting among the animals and infecting them.

How do you mean?

I mean that the father grows accustomed to descend to the level of his sons and to fear them, and the son is on a level with his father, he having no respect or reverence for either of his parents; and this is his freedom, and metic² is equal with the citizen and the citizen with the metic, and the stranger is quite as good as either.

Yes, he said, that is the way.

And these are not the only evils, I said—there are several lesser ones. In such a state of society the master fears and flatters his scholars, and the scholars despise their masters and tutors; young and old are all alike; and the young man is on a level with the old, and is ready to compete with him in word or deed; and old men condescend to the young and are full of pleasantry and gaiety; they are loth to be thought morose and authoritative, and therefore they adopt the manners of the young.

Quite true, he said.

The last extreme of popular liberty is when the slave bought with money, whether male or female, is just as free as his or her purchaser; nor must I forget to tell of the liberty and equality of the two sexes in relation to each other.

Why not, as Aeschylus says, utter the word which rises to our lips?

That is what I am doing, I replied; and I must add that no one who does not know would believe, how much greater is the liberty which the animals who are under the dominion of man have in a democracy than in any other state: for truly, the she-dogs, as the proverb says, are as good as their she-mistresses, and the horses and asses have a way of marching along with all the rights and dignities of freemen; and they

---

2. A foreigner living in an ancient Greek city who had some of the privileges of citizenship.

will run at anybody who comes in their way if he does not leave the road clear for them; and all things are just ready to burst with liberty.

When I take a country walk, he said, I often experience what you describe. You and I have dreamed the same thing.

And above all, I said, and as the result of all, see how sensitive the citizens become; they chafe impatiently at the least touch of authority and at length, as you know, they cease to care even for the laws, written or unwritten; they will have no one over them.

Yes, he said, I know it too well.

Such, my friend, I said, is the fair and glorious beginning out of which springs tyranny.

Glorious indeed, he said. But what is the next step?

The ruin of oligarchy is the ruin of democracy; the same disease magnified and intensified by liberty overmasters democracy—the truth being that the excessive increase of anything often causes a reaction in the opposite direction; and this is the case not only in the seasons and in vegetable and animal life, but above all in forms of government.

True.

The excess of liberty, whether in states or individuals, seems only to pass into excess of slavery.

Yes, the natural order.

And so tyranny naturally arises out of democracy, and the most aggravated form of tyranny and slavery out of the most extreme form of liberty?

As we might expect.

That, however, was not, as I believe, your question—you rather desired to know what is that disorder which is generated alike in oligarchy and democracy, and is the ruin of both?

Just so, he replied.

Well, I said, I meant to refer to the class of idle spendthrifts, of whom the more courageous are the leaders and the more timid the followers, the same whom we were comparing to drones, some stingless, and others having stings.

A very just comparison.

These two classes are the plagues of every city in which they are generated, being what phlegm and bile are to the body. And the good physician and lawgiver of the state ought, like the wise bee-master, to keep them at a distance and prevent, if possible, their ever coming in;

and if they have anyhow found a way in, then he should have them and their cells cut out as speedily as possible.

Yes, by all means, he said.

Then, in order that we may see clearly what we are doing, let us imagine democracy to be divided, as indeed it is, into three classes; for in the first place freedom creates rather more drones in the democratic than there were in the oligarchical state.

That is true.

And in the democracy they are certainly more intensified.

How so?

Because in the oligarchical state they are disqualified and driven from office, and therefore they cannot train or gather strength; whereas in a democracy they are almost the entire ruling power, and while the keener sort speak and act, the rest keep buzzing about the bema[3] and do not suffer a word to be said on the other side; hence in democracies almost everything is managed by the drones.

Very true, he said.

Then there is another class which is always being severed from the mass.

What is that?

They are the orderly class, which in a nation of traders sure to be the richest.

Naturally so.

They are the most squeezable persons and yield the largest amount of honey to the drones.

Why, he said, there is little to be squeezed out of people who have little.

And this is called the wealthy class, and the drones feed upon them.

That is pretty much the case, he said.

The people are a third class, consisting of those who work with their own hands; they are not politicians, and have not much to live upon. This, when assembled, is the largest and most powerful class in a democracy.

True, he said; but then the multitude is seldom willing to congregate unless they get a little honey.

And do they not share? I said. Do not their leaders deprive the rich

3. An elevated platform used as an orator's podium in ancient Athens.

of their estates and distribute them among the people; at the same time taking care to reserve the larger part for themselves?

Why, yes, he said, to that extent the people do share.

And the persons whose property is taken from them are compelled to defend themselves before the people as they best can?

What else can they do?

And then, although they may have no desire of change, the others charge them with plotting against the people and being friends of oligarchy? True.

And the end is that when they see the people, not of their own accord, but through ignorance, and because they are deceived by informers, seeking to do them wrong, then at last they are forced to become oligarchs in reality; they do not wish to be, but the sting of the drones torments them and breeds revolution in them.

That is exactly the truth.

Then come impeachments and judgments and trials of one another. True.

The people have always some champion whom they set over them and nurse into greatness.

Yes, that is their way.

This and no other is the root from which a tyrant springs; when he first appears above ground he is a protector.

Yes, that is quite clear.

How then does a protector begin to change into a tyrant? Clearly when he does what the man is said to do in the tale of the Arcadian temple of Lycaean Zeus.

What tale?

The tale is that he who has tasted the entrails of a single human victim minced up with the entrails of other victims is destined to become a wolf. Did you never hear it?

Oh, yes.

And the protector of the people is like him; having a mob entirely at his disposal, he is not restrained from shedding the blood of kinsmen; by the favourite method of false accusation he brings them into court and murders them, making the life of man to disappear, and with unholy tongue and lips tasting the blood of his fellow citizen; some he kills and others he banishes, at the same time hinting at the abolition of debts and partition of lands; and after this, what will be his destiny?

Must he not either perish at the hands of his enemies, or from being a man become a wolf—that is, a tyrant?

Inevitably.

This, I said, is he who begins to make a party against the rich?

The same.

After a while he is driven out, but comes back, in spite of his enemies, a tyrant full grown.

That is clear.

And if they are unable to expel him, or to get him condemned to death by a public accusation, they conspire to assassinate him.

Yes, he said, that is their usual way.

Then comes the famous request for a bodyguard, which is the device of all those who have got thus far in their tyrannical career. 'Let not the people's friend,' as they say, 'be lost to them.'

Exactly.

The people readily assent; all their fears are for him—they have none for themselves.

Very true.

And when a man who is wealthy and is also accused of being an enemy of the people sees this, then, my friend, as the oracle said to Croesus, 'By pebbly Hermus' shore he flees and rests not and is not ashamed to be a coward.' And quite right too, said he, for if he were, he would never be ashamed again.

But if he is caught he dies.

Of course.

And he, the protector of whom we spoke, is to be seen, not 'larding the plain' with his bulk, but himself the overthrower of many, standing up in the chariot of state with the reins in his hand, no longer protector, but tyrant absolute.

No doubt, he said.

And now let us consider the happiness of the man, and also of the state in which a creature like him is generated.

Yes, he said, let us consider that.

At first, in the early days of his power, he is full of smiles, and he salutes every one whom he meets—he to be called a tyrant, who is making promises in public, and also in private, liberating debtors, and distributing land to the people and his followers, and wanting to be so kind and good to every one!

Of course, he said.

But when he has disposed of foreign enemies by conquest or treaty, and there is nothing to fear from them, then he is always stirring up some war or other, in order that the people may require a leader.

To be sure.

Has he not also another object, which is that they may be impoverished by payment of taxes, and thus compelled to devote themselves to their daily wants and therefore less likely to conspire against him? Clearly.

And if any of them are suspected by him of having notions of freedom, and of resistance to his authority, he will have a good pretext for destroying them by placing them at the mercy of the enemy; and for all these reasons the tyrant must be always getting up a war.

He must.

Now he begins to grow unpopular.

A necessary result.

Then some of those who joined in setting him up, and who are in power, speak their minds to him and to one another, and the more courageous of them cast in his teeth what is being done.

Yes, that may be expected.

And the tyrant, if he means to rule, must get rid of them; he cannot stop while he has a friend or an enemy who is good for anything.

He cannot.

And therefore he must look about him and see who is valiant, who is high-minded, who is wise, who is wealthy; happy man, he is the enemy of them all, and must seek occasion against them whether he will or no, until he has made a purgation of the state.

Yes, he said, and a rare purgation.

Yes, I said, not the sort of purgation which the physicians make of the body; for they take away the worse and leave the better part, but he does the reverse.

If he is to rule, I suppose that he cannot help himself.

What a blessed alternative, I said—to be compelled to dwell only with the many bad, and to be by them hated, or not to live at all!

Yes, that is the alternative.

And the more detestable his actions are to the citizens the more satellites and the greater devotion in them will he require?

Certainly.

And who are the devoted band, and where will he procure them?

They will flock to him, he said, of their own accord, if he pays them.

By the dog! I said, here are more drones, of every sort and from every land.

Yes, he said, there are.

But will he not desire to get them on the spot?

How do you mean?

He will rob the citizens of their slaves; he will then set them free and enrol them in his bodyguard.

To be sure, he said; and he will be able to trust them best of all.

What a blessed creature, I said, must this tyrant be; he has put to death the others and has these for his trusted friends.

Yes, he said; they are quite of his sort.

Yes, I said, and these are the new citizens whom he has called into existence, who admire him and are his companions, while the good hate and avoid him.

Of course.

Verily, then, tragedy is a wise thing and Euripides a great tragedian.

Why so?

Why, because he is the author of the pregnant saying, 'Tyrants are wise by living with the wise'; and he clearly meant to say that they are the wise whom the tyrant makes his companions.

Yes, he said, and he also praises tyranny as godlike; and many other things of the same kind are said by him and by the other poets.

And therefore, I said, the tragic poets being wise men will forgive us and any others who live after our manner if we do not receive them into our state, because they are the eulogists of tyranny.

Yes, he said, those who have the wit will doubtless forgive us.

But they will continue to go to other cities and attract mobs, and hire voices fair and loud and persuasive, and draw the cities over to tyrannies and democracies.

Very true.

Moreover, they are paid for this and receive honour—the greatest honour, as might be expected, from tyrants, and the next greatest from democracies; but the higher they ascend our constitution hill, the more their reputation fails, and seems unable from shortness of breath to proceed further.

True.

But we are wandering from the subject: let us therefore return and inquire how the tyrant will maintain that fair and numerous and various and ever-changing army of his.

If, he said, there are sacred treasures in the city, he will confiscate and spend them; and in so far as the fortunes of attainted persons may suffice, he will be able to diminish the taxes which he would otherwise have to impose upon the people.

And when these fail?

Why, clearly, he said, then he and his boon companions, whether male or female, will be maintained out of his father's estate.

You mean to say that the people, from whom he has derived his being, will maintain him and his companions?

Yes, he said; they cannot help themselves.

But what if the people fly into a passion, and aver that a grown-up son ought not to be supported by his father, but that the father should be supported by the son? The father did not bring him into being, or settle him in life, in order that when his son became a man he should himself be the servant of his own servants and should support him and his rabble of slaves and companions; but that his son should protect him, and that by his help he might be emancipated from the government of the rich and aristocratic, as they are termed. And so he bids him and his companions depart, just as any other father might drive out of the house a riotous son and his undesirable associates.

By heaven, he said, then the parent will discover what a monster he has been fostering in his bosom; and, when he wants to drive him out, he will find that he is weak and his son strong.

Why, you do not mean to say that the tyrant will use violence? What! Beat his father if he opposes him?

Yes, he will, having first disarmed him.

Then he is a parricide, and a cruel guardian of an aged parent; and this is real tyranny, about which there can be no longer a mistake: as the saying is, the people who would escape the smoke which is the slavery of freemen, has fallen into the fire which is the tyranny of slaves. Thus liberty, getting out of all order and reason, passes into the harshest and bitterest form of slavery.

True, he said.

Very well; and may we not rightly say that we have sufficiently discussed the nature of tyranny, and the manner of the transition from democracy to tyranny?

Yes, quite enough, he said.

2

ARISTOTLE, POLITICS

INTRODUCTION

When Raphael painted 'The School of Athens', he depicted at the centre of the fresco Plato and Aristotle deep in conversation as they stroll forward towards the viewer. Plato is rendered as a wise old man pointing upwards toward the heavens, while next to him appears a younger, virile-looking Aristotle with hand held out horizontally in front, in an arrangement that represents figuratively the otherworldly idealism of the former and the this-worldly empiricism of the latter. Developing the contrast, Raphael shows Plato bearing his *Timaeus*, a work of abstract metaphysics, whereas Aristotle holds his *Nicomachean Ethics*, a guidebook on living well. The artist's insight into the respective orientations of these two great ancient philosophers is, however, just as instructive for our understanding of their political philosophies as it for their philosophies generally: for where Plato dreamed of utopia in his *Republic*, Aristotle provides in his *Politics* one of the most down-to-earth accounts of politics in practice.

Aristotle was born around 384 BC at Stagira, in Thrace, and came to Athens at about the age of eighteen to become a pupil of Plato. He stayed at the Academy for nearly twenty years until the death of his tutor, at which point he accompanied Xenocrates to Lesbos, where he received the welcome of his friend the tyrant (and former slave) Hermias, whose adoptive daughter, Pythias, he later married. In around 343 BC, Aristotle was invited by Philip of Macedon to become tutor to his son Alexander, later to be known as Alexander the Great. Returning to Athens in 335 BC, Aristotle founded his own school, the Lyceum, and over the course of the next twelve years wrote most of his books. Upon the death of Alexander in 323 BC, however, Athens rebelled, and the situation became untenable for Alexander's former tutor. Indicted for impiety, he fled to avoid punishment—in stark contrast to the conduct of Plato's own mentor, Socrates, in the face of similar difficulties—and died in the following year.

At the heart of Aristotle's *Politics* is the crucial realization that man is intended, by nature, to live in the state: the state is the highest kind of community and aims at the highest good, and it is through the state that man can best fulfil his purpose and potential.

Aristotle's doctrine of the 'four causes' provided that natural phenomenon—such as the behaviour of plants, animals, persons, and institutions—are to be explained by their *telos* or 'end' (i.e. purpose) as much as by purely physical causation. A man cannot fulfil his purpose or end separately from the state, thought Aristotle, in the same way that a hand cannot fulfil its purpose separate from the body. Political society exists for the sake of enabling and facilitating the full development and 'noble action' of its members—and not merely for companionship, or trade, or the prevention of crime, although it is certainly also true, he held, that without law man is the worst of animals, and without the state there is no law. The state, thought Aristotle, is therefore prior to the individual—a startling proposition to the contemporary reader, trained conceptually to always put the individual first, but one that serves as a valuable counterpoise to the excesses of the individualistic philosophies that insist, absurdly, that each man's achievements are his alone, owing nothing to his ancestors, his patrons, his associates, or his community.

Aristotle identified three kinds of 'good' government, being governments aiming at the good of the whole community: these are monarchy, aristocracy, and constitutional government (or polity), in which one, few, or many respectively exercise power for the benefit of the whole community. Similarly, there are three kinds of 'bad' government, namely tyranny, oligarchy, and democracy, in which the one, few, and the many exercise power for the benefit only of themselves. Monarchy is preferable to aristocracy and aristocracy is preferable to constitutional government; conversely, since corruption of what is best is the worst, tyranny (a corruption of monarchy) is worse than oligarchy, and oligarchy (a corruption of aristocracy) worse than democracy. Since in reality most governments are bad, the best form of government we are likely to encounter in practice is the democratic one.

That appears to be faint praise for the democratic regimes many of us live under today, but we must remember that for Aristotle democracies are those systems under which public officials are appointed by lot; to elect those officials was, for him, the hallmark of that still less attractive form of government known as oligarchy. And while neither democracy nor oligarchy is as disfavourable as tyranny, both are prone to instability, democracies because their inhabitants think that they are equal in some respects (i.e. equal in freedom) and should, therefore, be equal in all, and oligarchies because certain of their inhabitants think that they are superior in some respects (i.e. in property) and should be superior in all. There is a fundamental error in all this that persists today: it is the idea that equality, superiority, and inferiority must pertain the one or the other uniformly across all aspects of life, and the concomitant failure to accept that we may be equal in one respect, as in our civil rights and equality before the law, while being at the same time unequal in many others—and this without the least injustice.

The prevalence of imperfect oligarchical and democratic regimes being accepted, is there nevertheless any way we can render them better vehicles for the wellbeing of their inhabitants?

The *Politics* suggests several answers to this question.

Among the most important must be what Aristotle refers to as 'justice and proportionate equality'. It is clear that for Aristotle equality is not an absolute and independent political good; but it is likewise clear that equality in a qualified or more tightly defined sense is, nevertheless, a precondition for the well-governed state. What is necessary is 'proportionate' equality—proportionate, it has been understood, to virtue. Advocates of 'absolute' equality have, of course, observed that the notion of proportionate equality poses dangers in practice: who, after all, is in a position to define virtue, and determine which of the citizens are held to possess it, if not those who already (and for some other reason) hold power in the state? What is equally clear, however, is that all political structures allocate unequal powers, and that wholly equal societies have never come into being. Even—and perhaps especially—when it has been proclaimed that all men are equal, there have always been some who have been more equal than others. Since a certain degree of inequality appears to be a necessary and unavoidable characteristic of complex societies, then, would it not make sense to at least attempt, following Aristotle, to allocate power and responsibility on the basis of virtue?

The state should, Aristotle suggests, be composed, as far as possible, of 'equals and similars', these generally being citizens of the middling sort. The middle classes do not covet the goods of their neighbours, as do the poor, nor do their neighbours covet theirs; they do not plot against others, nor are they themselves plotted against. They are the least likely to shrink from rule, and the least likely to be over-eager for it: the best legislators, says Aristotle, have been of the middle condition. Where extremes of wealth are found, on the other hand, despotism soon follows, for those of exceptional wealth know only how to command, while those handicapped by extreme poverty know only how to obey. It goes without saying that Aristotle, in stark contrast to his teacher Plato, fully appreciated the advantages of being a member of a property-owning society: personal ownership, he explains, gives us a stake in maintaining and improving property, whereas property held in common is subject to what has been called the 'tragedy of the commons', a phenomenon that occurs when private individuals exploit shared resources for personal benefit contrary the collective good. All the same, people should be trained in benevolence and encouraged to make available their property for the benefit of the community as a whole—but as a matter of moral duty rather than political obligation.

Citizenship was not, by any means, to be open to all. For Aristotle, it was a prerequisite for citizenship that a person was in a position 'to rule and be ruled'—competent to participate in the affairs of state and to subrogate his conduct to such measures as the state might effect. The citizen should, therefore, be an economically independent, free, native male. It is on this basis that Aristotle would exclude from citizenship not only women, foreigners, and slaves, but also men employed as manual labourers. This did not mean that those groups would fall outside the protection of the law, but it did mean that they would not be entitled to exercise the full range of political rights of the citizen. Of course, it is unthinkable that anyone today would argue for citizenship to be restricted on the lines suggested by Aristotle in the fourth century BC. Nevertheless, the principle he was advancing—that the citizen ought to be in a fundamental sense *autonomous* as a precondition of exercising the full rights and privileges of citizenship—is more powerful and relevant today than ever.

The last—but by no means least—of the extracts provided below is Aristotle's brief outline of the characteristic methods by which tyrants subjugate the peoples over whom they purport to rule. Tyranny, in Aristotle's analysis, operates primarily through demoralization of its subjects: they are humiliated, encouraged to distrust one another, and made to feel incapable of action. The tyrant makes war to ensure that his subjects may have something to do and be always in want of a leader; citizens are spied upon and made to feel afraid to express their true thoughts. The tyrant elevates bad men because bad men can be used for bad purposes. Foreigners are preferred over citizens because they are no rival to the tyrant and pose no threat. And the tyrant raises taxes and impoverishes his people so that they have to keep hard at work and have no time to conspire. If, having read this account of tyranny, you are still in doubt about the relevance of Aristotle today, then there is nothing more that can be done to persuade you.

For the modern man, Aristotle's work raises many important and disturbing questions, and challenges us to rethink many of our most fundamental assumptions. We don't have to agree with everything he says; but we do owe it to our intellectual forebears, and more importantly to ourselves, to think beyond the rather narrow intellectual horizons of our current era.

BOOK II, PART V

[PRIVATE PROPERTY]

Next let us consider what should be our arrangements about property: should the citizens of the perfect state have their possessions in common or not? This question may be discussed separately from the enactments about women and children. Even supposing that the women and children belong to individuals, according to the custom which is at present universal, may there not be an advantage in having and using possessions in common? Three cases are possible: (1) the soil may be appropriated, but the produce may be thrown for consumption into the common stock; and this is the practice of some nations. Or (2), the soil may be common, and may be cultivated in common, but the produce divided among individuals for their private use; this is a form of common property which is said to exist among certain barbarians. Or (3), the soil and the produce may be alike common.

When the husbandmen are not the owners, the case will be different and easier to deal with; but when they till the ground for themselves the question of ownership will give a world of trouble. If they do not share equally enjoyments and toils, those who labour much and get little will necessarily complain of those who labour little and receive or consume much. But indeed there is always a difficulty in men living together and having all human relations in common, but especially in their having common property. The partnerships of fellow-travellers are an example to the point; for they generally fall out over everyday matters and quarrel about any trifle which turns up. So with servants: we are most able to take offence at those with whom we most frequently come into contact in daily life.

These are only some of the disadvantages which attend the community of property; the present arrangement, if improved as it might be by good customs and laws, would be far better, and would have the advantages of both systems. Property should be in a certain sense common, but, as a general rule, private; for, when everyone has a distinct interest, men will not complain of one another, and they will make more progress, because everyone will be attending to his own business. And yet by reason of goodness, and in respect of use, 'friends,' as the proverb says, 'will have all things common.' Even now there are traces of such a principle, showing that it is not impracticable, but, in well-ordered states, exists already to a certain extent and may be carried further. For, although every man has his own property, some things he will place at the disposal of his friends, while of others he shares the use with them. The Lacedaemonians, for example, use one another's slaves, and horses, and dogs, as if they were their own; and when they lack provisions on a journey, they appropriate what they find in the fields throughout the country. It is clearly better that property should be private, but the use of it common; and the special business of the legislator is to create in men this benevolent disposition. Again, how immeasurably greater is the pleasure, when a man feels a thing to be his own; for surely the love of self is a feeling implanted by nature and not given in vain, although selfishness is rightly censured; this, however, is not the mere love of self, but the love of self in excess, like the miser's love of money; for all, or almost all, men love money and other such objects in a measure. And further, there is the greatest pleasure in doing a kindness or service to friends or guests or companions, which can only be rendered when a man has private property. These advantages are lost by excessive unification of the state. The exhibition of two virtues, besides, is visibly annihilated in such a state: first, temperance towards women (for it is an honourable action to abstain from another's wife for temperance's sake); secondly, liberality in the matter of property. No one, when men have all things in common, will any longer set an example of liberality or do any liberal action; for liberality consists in the use which is made of property.

Such legislation may have a specious appearance of benevolence; men readily listen to it, and are easily induced to believe that in some wonderful manner everybody will become everybody's friend, especially when someone is heard denouncing the evils now existing in states, suits about contracts, convictions for perjury, flatteries of rich men and the like, which are said to arise out of the possession of private property. These evils, however, are due to a very different cause—the wickedness of human nature. Indeed, we see that there is much more quarrelling among those who have all things in common, though there are not many of them when compared with the vast numbers who have private property.

Again, we ought to reckon, not only the evils from which the citizens will be saved, but also the advantages which they will lose. The life which they are to lead appears to be quite impracticable. The error of Socrates must be attributed to the false notion of unity from which he starts. Unity there should be, both of the family and of the state, but in some respects only. For there is a point at which a state may attain such a degree of unity as to be no longer a state, or at which, without actually ceasing to exist, it will become an inferior state, like harmony passing into unison, or rhythm which has been reduced to a single foot. The state, as I was saying, is a plurality which should be united and made into a community by education; and it is strange that the author of a system of education which he thinks will make the state virtuous, should expect to improve his citizens by regulations of this sort, and not by philosophy or by customs and laws, like those which prevail at Sparta and Crete respecting common meals, whereby the legislator has made property common. Let us remember that we should not disregard the experience of ages; in the multitude of years these things, if they were good, would certainly not have been unknown; for almost everything has been found out, although sometimes they are not put together; in other cases men do not use the knowledge which they have. Great light would be thrown on this subject if we could see such a form of government in the actual process of construction; for the legislator could not form a state at all without distributing and dividing its constituents into associations for common meals, and into phratries[1] and tribes. But all this legislation ends only in forbidding agriculture to the guardians, a prohibition which the Lacedaemonians try to enforce already. ...

BOOK III, PART V

[CITIZENS]

There still remains one more question about the citizen: Is he only a true citizen who has a share of office, or is the mechanic to be included? If they who hold no office are to be deemed citizens, not every citizen can have this virtue of ruling and obeying; for this man is a citizen. And if none of the lower class are citizens, in which part of the state are they to be placed? For they are not resident aliens, and they are not foreigners. May we not reply, that as far as this objection goes there is no more absurdity in excluding them than in excluding slaves and freedmen from any of the above-mentioned classes? It must be admitted that we cannot consider all those to be citizens who are necessary to the existence of the state; for example, children are not citizen equally with grown-up men, who are citizens absolutely, but children, not being grown up, are only citizens on a certain assumption. Nay, in ancient times, and among some nations the artisan class were slaves or foreigners, and therefore the majority of them are so now. The best form of state will not admit them to citizenship; but if

---

1. Groups of people within a tribe who have a common ancestor.

they are admitted, then our definition of the virtue of a citizen will not apply to every citizen nor to every free man as such, but only to those who are freed from necessary services. The necessary people are either slaves who minister to the wants of individuals, or mechanics and labourers who are the servants of the community. These reflections carried a little further will explain their position; and indeed what has been said already is of itself, when understood, explanation enough.

Since there are many forms of government there must be many varieties of citizen and especially of citizens who are subjects; so that under some governments the mechanic and the laborer will be citizens, but not in others, as, for example, in aristocracy or the so-called government of the best (if there be such a one), in which honours are given according to virtue and merit; for no man can practice virtue who is living the life of a mechanic or laborer. In oligarchies the qualification for office is high, and therefore no labourer can ever be a citizen; but a mechanic may, for an actual majority of them are rich. At Thebes there was a law that no man could hold office who had not retired from business for ten years. But in many states the law goes to the length of admitting aliens; for in some democracies a man is a citizen though his mother only be a citizen; and a similar principle is applied to illegitimate children; the law is relaxed when there is a dearth of population. But when the number of citizens increases, first the children of a male or a female slave are excluded; then those whose mothers only are citizens; and at last the right of citizenship is confined to those whose fathers and mothers are both citizens.

Hence, as is evident, there are different kinds of citizens; and he is a citizen in the highest sense who shares in the honours of the state. Compare Homer's words, 'like some dishonoured stranger'; he who is excluded from the honours of the state is no better than an alien. But when his exclusion is concealed, then the object is that the privileged class may deceive their fellow inhabitants. ...

BOOK III, PART VII

[FORMS OF GOVERNMENT]

Having determined these points, we have next to consider how many forms of government there are, and what they are; and in the first place what are the true forms, for when they are determined the perversions of them will at once be apparent. The words constitution and government have the same meaning, and the government, which is the supreme authority in states, must be in the hands of one, or of a few, or of the many. The true forms of government, therefore, are those in which the one, or the few, or the many, govern with a view to the common interest; but governments which rule with a view to the private interest, whether of the one or of the few, or of the many, are perversions. For the members of a state, if they are truly citizens, ought to participate in its advantages. Of forms of government in which one rules, we call that which regards the common interests, kingship or royalty; that in which more than one, but not many, rule, aristocracy; and it is so called, either because the rulers are the best men, or because they have at heart the best interests of the state and of the citizens. But when the citizens at large administer the state for the common interest, the government is called by the generic name—a constitution. And there is a reason for this use of language. One man or a few may excel in virtue; but as the number increases it becomes more difficult for them to attain perfection in every kind of virtue, though they may in military virtue, for this is found in the masses. Hence in a constitutional government the fighting men have the supreme power, and those who possess arms are the citizens.

Of the above-mentioned forms, the perversions are as follows: of royalty, tyranny; of aristocracy, oligarchy; of constitutional government, democracy. For tyranny is a kind of monarchy which has in view the interest of the monarch only; oligarchy has in view the interest of the wealthy; democracy, of the needy: none of them the common good of all.

BOOK III, PART IX

[THE PURPOSE OF THE STATE AND POLITICAL SOCIETY]

Let us begin by considering the common definitions of oligarchy and democracy, and what is justice oligarchical and democratical. For all men cling to justice of some kind, but their conceptions are imperfect and they do not express the whole idea. For example, justice is thought by them to be, and is, equality, not, however, for all, but only for equals.

And inequality is thought to be, and is, justice; neither is this for all, but only for unequals. When the persons are omitted, then men judge erroneously. The reason is that they are passing judgment on themselves, and most people are bad judges in their own case. And whereas justice implies a relation to persons as well as to things, and a just distribution, as I have already said in the *Ethics*, implies the same ratio between the persons and between the things, they agree about the equality of the things, but dispute about the equality of the persons, chiefly for the reason which I have just given—because they are bad judges in their own affairs; and secondly, because both the parties to the argument are speaking of a limited and partial justice, but imagine themselves to be speaking of absolute justice. For the one party, if they are unequal in one respect, for example wealth, consider themselves to be unequal in all; and the other party, if they are equal in one respect, for example free birth, consider themselves to be equal in all. But they leave out the capital point. For if men met and associated out of regard to wealth only, their share in the state would be proportioned to their property, and the oligarchical doctrine would then seem to carry the day. It would not be just that he who paid one mina should have the same share of a hundred minae, whether of the principal or of the profits, as he who paid the remaining ninety-nine. But a state exists for the sake of a good life, and not for the sake of life only: if life only were the object, slaves and brute animals might form a state, but they cannot, for they have no share in happiness or in a life of free choice. Nor does a state exist for the sake of alliance and security from injustice, nor yet for the sake of exchange and mutual intercourse; for then the Tyrrhenians and the Carthaginians, and all who have commercial treaties with one another, would be the citizens of one state. True, they have agreements about imports, and engagements that they will do no wrong to one another, and written articles of alliance. But there are no magistrates common to the contracting parties who will enforce their engagements; different states have each their own magistracies. Nor does one state take care that the citizens of the other are such as they ought to be, nor see that those who come under the terms of the treaty do no wrong or wickedness at all, but only that they do no injustice to one another. Whereas, those who care for good government take into consideration virtue and vice in states. Whence it may be further inferred that virtue must be the care of a state which is truly so called, and not merely enjoys the name: for without this end the community becomes a mere alliance which differs only in place from alliances of which the members live apart; and law is only a convention, 'a surety to one another of justice,' as the sophist Lycophron says, and has no real power to make the citizens good and just.

This is obvious; for suppose distinct places, such as Corinth and Megara, to be brought together so that their walls touched, still they would not be one city, not even if the citizens had the right to intermarry, which is one of the rights peculiarly characteristic of states. Again, if men dwelt at a distance from one another, but not so far off as to have no intercourse, and there were laws among them that they should not wrong each other in their exchanges, neither would this be a state. Let us suppose that one man is a carpenter, another a husbandman, another a shoemaker, and so on, and that their number is ten thousand: nevertheless, if they have nothing in common but exchange, alliance, and the like, that would not constitute a state. Why is this? Surely not because they are at a distance from one another: for even supposing that such a community were to meet in one place, but that each man had a house of his own, which was in a manner his state, and that they made alliance with one another, but only against evil-doers; still an accurate thinker would not deem this to be a state, if their intercourse with one another was of the same character after as before their union. It is clear then that a state is not a mere society, having a common place, established for the prevention of mutual crime and for the sake of exchange. These are conditions without which a state cannot exist; but all of them together do not constitute a state, which is a community of families and aggregations of families in well-being, for the sake of a perfect and self-sufficing life. Such a community can only be established among those who live in the same place and intermarry. Hence arise in cities family connections, brotherhoods, common sacrifices, amusements which draw men together. But these are created by friendship, for the will to live together is friendship. The end of the state is the good life, and these are the means towards it. And the state is the union of families and villages in a perfect and self-sufficing life, by which we mean a happy and honourable life.

Our conclusion, then, is that political society exists for the sake of noble actions, and not of mere companionship. Hence they who contribute most to such a society have a greater share in it than those who have the same or a greater freedom or nobility of birth but are inferior to them in political virtue; or than those who exceed them in wealth but are surpassed by them in virtue.

From what has been said it will be clearly seen that all the partisans of different forms of government speak of a part of justice only.

BOOK IV, PART XI

[THE MIDDLING SORTS]

We have now to inquire what is the best constitution for most states, and the best life for most men, neither assuming a standard of virtue which is above ordinary persons, nor an education which is exceptionally favored by nature and circumstances, nor yet an ideal state which is an aspiration only, but having regard to the life in which the majority are able to share, and to the form of government which states in general can attain. As to those aristocracies, as they are called, of which we were just now speaking, they either lie beyond the possibilities of the greater number of states, or they approximate to the so-called constitutional government, and therefore need no separate discussion. And in fact the conclusion at which we arrive respecting all these forms rests upon the same grounds. For if what was said in the ethics is true, that the happy life is the life according to virtue lived without impediment, and that virtue is a mean, then the life which is in a mean, and in a mean attainable by every one, must be the best. And the same principles of virtue and vice are characteristic of cities and of constitutions; for the constitution is in a figure the life of the city.

Now in all states there are three elements: one class is very rich, another very poor, and a third in a mean. It is admitted that moderation and the mean are best, and therefore it will clearly be best to possess the gifts of fortune in moderation; for in that condition of life men are most ready to follow rational principle. But he who greatly excels in beauty, strength, birth, or wealth, or on the other hand who is very poor, or very weak, or very much disgraced, finds it difficult to follow rational principle. Of these two the one sort grow into violent and great criminals, the others into rogues and petty rascals. And two sorts of offences correspond to them, the one committed from violence, the other from roguery. Again, the middle class is least likely to shrink from rule, or to be over-ambitious for it; both of which are injuries to the state. Again, those who have too much of the goods of fortune, strength, wealth, friends, and the like, are neither willing nor able to submit to authority. The evil begins at home; for when they are boys, by reason of the luxury in which they are brought up, they never learn, even at school, the habit of obedience. On the other hand, the very poor, who are in the opposite extreme, are too degraded. So that the one class cannot obey, and can only rule despotically; the other knows not how to command and must be ruled like slaves. Thus arises a city, not of freemen, but of masters and slaves, the one despising, the other envying; and nothing can be more fatal to friendship and good fellowship in states than this: for good fellowship springs from friendship; when men are at enmity with one another, they would rather not even share the same path. But a city ought to be composed, as far as possible, of equals and similars; and these are generally the middle classes. Wherefore the city which is composed of middle-class citizens is necessarily best constituted in respect of the elements of which we say the fabric of the state naturally consists. And this is the class of citizens which is most secure in a state, for they do not, like the poor, covet their neighbours' goods; nor do others covet theirs, as the poor covet the goods of the rich; and as they neither plot against others, nor are themselves plotted against, they pass through life safely. Wisely then did Phocylides pray—'Many things are best in the mean; I desire to be of a middle condition in my city.'

Thus it is manifest that the best political community is formed by citizens of the middle class, and that those states are likely to be well-administered in which the middle class is large, and stronger if possible than both the other classes, or at any rate than either singly; for the addition of the middle class turns the scale, and prevents either of the extremes from being dominant. Great then is the good fortune of a state in which the citizens have a moderate and sufficient property; for where some possess much, and the others nothing, there may arise an extreme democracy, or a pure oligarchy; or a tyranny may grow out of either extreme—either out of the most rampant democracy, or out of an oligarchy; but it is not so likely to arise out of the middle constitutions and those akin to them. I will explain the reason of this hereafter, when I speak of the revolutions of states. The mean condition of states is clearly best, for no other is free from faction; and where the middle class is large, there are least likely to be factions and dissensions. For a similar reason large states are less liable to faction than small ones, because in them the middle class is large; whereas in small states it is easy to divide all the citizens into two classes who are either rich or poor, and to leave nothing in the middle. And democracies are safer and more permanent than oligarchies, because they have a middle class which is more numerous and has a greater share in the government; for when there is no middle class, and the poor greatly exceed in number, troubles arise, and the state soon comes to an end. A proof of the superiority of the middle class is that the best legislators have been of a middle condition; for example, Solon, as his own verses testify; and Lycurgus, for he was not a king; and Charondas, and almost all legislators.

These considerations will help us to understand why most governments are either democratical or oligarchical. The reason is that the middle class is seldom numerous in them, and whichever party, whether the rich or the common people, transgresses the mean and predominates, draws the constitution its own way, and thus arises either oligarchy or democracy. There is another reason—the poor and the rich quarrel with one another, and whichever side gets the better, instead of establishing a just or popular government, regards political supremacy as the prize of victory, and the one party sets up a democracy and the other an oligarchy. Further, both the parties which had the supremacy in Hellas looked only to the interest of their own form of government, and established in states, the one, democracies, and the other, oligarchies; they thought of their own advantage, of the public not at all. For these reasons the middle form of government has rarely, if ever, existed, and among a very few only. One man alone of all who ever ruled in Hellas was induced to give this middle constitution to states. But it has now become a habit among the citizens of states, not even to care about equality; all men are seeking for dominion, or, if conquered, are willing to submit.

What then is the best form of government, and what makes it the best, is evident; and of other constitutions, since we say that there are many kinds of democracy and many of oligarchy, it is not difficult to see which has the first and which the second or any other place in the order of excellence, now that we have determined which is the best.

For that which is nearest to the best must of necessity be better, and that which is furthest from it worse, if we are judging absolutely and not relatively to given conditions: I say 'relatively to given conditions,' since a particular government may be preferable, but another form may be better for some people.

BOOK V, PART I

The design which we proposed to ourselves is now nearly completed. Next in order follow the causes of revolution in states, how many, and of what nature they are; what modes of destruction apply to particular states, and out of what, and into what they mostly change; also what are the modes of preservation in states generally, or in a particular state, and by what means each state may be best preserved: these questions remain to be considered.

In the first place we must assume as our starting point that in the many forms of government which have sprung up there has always been an acknowledgment of justice and proportionate equality, although mankind fail attaining them, as I have already explained. Democracy, for example, arises out of the notion that those who are equal in any respect are equal in all respects; because men are equally free, they claim to be absolutely equal. Oligarchy is based on the notion that those who are unequal in one respect are in all respects unequal; being unequal, that is, in property, they suppose themselves to be unequal absolutely. The democrats think that as they are equal they ought to be equal in all things; while the oligarchs, under the idea that they are unequal, claim too much, which is one form of inequality. All these forms of government have a kind of justice, but, tried by an absolute standard, they are faulty; and, therefore, both parties, whenever their share in the government does not accord with their preconceived ideas, stir up revolution. Those who excel in virtue have the best right of all to rebel (for they alone can with reason be deemed absolutely unequal), but then they are of all men the least inclined to do so. There is also a superiority which is claimed by men of rank; for they are thought noble because they spring from wealthy and virtuous ancestors. Here then, so to speak, are opened the very springs and fountains of revolution; and hence arise two sorts of changes in governments; the one affecting the constitution, when men seek to change from an existing form into some other, for example, from democracy into oligarchy, and from oligarchy into democracy, or from either of them into constitutional government or aristocracy, and conversely; the other not affecting the constitution, when, without disturbing the form of government, whether oligarchy, or monarchy, or any other, they try to get the administration into their own hands. Further, there is a question of degree: an oligarchy, for example, may become more or less oligarchical, and a democracy more or less democratical; and in like manner the characteristics of the other forms of government may be more or less strictly maintained. Or the revolution may be directed against a portion of the constitution only, e.g. the establishment or overthrow of a particular office: as at Sparta it is said that Lysander attempted to overthrow the monarchy, and King Pausanias, the Ephoralty.[2] At Epidamnus, too, the change was partial. For instead of phylarchs or heads of tribes, a council was appointed; but to this day the magistrates are the only members of the ruling class who are compelled to go to the Heliaea when an election takes place, and the office of the single archon[3] was another oligarchical feature. Everywhere inequality is a cause of revolution, but an inequality in which there is no proportion—for instance, a perpetual monarchy among equals; and always it is the desire of equality which rises in rebellion.

Now equality is of two kinds, numerical and proportional: by the first I mean sameness or equality in number or size; by the second, equality of ratios. For example, the excess of three over two is numerically equal to the excess of two over one; whereas four exceeds two in the same ratio in which two exceeds one, for two is the same part of four that one is of two, namely, the half. As I was saying before, men agree that justice in the abstract is proportion, but they differ in that some think that if they are equal in any respect they are equal absolutely, others that if they are unequal in any respect they should be unequal in all. Hence there are two principal forms of government, democracy and oligarchy; for good birth and virtue are rare, but wealth and numbers are more common. In what city shall we find a hundred

2. A body of five magistrates annually elected by the people of Sparta.
3. One of the chief magistrates of ancient Athens.

persons of good birth and of virtue? whereas the rich everywhere abound. That a state should be ordered, simply and wholly, according to either kind of equality, is not a good thing; the proof is the fact that such forms of government never last. They are originally based on a mistake, and, as they begin badly, cannot fail to end badly. The inference is that both kinds of equality should be employed: numerical in some cases, and proportionate in others.

Still democracy appears to be safer and less liable to revolution than oligarchy. For in oligarchies there is the double danger of the oligarchs falling out among themselves and also with the people; but in democracies there is only the danger of a quarrel with the oligarchs. No dissension worth mentioning arises among the people themselves. And we may further remark that a government which is composed of the middle class more nearly approximates to democracy than to oligarchy, and is the safest of the imperfect forms of government.

BOOK V, PART XI

[HOW TYRANNIES ARE PRESERVED]

...As to (2) tyrannies, they are preserved in two most opposite ways. One of them is the old traditional method in which most tyrants administer their government. Of such arts Periander of Corinth is said to have been the great master, and many similar devices may be gathered from the Persians in the administration of their government. There are firstly the prescriptions mentioned some distance back for the preservation of a tyranny, in so far as this is possible: viz., that the tyrant should lop off those who are too high; he must put to death men of spirit; he must not allow common meals, clubs, education, and the like; he must be upon his guard against anything which is likely to inspire either courage or confidence among his subjects; he must prohibit literary assemblies or other meetings for discussion, and he must take every means to prevent people from knowing one another (for acquaintance begets mutual confidence). Further, he must compel all persons staying in the city to appear in public and live at his gates; then he will know what they are doing: if they are always kept under, they will learn to be humble. In short, he should practice these and the like Persian and barbaric arts, which all have the same object. A tyrant should also endeavour to know what each of his subjects says or does, and should employ spies, like the 'female detectives' at Syracuse, and the eavesdroppers whom Hiero was in the habit of sending to any place of resort or meeting; for the fear of informers prevents people from speaking their minds, and if they do, they are more easily found out. Another art of the tyrant is to sow quarrels among the citizens; friends should be embroiled with friends, the people with the notables, and the rich with one another. Also he should impoverish his subjects; he thus provides against the maintenance of a guard by the citizen, and the people, having to keep hard at work, are prevented from conspiring. The Pyramids of Egypt afford an example of this policy; also the offerings of the family of Cypselus, and the building of the temple of Olympian Zeus by the Peisistratidae, and the great Polycratean monuments at Samos; all these works were alike intended to occupy the people and keep them poor. Another practice of tyrants is to multiply taxes, after the manner of Dionysius at Syracuse, who contrived that within five years his subjects should bring into the treasury their whole property. The tyrant is also fond of making war in order that his subjects may have something to do and be always in want of a leader. And whereas the power of a king is preserved by his friends, the characteristic of a tyrant is to distrust his friends, because he knows that all men want to overthrow him, and they above all have the power.

Again, the evil practices of the last and worst form of democracy are all found in tyrannies. Such are the power given to women in their families in the hope that they will inform against their husbands, and the license which is allowed to slaves in order that they may betray their masters; for slaves and women do not conspire against tyrants; and they are of course friendly to tyrannies and also to democracies, since under them they have a good time. For the people too would fain be a monarch, and therefore by them, as well as by the tyrant, the flatterer is held in honour; in democracies he is the demagogue; and the tyrant also has those who associate with him in a humble spirit, which is a work of flattery.

Hence tyrants are always fond of bad men, because they love to be flattered, but no man who has the spirit of a freeman in him will lower himself by flattery; good men love others, or at any rate do not flatter them. Moreover, the bad are useful for bad purposes; 'nail knocks out nail', as the proverb says. It is characteristic of a tyrant to dislike everyone who has dignity or independence; he wants to be alone in his glory, but anyone who claims a like dignity or asserts his independence encroaches upon his prerogative, and is hated by him as an enemy to his power. Another mark of a tyrant is that he likes foreigners better than citizens, and lives with them and invites them to his table; for the one are enemies, but the others enter into no rivalry with him.

Such are the notes of the tyrant and the arts by which he preserves his power; there is no wickedness too great for him. All that we have said may be summed up under three heads, which answer to the three aims of the tyrant. These are, (1) the humiliation of his subjects; he knows that a mean-spirited man will not conspire against anybody; (2) the creation of mistrust among them; for a tyrant is not overthrown until men begin to have confidence in one another; and this is the reason why tyrants are at war with the good; they are under the idea that their power is endangered by them, not only because they would not be ruled despotically but also because they are loyal to one another, and to other men, and do not inform against one another or against other men; (3) the tyrant desires that his subjects shall be incapable of action, for no one attempts what is impossible, and they will not attempt to overthrow a tyranny if they are powerless. Under these three heads the whole policy of a tyrant may be summed up, and to one or other of them all his ideas may be referred: (1) he sows distrust among his subjects; (2) he takes away their power; (3) he humbles them. ...

3

NICCOLÒ MACHIAVELLI, THE PRINCE & DISCOURSES

INTRODUCTION

Niccolò Machiavelli, the pre-eminent political thinker of the Italian Renaissance, is often considered to be a master of the dark arts of statecraft. His most infamous work, *The Prince*, is a guidebook on how princes may obtain and hold onto power; his lesser-read but no less thought-provoking *Discourses,* nominally a commentary on the work of Roman historian Livy, is an inquiry into the establishment of a republic, the manner in which such republic may be best organized, and the type of political leadership most conducive to its well-being. Underlying the two works is, in fact, a common approach based upon the extraction of general political principles and practical political wisdom from ancient and modern history. What makes Machiavelli's work uniquely valuable to the modern man is his unapologetic real-talk and his uncompromising real-world focus: if you want to obtain and consolidate power, says Machiavelli, I will show you how it is done.

Machiavelli (1469-1527) was born into a prominent and wealthy Florentine family, although his father, a lawyer, was one of its poorest members. In his twenties, Machiavelli observed in Florence the remarkable rise to prominence of Savonarola, a Dominican friar who dominated the city-state as de facto ruler on a reforming mission against tyrannical rulers and a corrupt clergy, until he was hanged as

47

a heretic and his body burned in the public square. Shortly thereafter Machiavelli obtained a post in the government of Florentine Republic as head of the second chancery, putting him in charge of the Republic's foreign affairs in subject territories. He undertook diplomatic and military missions to the court of Louis XII in France, to Cesare Borgia in the Romagna, to Pope Julius II in Rome, and to the court of Holy Roman Emperor Maximilian I. Upon the restoration of the Medici in Florence in 1512, Machiavelli—who was suspected of conspiring against them—was imprisoned and tortured, before being sent into exile in 1513 to his farm at Percussina just south of Florence. It was here in enforced retirement that Machiavelli wrote his major works, *The Prince* and *Discourses*, neither of which were published until after his death in 1527, the same year in which the armies of Charles V sacked Rome.

Machiavelli brought a strongly pragmatic element into Western political philosophy: his works bridge the gap between how rulers in fact conducted their political affairs, as a matter of practical necessity, and what it was possible for thinkers, like Machiavelli, to say about this. He is open about his approach in *The Prince*: we could talk about an imaginary world in which princes are possessed of all the virtues and free of all vices, he says, but this would be pointless; far better to face up to the fact that no prince is wholly virtuous and that no wholly virtuous prince would be likely to hold onto power for long. A prince must, in fact, 'know how to do wrong'. Of course, it is preferable to *seem* virtuous, and indeed a prince should avoid by all means the vices that cause harm to his state; he should even (as far as possible) avoid those vices that are inconsequential to it. But there are certain vices 'without which the state can only be saved with difficulty'—certain vices that positively assist in ruling the state—and in respect of these the prince need feel no compunction or remorse.

This is, lest the reader misunderstand, a philosophy every bit as applicable to the saint as it is to the sinner. It is true, of course, that Machiavelli has not ordinarily been viewed as being on the side of the angels: the Catholic Church went as far as to ban *The Prince* by putting it on the Index Librorum Prohibitorum (the list of forbidden books), and even today 'Machiavellian' is routinely used as a synonym for 'unscrupulous'. But this is unfair. In fact, Machiavelli communicated two insights of enduring value: first, that the art and craft of political action could be studied empirically from its historical *exempla* in order to extract principles and practices that were, in themselves, morally neutral, and capable of being applied equally in the cause of good or of evil; and second, that it is necessary for the good man to master this art in order to overcome the evil in the world that will otherwise deprive him of his power—and hence his capacity to do good—before destroying him completely.

The ruler, then, must engender and release something of the animal within himself in order to survive: he must be as cunning as the fox and as ferocious as the lion. Cultivate appearances, counsels Machiavelli, since men are credible and easily fooled: show yourself to be merciful, faithful, humane, religious, and upright—but have a mind framed so that you may change to the opposite when necessary. Be open-handed when you need to buy your way into power or when you can spend money extracted from citizens of other nations; otherwise, liberality is best avoided, as it risks weighing down on the people through taxes, or arousing their contempt for your poverty once you are spent up. And, while it would be better to be loved as well as feared, if you have to choose one, choose the latter. Men, in general, are contemptible creatures, who will offer blood, property, life, and children in your support when you are successful, but when you need their help they will turn against you. Fear, on the other hand, has a more prolonged effect: it protects and preserves you by a dread of punishment that never fails.

Powerful as *The Prince* certainly is, it is Machiavelli's *Discourses* that establish him most securely in the firmament of great European political thinkers. It is in this work that Machiavelli presents an affirmative political ethos in support of national independence, security, and a well-ordered constitution.[1] In doing so he brings together what he perceives to be the best of the ancient past with a vision for the future: he is an enthusiastic advocate, for example, of a doctrine of constitutional checks and balances whereby princes, nobles, and commons keep each other reciprocally in check, as did the consuls, senate, and commons (represented by the tribunes) of the Roman Republic.

The greatest gift, however, that Machiavelli can offer the modern man is his thoroughgoing consciousness that the state is a moral entity

---

1. Bertrand Russell, *History of Western Philosophy* (London and New York: Routledge, 2000), 496.

held together by the overall ethical level of the nation and the personal virtue of its citizens. Great nations, like great men, preserve their spirit and bearing through every change of fortune: it is this that ensures that they behave with dignity and graciousness in victory, and resolution in defeat, with the consequence that fortune has no dominion over them and their onward progress will be assured. A nation can be great irrespective of its economic prosperity, just as Rome had been great even while its citizens were still poor: the state is there to be served by its economic functions, and it is only insofar as those functions contribute to the well-being and improvement of its inhabitants as a whole that they have significance. Machiavelli would have rejected, then, and without a moment's hesitation, the particular insanity of the modern age of viewing the state as a vehicle whose main role and justification is the accumulation of paper wealth and the expansion of production or trade irrespective of the overall cultural and ethical level and general well-being of its inhabitants. Follow the Romans, he suggests, in ensuring that the prospects of advancement are open to all, and that merit is preferred wherever it is found, since this renders wealth of less significance, at the same time as rendering honour all the more the proper object of aspiration.

THE PRINCE

CHAPTER 15

CONCERNING THINGS FOR WHICH MEN, AND ESPECIALLY PRINCES, ARE PRAISED OR BLAMED

It remains now to see what ought to be the rules of conduct for a prince towards subject and friends. And as I know that many have written on this point, I expect I shall be considered presumptuous in mentioning it again, especially as in discussing it I shall depart from the methods of other people. But, it being my intention to write a thing which shall be useful to him who apprehends it, it appears to me more appropriate to follow up the real truth of the matter than the imagination of it; for many have pictured republics and principalities which in fact have never been known or seen, because how one lives is so far distant from how one ought to live, that he who neglects what is done for what ought to be done, sooner effects his ruin than his preservation; for a man who wishes to act entirely up to his professions of virtue soon meets with what destroys him among so much that is evil.

Hence it is necessary for a prince wishing to hold his own to know how to do wrong, and to make use of it or not according to necessity. Therefore, putting on one side imaginary things concerning a prince, and discussing those which are real, I say that all men when they are spoken of, and chiefly princes for being more highly placed, are remarkable for some of those qualities which bring them either blame or praise; and thus it is that one is reputed liberal, another miserly, using a Tuscan term (because an avaricious person in our language is still he who desires to possess by robbery, whilst we call one miserly who deprives himself too much of the use of his own); one is reputed generous, one rapacious; one cruel, one compassionate; one faithless, another faithful; one effeminate and cowardly, another bold and brave; one affable, another haughty; one lascivious, another chaste; one sincere, another cunning; one hard, another easy; one grave, another frivolous; one religious, another unbelieving, and the like. And I know that everyone will confess that it would be most praiseworthy in a prince to exhibit all the above qualities that are considered good; but because they can neither be entirely possessed nor observed, for human conditions do not permit it, it is necessary for him to be sufficiently prudent that he may know how to avoid the reproach of those vices which would lose him his state; and also to keep himself, if it be possible, from those which would not lose him it; but this not being possible, he may with less hesitation abandon himself to them. And again, he need not make himself uneasy at incurring a reproach for those vices without which the state can only be saved with difficulty, for if everything is considered carefully, it will be found that something which looks like virtue, if followed, would be his ruin; whilst something else, which looks like vice, yet followed brings him security and prosperity.

CHAPTER 17

CONCERNING CRUELTY AND CLEMENCY, AND WHETHER IT IS BETTER TO

BE LOVED THAN FEARED

Coming now to the other qualities mentioned above, I say that every prince ought to desire to be considered clement and not cruel. Nevertheless, he ought to take care not to misuse this clemency. Cesare Borgia was considered cruel; notwithstanding, his cruelty reconciled the Romagna, unified it, and restored it to peace and loyalty. And if this be rightly considered, he will be seen to have been much more merciful than the Florentine people, who, to avoid a reputation for cruelty, permitted Pistoia to be destroyed. Therefore a prince, so long as he keeps his subjects united and loyal, ought not to mind the reproach of cruelty; because with a few examples he will be more merciful than those who, through too much mercy, allow disorders to arise, from which follow murders or robberies; for these are wont to injure the whole people, whilst those executions which originate with a prince offend the individual only.

And of all princes, it is impossible for the new prince to avoid the imputation of cruelty, owing to new states being full of dangers. Hence Virgil, through the mouth of Dido, excuses the inhumanity of her reign owing to its being new, saying:

'Res dura, et regni novitas me talia cogunt
Moliri, et late fines custode tueri.'

[*'. . . against my will, my fate*
A throne unsettled, and an infant state,
Bid me defend my realms with all my pow'rs,
And guard with these severities my shores.]

Nevertheless, he ought to be slow to believe and to act, nor should he himself show fear, but proceed in a temperate manner with prudence and humanity, so that too much confidence may not make him incautious and too much distrust render him intolerable.

Upon this, a question arises: whether it be better to be loved than feared or feared than loved? It may be answered that one should wish to be both, but, because it is difficult to unite them in one person, it is much safer to be feared than loved, when, of the two, either must be dispensed with. Because this is to be asserted in general of men, that they are ungrateful, fickle, false, cowardly, covetous, and as long as you succeed they are yours entirely; they will offer you their blood, property, life, and children, as is said above, when the need is far distant; but when it approaches they turn against you. And that prince who, relying entirely on their promises, has neglected other precautions, is ruined; because friendships that are obtained by payments, and not by greatness or nobility of mind, may indeed be earned, but they are not secured, and in time of need cannot be relied upon; and men have less scruple in offending one who is beloved than one who is feared, for love is preserved by the link of obligation which, owing to the baseness of men, is broken at every opportunity for their advantage; but fear preserves you by a dread of punishment which never fails.

Nevertheless, a prince ought to inspire fear in such a way that, if he does not win love, he avoids hatred; because he can endure very well being feared whilst he is not hated, which will always be as long as he abstains from the property of his citizens and subjects and from their women. But when it is necessary for him to proceed against the life of someone, he must do it on proper justification and for manifest cause, but above all things he must keep his hands off the property of others, because men more quickly forget the death of their father than the loss of their patrimony. Besides, pretexts for taking away the property are never wanting; for he who has once begun to live by robbery will always find pretexts for seizing what belongs to others; but reasons for taking life, on the contrary, are more difficult to find and sooner lapse. But when a prince is with his army, and has under control a multitude of soldiers, then it is quite necessary for him to disregard the reputation of cruelty, for without it he would never hold his army united or disposed to its duties.

Among the wonderful deeds of Hannibal this one is enumerated: that having led an enormous army, composed of many various races of men, to fight in foreign lands, no dissensions arose either among them or against the prince, whether in his bad or in his good fortune. This arose from nothing else than his inhuman cruelty, which, with his boundless valour, made him revered and terrible in the sight of his soldiers, but without that cruelty, his other virtues were not sufficient to produce this effect. And shortsighted writers admire his deeds from one point of view and from another condemn the principal cause of them. That it is true his other virtues would not have been sufficient for him may be proved by the case of Scipio, that most excellent man, not only of his own times but within the memory of man, against whom, nevertheless, his army rebelled in Spain; this arose from nothing but his too great forbearance, which gave his soldiers more license than is consistent with military discipline. For this, he was upbraided in the Senate by Fabius Maximus, and called the corrupter of the Roman soldiery. The Locrians were laid waste by a legate of Scipio, yet they were not avenged by him, nor was the insolence of the legate punished, owing entirely to his easy nature. Insomuch that someone in the Senate, wishing to excuse him, said there were many men who knew much better how not to err than to correct the errors of others. This disposition, if he had been continued in the command, would have destroyed in time the fame and glory of Scipio; but, he being under the control of the Senate, this injurious characteristic not only concealed itself but contributed to his glory.

Returning to the question of being feared or loved, I come to the conclusion that men loving according to their own will and fearing according to that of the prince, a wise prince should establish himself on that which is in his own control and not in that of others; he must endeavour only to avoid hatred, as is noted.

CHAPTER 18

CONCERNING THE WAY IN WHICH PRINCES SHOULD KEEP FAITH

Everyone admits how praiseworthy it is in a prince to keep faith, and to live with integrity and not with craft. Nevertheless our experience has been that those princes who have done great things have held good faith of little account, and have known how to circumvent the intellect of men by craft, and in the end have overcome those who have relied on their word. You must know there are two ways of contesting, the one by the law, the other by force; the first method is proper to men, the second to beasts; but because the first is frequently not sufficient, it is necessary to have recourse to the second. Therefore it is necessary for a prince to understand how to avail himself of the beast and the man. This has been figuratively taught to princes by ancient writers, who describe how Achilles and many other princes of old were given to the Centaur Chiron to nurse, who brought them up in his discipline;

which means solely that, as they had for a teacher one who was half beast and half man, so it is necessary for a prince to know how to make use of both natures, and that one without the other is not durable. A prince, therefore, being compelled knowingly to adopt the beast, ought to choose the fox and the lion; because the lion cannot defend himself against snares and the fox cannot defend himself against wolves. Therefore, it is necessary to be a fox to discover the snares and a lion to terrify the wolves. Those who rely simply on the lion do not understand what they are about. Therefore a wise lord cannot, nor ought he to, keep faith when such observance may be turned against him, and when the reasons that caused him to pledge it exist no longer. If men were entirely good this precept would not hold, but because they are bad, and will not keep faith with you, you too are not bound to observe it with them. Nor will there ever be wanting to a prince legitimate reasons to excuse this non-observance. Of this endless modern examples could be given, showing how many treaties and engagements have been made void and of no effect through the faithlessness of princes; and he who has known best how to employ the fox has succeeded best.

But it is necessary to know well how to disguise this characteristic, and to be a great pretender and dissembler; and men are so simple, and so subject to present necessities, that he who seeks to deceive will always find someone who will allow himself to be deceived. One recent example I cannot pass over in silence. Alexander the Sixth did nothing else but deceive men, nor ever thought of doing otherwise, and he always found victims; for there never was a man who had greater power in asserting, or who with greater oaths would affirm a thing, yet would observe it less; nevertheless his deceits always succeeded according to his wishes, because he well understood this side of mankind.

Therefore it is unnecessary for a prince to have all the good qualities I have enumerated, but it is very necessary to appear to have them. And I shall dare to say this also, that to have them and always to observe them is injurious, and that to appear to have them is useful; to appear merciful, faithful, humane, religious, upright, and to be so, but with a mind so framed that should you require not to be so, you may be able and know how to change to the opposite.

And you have to understand this, that a prince, especially a new one, cannot observe all those things for which men are esteemed, being often forced, in order to maintain the state, to act contrary to fidelity, friendship, humanity, and religion. Therefore it is necessary for him to have a mind ready to turn itself accordingly as the winds and variations of fortune force it, yet, as I have said above, not to diverge from the good if he can avoid doing so, but, if compelled, then to know how to set about it.

For this reason, a prince ought to take care that he never lets anything slip from his lips that is not replete with the above-named five qualities, that he may appear to him who sees and hears him altogether merciful, faithful, humane, upright, and religious. There is nothing more necessary to appear to have than this last quality, inasmuch as men judge generally more by the eye than by the hand, because it belongs to everybody to see you, to few to come in touch with you. Everyone sees what you appear to be, few really know what you are, and those few dare not oppose themselves to the opinion of the many, who have the majesty of the state to defend them; and in the actions of all men, and especially of princes, which it is not prudent to challenge, one judges by the result.

For that reason, let a prince have the credit of conquering and holding his state, the means will always be considered honest, and he will be praised by everybody; because the vulgar are always taken by what a thing seems to be and by what comes of it; and in the world there are only the vulgar, for the few find a place there only when the many have no ground to rest on.

One prince[2] of the present time, whom it is not well to name, never preaches anything else but peace and good faith, and to both he is most hostile, and either, if he had kept it, would have deprived him of reputation and kingdom many a time.

CHAPTER 25

WHAT FORTUNE CAN EFFECT IN HUMAN AFFAIRS AND HOW TO WITHSTAND HER

It is not unknown to me how many men have had, and still have, the opinion that the affairs of the world are in such wise governed by

---

2. Ferdinand of Aragon.

fortune and by God that men with their wisdom cannot direct them and that no one can even help them; and because of this they would have us believe that it is not necessary to labour much in affairs, but to let chance govern them. This opinion has been more credited in our times because of the great changes in affairs which have been seen, and may still be seen, every day, beyond all human conjecture. Sometimes pondering over this, I am in some degree inclined to their opinion. Nevertheless, not to extinguish our free will, I hold it to be true that Fortune is the arbiter of one-half of our actions,[3] but that she still leaves us to direct the other half, or perhaps a little less.

I compare her to one of those raging rivers, which when in flood overflows the plains, sweeping away trees and buildings, bearing away the soil from place to place; everything flies before it, all yield to its violence, without being able in any way to withstand it; and yet, though its nature be such, it does not follow therefore that men, when the weather becomes fair, shall not make provision, both with defences and barriers, in such a manner that, rising again, the waters may pass away by canal, and their force be neither so unrestrained nor so dangerous. So it happens with fortune, who shows her power where valour has not prepared to resist her, and thither she turns her forces where she knows that barriers and defences have not been raised to constrain her.

And if you will consider Italy, which is the seat of these changes, and which has given to them their impulse, you will see it to be an open country without barriers and without any defence. For if it had been defended by proper valour, as are Germany, Spain, and France, either this invasion would not have made the great changes it has made or it would not have come at all. And this I consider enough to say concerning resistance to fortune in general.

But confining myself more to the particular, I say that a prince may be seen happy today and ruined tomorrow without having shown any change of disposition or character. This, I believe, arises firstly from causes that have already been discussed at length, namely, that the prince who relies entirely on fortune is lost when it changes. I believe also that he will be successful who directs his actions according to the

---

3. Frederick the Great was accustomed to say: 'The older one gets the more convinced one becomes that his Majesty King Chance does three-quarters of the business of this miserable universe.' Sorel's 'Eastern Question'.

spirit of the times, and that he whose actions do not accord with the times will not be successful. Because men are seen, in affairs that lead to the end which every man has before him, namely, glory and riches, to get there by various methods; one with caution, another with haste; one by force, another by skill; one by patience, another by its opposite; and each one succeeds in reaching the goal by a different method. One can also see of two cautious men the one attain his end, the other fail; and similarly, two men by different observances are equally successful, the one being cautious, the other impetuous; all this arises from nothing else than whether or not they conform in their methods to the spirit of the times. This follows from what I have said, that two men working differently bring about the same effect, and of two working similarly, one attains his object and the other does not.

Changes in estate also issue from this, for if, to one who governs himself with caution and patience, times and affairs converge in such a way that his administration is successful, his fortune is made; but if times and affairs change, he is ruined if he does not change his course of action. But a man is not often found sufficiently circumspect to know how to accommodate himself to the change, both because he cannot deviate from what nature inclines him to do, and also because, having always prospered by acting in one way, he cannot be persuaded that it is well to leave it; and, therefore, the cautious man, when it is time to turn adventurous, does not know how to do it, hence he is ruined; but had he changed his conduct with the times fortune would not have changed.

Pope Julius the Second went to work impetuously in all his affairs, and found the times and circumstances conform so well to that line of action that he always met with success. Consider his first enterprise against Bologna, Messer Giovanni Bentivogli being still alive. The Venetians were not agreeable to it, nor was the King of Spain, and he had the enterprise still under discussion with the King of France; nevertheless he personally entered upon the expedition with his accustomed boldness and energy, a move which made Spain and the Venetians stand irresolute and passive, the latter from fear, the former from desire to recover the kingdom of Naples; on the other hand, he drew after him the King of France, because that king, having observed the movement, and desiring to make the Pope his friend so as to humble the Venetians, found it impossible to refuse him. Therefore

Julius with his impetuous action accomplished what no other pontiff with simple human wisdom could have done; for if he had waited in Rome until he could get away, with his plans arranged and everything fixed, as any other pontiff would have done, he would never have succeeded. Because the King of France would have made a thousand excuses, and the others would have raised a thousand fears.

I will leave his other actions alone, as they were all alike, and they all succeeded, for the shortness of his life did not let him experience the contrary; but if circumstances had arisen which required him to go cautiously, his ruin would have followed, because he would never have deviated from those ways to which nature inclined him.

I conclude, therefore, that fortune being changeful and mankind steadfast in his ways, so long as the two are in agreement men are successful, but unsuccessful when they fall out. For my part I consider that it is better to be adventurous than cautious, because fortune is a woman, and if you wish to keep her under it is necessary to beat and ill-use her; and it is seen that she allows herself to be mastered by the adventurous rather than by those who go to work more coldly. She is, therefore, always, woman-like, a lover of young men, because they are less cautious, more violent, and with more audacity command her.

Discourses on Livy

Book III, Chapter 25

OF THE POVERTY OF CINCINNATUS AND OF MANY OTHER ROMAN CITIZENS

Elsewhere I have shown that no ordinance is of such advantage to a commonwealth as one which enforces poverty on its citizens. And although it does not appear what particular law it was that had this operation in Rome (especially since we know the agrarian law to have been stubbornly resisted), we find, as a fact, that four hundred years after the city was founded, great poverty still prevailed there; and may assume that nothing helped so much to produce this result as the knowledge that the path to honours and preferment was closed to none, and that merit was sought after wheresoever it was to be found; for this manner of conferring honours made riches the less courted. In proof whereof I shall cite one instance only.

When the consul Minutius was beset in his camp by the Equians, the Roman people were filled with such alarm lest their army should be destroyed, that they appointed a dictator, always their last stay in seasons of peril. Their choice fell on Lucius Quintius Cincinnatus, who at the time was living on his small farm of little more than four acres, which he tilled with his own hand. The story is nobly told by Titus Livius where he says: 'This is worth listening to by those who contemn all things human as compared with riches, and think that glory and excellence can have no place unless accompanied by lavish wealth.' Cincinnatus, then, was ploughing in his little field, when there arrived from Rome the messengers sent by the senate to tell him he had been made dictator, and inform him of the dangers which threatened the Republic. Putting on his gown, he hastened to Rome, and getting together an army, marched to deliver Minutius. But when he had defeated and spoiled the enemy, and released Minutius, he would not suffer the army he had rescued to participate in the spoils, saying, 'I will not have you share in the plunder of those to whom you had so nearly fallen a prey.' Minutius he deprived of his consulship, and reduced to be a subaltern, in which rank he bade him remain till he had learned how to command. And before this he had made Lucius Tarquininus, although forced by his poverty to serve on foot, his master of the knights.

Here, then, we see what honour was paid in Rome to poverty, and how four acres of land sufficed to support so good and great a man as Cincinnatus. We find the same poverty still prevailing in the time of Marcus Regulus, who when serving with the army in Africa sought leave of senate to return home that he might look after his farm which his labourers had suffered to run to waste. Here again we learn two things worthy our attention: first, the poverty of these men and their contentment under it, and how their sole study was to gain renown from war, leaving all its advantages to the state. For had they thought of enriching themselves by war, it had given them little concern that their fields were running to waste. Further, we have to remark the magnanimity of these citizens, who when placed at the head of armies surpassed all princes in the loftiness of their spirit, who cared neither for king nor for commonwealth, and whom nothing could daunt or dismay; but who, on returning to private life, became once more so humble, so frugal, so careful of their slender means, and so submissive to the magistrates and reverential to their superiors, that it might seem impossible for the human mind to undergo so violent a change.

This poverty prevailed down to the days of Paulus Emilius, almost the last happy days for this republic wherein a citizen, while enriching Rome by his triumphs, himself remained poor. And yet so greatly was poverty still esteemed at this time, that when Paulus, in conferring rewards on those who had behaved well in the war, presented his own son-in-law with a silver cup, it was the first vessel of silver ever seen in his house.

I might run on to a great length pointing out how much better are the fruits of poverty than those of riches, and how poverty has brought cities, provinces, and nations to honour, while riches have wrought their ruin, had not this subject been often treated by others.

BOOK III, CHAPTER 31

THAT STRONG REPUBLICS AND VALIANT MEN PRESERVE THROUGH EVERY CHANGE THE SAME SPIRIT AND BEARING

Among other high sayings which our historian ascribes to Camillus, as showing of what stuff a truly great man should be made, he puts in his mouth the words, '*My courage came not with my dictatorship nor went with my exile*'; for by these words we are taught that a great man is constantly the same through all vicissitudes of Fortune; so that although she change, now exalting, now depressing, he remains unchanged, and retains always a mind so unmoved, and in such complete accordance with his nature as declares to all that over him Fortune has no dominion.

Very different is the behaviour of those weak-minded mortals who, puffed up and intoxicated with their success, ascribe all their felicity to virtues which they never knew, and thus grow hateful and insupportable to all around them. Whence also the changes in their fortunes. For whenever they have to look adversity in the face, they suddenly pass to the other extreme, becoming abject and base. And thus it happens that feeble-minded princes, when they fall into difficulties, think rather of flight than of defence, because, having made bad use of their prosperity, they are wholly unprepared to defend themselves.

The same merits and defects which I say are found in individual men, are likewise found in republics, whereof we have example in the case of Rome and of Venice. For no reverse of fortune ever broke the spirit of the Roman people, nor did any success ever unduly elate them; as we see plainly after their defeat at Cannae, and after the victory they had over Antiochus. For the defeat at Cannae, although most momentous, being the third they had met with, no whit daunted them; so that they continued to send forth armies, refused to ransom prisoners as contrary to their custom, and dispatched no envoy to Hannibal or to Carthage to sue for peace; but without ever looking back on past humiliations, thought always of war, though in such straits for soldiers that they had to arm their old men and slaves. Which facts being made known to Hanno the Carthaginian, he, as I have already related, warned the Carthaginian senate not to lay too much stress upon their victory. Here, therefore, we see that in times of adversity the Romans were neither cast down nor dismayed. On the other hand, no prosperity ever made them arrogant. Before fighting the battle wherein he was finally routed, Antiochus sent messengers to Scipio to treat for an accord; when Scipio offered peace on condition that he withdrew at once into Syria, leaving all his other dominions to be dealt with by the Romans as they thought fit. Antiochus refusing these terms, fought and was defeated, and again sent envoys to Scipio, enjoining them to accept whatever conditions the victor might be pleased to impose. But Scipio proposed no different terms from those he had offered before saying that 'the Romans, as they lost not heart on defeat, so waxed not insolent with success.'

The contrary of all this is seen in the behaviour of the Venetians, who thinking their good fortune due to valour of which they were devoid, in their pride addressed the French king as 'Son of St Mark'; and making no account of the Church, and no longer restricting their ambition to the limits of Italy, came to dream of founding an empire like the Roman. But afterwards, when their good fortune deserted them, and they met at Vailà a half-defeat at the hands of the French king, they lost their whole dominions, not altogether from revolt, but mainly by a base and abject surrender to the Pope and the King of

Spain. Nay, so low did they stoop as to send ambassadors to the Emperor offering to become his tributaries, and to write letters to the Pope, full of submission and servility, in order to move his compassion. To such abasement were they brought in four days' time by what was in reality only a half-defeat. For on their flight after the battle of Vailà only about a half of their forces were engaged, and one of their two *provedditori* escaped to Verona with five and twenty thousand men, horse and foot. So that had there been a spark of valour in Venice, or any soundness in her military system, she might easily have renewed her armies, and again confronting fortune have stood prepared either to conquer, or, if she must fall, to fall more gloriously; and at any rate might have obtained for herself more honourable terms. But a pusillanimous spirit, occasioned by the defects of her ordinances in so far as they relate to war, caused her to lose at once her courage and her dominions. And so will it always happen with those who behave like the Venetians. For when men grow insolent in good fortune, and abject in evil, the fault lies in themselves and in the character of their training, which, when slight and frivolous, assimilates them to itself; but when otherwise, makes them of another temper, and giving them better acquaintance with the world, causes them to be less disheartened by misfortunes and less elated by success.

And while this is true of individual men, it holds good also of a concourse of men living together in one republic, who will arrive at that measure of perfection which the institutions of their state permit. And although I have already said on another occasion that a good militia is the foundation of all states, and where that is wanting there can neither be good laws, nor aught else that is good, it seems to me not superfluous to say the same again; because in reading this history of Titus Livius the necessity of such a foundation is made apparent in every page. It is likewise shown that no army can be good unless it be thoroughly trained and exercised, and that this can only be the case with an army raised from your own subjects. For as a state is not and cannot always be at war, you must have opportunity to train your army in times of peace; but this, having regard to the cost, you can only have in respect of your own subjects.

When Camillus, as already related, went forth to meet the Etruscans, his soldiers on seeing the great army of their enemy, were filled with fear, thinking themselves too weak to withstand its onset.

This untoward disposition being reported to Camillus, he showed himself to his men and by visiting their tents, and conversing with this and the other among them, was able to remove their misgivings; and, finally, without other word of command, he bade them '*each do his part as he had learned and been accustomed.*' Now, anyone who well considers the methods followed by Camillus, and the words spoken by him to encourage his soldiers to face their enemy, will perceive that these words and methods could never have been used with an army which had not been trained and disciplined in time of peace as well as of war. For no captain can trust to untrained soldiers or look for good service at their hands; nay, though he were another Hannibal, with such troops his defeat were certain. For, as a captain cannot be present everywhere while a battle is being fought, unless he have taken all measures beforehand to render his men of the same temper as himself, and have made sure that they perfectly understand his orders and arrangements, he will inevitably be destroyed.

When a city therefore is armed and trained as Rome was, and when its citizens have daily opportunity, both singly and together, to make trial of their valour and learn what fortune can effect, it will always happen, that at all times, and whether circumstances be adverse or favourable, they will remain of unaltered courage and preserve the same noble bearing. But when its citizens are unpractised in arms, and trust not to their own valour but wholly to the arbitration of Fortune, they will change their temper as she changes, and offer always the same example of behaviour as was given by the Venetians.

4

THOMAS HOBBES, LEVIATHAN

INTRODUCTION

Of Thomas Hobbes' several contributions to philosophical inquiry, probably his most challenging and certainly his most influential is *Leviathan* (1651)—a stunning account of the state of nature as 'war of all against all' and unabashed justification of absolute sovereign power.

Hobbes was born on Good Friday 1588 in Malmesbury, Wiltshire, the son of a local clergyman. He went to Oxford at fifteen, where he studied Aristotle and scholastic logic, and upon graduation in 1608 was recommended by the Principal of Magdalen Hall to Sir William Cavendish to be tutor and travelling companion to his eldest son (later second Earl of Devonshire). Remarkably for someone who would go on to be so prolific, in the next thirty years Hobbes published nothing but a translation of Thucydides' *History of the Peloponnesian War*. These were not, however, wasted years: in addition to learning from Thucydides the 'enduring lesson' that Athenian democracy 'was ultimately incapable of imposing the unity of organization and the continuity of purpose required for the successful prosecution of policies needed for the long-term preservation of the commonwealth', Hobbes obtained insight into practical politics through his continuous contact with men of great power in the state, including the Cavendishes and Francis Bacon (for whom Hobbes had acted as

1. J.C.A. Gaskin, 'Introduction,' in Thomas Hobbes, *Leviathan*, ed. J.C.A. Gaskin (Oxford: Oxford University Press, 1996), xv.

secretary in the early 1620s). Aware that civil war was brewing, Hobbes fled England for Paris in 1640, where he associated with mathematicians, scientists, and Royalist refugees. King Charles I was put on trial in England and executed on 30 January 1650. Hobbes published *Leviathan* the following year, went home, made submission to Cromwell's Council of State, and swore allegiance to the new government. At the Restoration in 1660, Charles II, evidently willing to let bygones be bygones, invited Hobbes to court, awarding him a pension of £100 per annum. In the context of the plague and Great Fire of 1666, however, the House of Commons ordered an inquiry into atheistical writings, Hobbes being specifically mentioned, which terrified the old philosopher, and he retired to the countryside to be sheltered by the Cavendish family at Chatsworth. He died in 1679 at the age of ninety-one. After his death, the University of Oxford condemned his works and had them burned in the quadrangle of the Bodleian Library.

To understand Hobbes' political philosophy we first need to understand his view of human nature. Humans are, he says, complex physical systems, or natural automata, endowed with sense, reason, and passions. Motion of thought or imagination toward something, we call *desire*; and motion away from something, we call *aversion*. Through deliberation, namely the succession of contrary appetites, we arrive upon final appetite or aversion prior to taking (or refraining from taking) action—this is the *will*. This mechanical and deterministic process leaves little room for authentic free-will in the sense of unconstrained voluntariness: 'a man can no more say that he will will, than he will will will, and so make an infinite repetition of the word will,' says Hobbes. Happiness, nevertheless, is found in prospering and continuing to prosper through continued and renewed satisfactions of the will. This means that there is no such thing as static happiness, and no escape from continual striving in a world in which all other men are continually striving too.

A fundamental plank of Hobbes' thinking is that all men are naturally equal. Hobbes is no egalitarian so it is important to appreciate what he means by this. He accepts, as any unbiased observer would be bound to, that there may be found one man manifestly stronger in body or of quicker mind than another. He also accepts that men may reach differing levels of wisdom in different fields, although he considers that this is simply an effect of some men spending more time on certain matters than others. What is most important, however, is that none of the differences between men amount to very much. There is nothing that one man can claim that another cannot make claim as much as he. Crucially, Hobbes observes, even the weakest has strength enough to kill the strongest, either by secret machination or by confederacy with others.

It is because we are all, in the most significant respects, broadly equal in ability that we cannot—in a state of nature—be at peace. In the first place, natural equality leads to competition, because one man (whether alone or in conjunction with others) is always capable of being displaced by others ('invaders'), not only of the fruits of his labour, but also of his life or liberty, especially if he has established some favourable possession or position for himself. It gets worse than that, however, for humankind is further troubled by what Hobbes refers to as 'diffidence' (a word retaining here much of the meaning of its Latin root, *diffidentia*, or 'distrust'): men are distrustful of one another, and even those who would be content to live within modest bounds fear that, if they do not act first, they will remain vulnerable to attack; in these circumstances, the natural reaction is to take preemptive measures and, by striking first, to expand dominion over those who might otherwise pose a threat. Finally, men fall to war about 'glory': they want to be valued by others at the same rate as they value themselves, and when that fails to occur, they extract recognition from their contemnors by harming them, and from onlookers by making an example.

Competition, diffidence, and glory are the hallmarks of the state of nature, which is a state of 'perpetual war of all against all', and in which the life of man is 'solitary, poor, nasty, brutish, and short'. In such a state there is no place for industry, because the fruit thereof is uncertain; there is no culture of the earth; no navigation and no use of such commodities as may be imported by sea; no building of comfortable homes; no knowledge of the world; no account of time; no arts; no letters; and no society.

We are brought out of the state of nature by means of a 'covenant' between men whereby each agrees with the others to choose a sovereign, or a sovereign body, to exercise authority over them all. Once the sovereign has been chosen the citizens are to retain only such rights as the sovereign thinks fit to grant, subject to very limited exceptions. It is important to note that this is not a covenant between the citizens and the sovereign but between the citizens and each other; it does not, therefore, bind or otherwise impose obligations on that sovereign. The sovereign's powers are unlimited and indivisible: all subjects, including any previously dissenting minorities, must submit to the sovereign that has been declared by the majority, or else justly be destroyed; the sovereign is the sole judge of what is necessary for peace, including what opinions and doctrines may or may not be allowable as conducing thereto; the laws of property are entirely a matter for the sovereign, since property rights are created in the first place by the state; and, in general, the sovereign may legislate and govern as it sees fit. There is no right of rebellion under any circumstances. The sole right preserved by the subject is the right of self-preservation—the right to self-defence (even against the sovereign), the right to refuse to fight and lay down his life for the sovereign, and the right to protect himself when the sovereign is no longer able to do so.

This is not as unattractive a condition as it appears on first glance. First, the sovereign provides to the subject the security without which his life and liberty and the fruits of all his labour would be constantly exposed to predation. It is worthwhile observing that if the sovereign fails in this basic task—as, arguably Charles I had done in England prior to the ascension of Oliver Cromwell—then the subject will be discharged and free to enter into a new covenant instituting a new ruler. Secondly, while the subject has no rights against the sovereign except those that the sovereign concedes to him, he remains free insofar as the sovereign has not enacted laws that interfere with his conduct. The absolute authority of the sovereign is authority *in potentia*; whether and to what extent it is, in fact, exercised over particular aspects of life or fields of activity is a different matter. And finally, although Hobbes is clear that the sovereign is entitled to legislate on all matters, it is also open to the sovereign to do so sparingly in order to leave as much latitude to its subjects as is consistent with peace and security. 'The greatest liberty of the subjects,' Hobbes explained, 'depends on silence of the law.'

A final question arises as to why absolutism should be any less fearful to the common man than anarchy: John Locke would later ask, famously, why men should take care to avoid mischiefs done by polecats and foxes but be content to be devoured by lions. This is, however, to wilfully turn away from one central justification for absolute sovereignty: when sovereignty is absolute, the interests of the sovereign are identical with those of his subjects—he is richer if they are richer, he is stronger if they are stronger, and he is at peace if they are at peace. It is not strictly speaking necessary that the absolute authority take the form of monarchy: Hobbes expressly conceives of absolute aristocracy and absolute democracy, and, as we know, Hobbes himself came to terms with the revolutionary government under Cromwell after the demise of Charles I. But monarchy, in Hobbes' view, had several additional benefits. The monarch, in contrast to an assembly, can receive counsel from whomsoever he chooses; his resolutions are subject to no inconstancy other than those of human nature; he cannot disagree with himself out of envy, or interest, and so precipitate civil war; and whereas the favourites of assemblies are many, the favourites of monarchs are few.

Hobbes' philosophy, I suggest, has a particular value for the modern man. We live in an era where it appears to many that the democratic regimes have neglected many of the basic security concerns of their citizens, and have been compromised by unprincipled bartering for votes, or have been 'captured' by special interests. Of course, nobody is seriously suggesting that we either can, or should, make a return to seventeenth-century absolutism. But it is worthwhile revisiting, on occasion, the roots of our own particular prejudices and asking, with Hobbes, what is the true basis and nature of our constitutional and political system, whether there are other better options, and how we can bring the interests of our rulers better into line with the interests of the people over whom they purport to rule.

PART I, CHAPTER XIII

OF THE NATURAL CONDITION OF MANKIND AS CONCERNING THEIR FELICITY AND MISERY

Nature hath made men so equal in the faculties of body and mind as that, though there be found one man sometimes manifestly stronger in body or of quicker mind than another, yet when all is reckoned together the difference between man and man is not so considerable as that one man can thereupon claim to himself any benefit to which another may not pretend as well as he. For as to the strength of body, the weakest has strength enough to kill the strongest, either by secret machination or by confederacy with others that are in the same danger with himself.

And as to the faculties of the mind, setting aside the arts grounded upon words, and especially that skill of proceeding upon general and infallible rules, called science, which very few have and but in few things, as being not a native faculty born with us, nor attained, as prudence, while we look after somewhat else, I find yet a greater equality amongst men than that of strength. For prudence is but experience, which equal time equally bestows on all men in those things they equally apply themselves unto. That which may perhaps make such equality incredible is but a vain conceit of one's own wisdom, which almost all men think they have in a greater degree than the vulgar; that is, than all men but themselves, and a few others, whom by fame, or for concurring with themselves, they approve. For such is the nature of men that howsoever they may acknowledge many others to be more witty, or more eloquent or more learned, yet they will hardly believe there be many so wise as themselves; for they see their own wit at hand, and other men's at a distance. But this proveth rather that men are in that point equal, than unequal. For there is not ordinarily a greater sign of the equal distribution of anything than that every man is contented with his share.

FROM EQUALITY PROCEEDS DIFFIDENCE

From this equality of ability ariseth equality of hope in the attaining of our ends. And therefore if any two men desire the same thing, which nevertheless they cannot both enjoy, they become enemies; and in the way to their end (which is principally their own conservation, and sometimes their delectation only) endeavour to destroy or subdue one another. And from hence it comes to pass that where an invader hath no more to fear than another man's single power, if one plant, sow, build, or possess a convenient seat, others may probably be expected to come prepared with forces united to dispossess and deprive him, not only of the fruit of his labour, but also of his life or liberty. And the invader again is in the like danger of another.

And from this diffidence of one another, there is no way for any man to secure himself so reasonable as anticipation; that is, by force, or wiles, to master the persons of all men he can so long till he see no other power great enough to endanger him: and this is no more than his own conservation requireth, and is generally allowed. Also, because there be some that, taking pleasure in contemplating their own power in the acts of conquest, which they pursue farther than their security requires, if others, that otherwise would be glad to be at ease within modest bounds, should not by invasion increase their power, they would not be able, long time, by standing only on their defence, to subsist. And by consequence, such augmentation of dominion over men being necessary to a man's conservation, it ought to be allowed him.

Again, men have no pleasure (but on the contrary a great deal of grief) in keeping company where there is no power able to overawe them all. For every man looketh that his companion should value him at the same rate he sets upon himself, and upon all signs of contempt or undervaluing naturally endeavours, as far as he dares (which amongst them that have no common power to keep them in quiet is far enough to make them destroy each other), to extort a greater value from his contemners, by damage; and from others, by the example.

So that in the nature of man, we find three principal causes of quarrel. First, competition; secondly, diffidence; thirdly, glory.

The first maketh men invade for gain; the second, for safety; and the third, for reputation. The first use violence, to make themselves masters of other men's persons, wives, children, and cattle; the second, to defend them; the third, for trifles, as a word, a smile, a different opinion, and any other sign of undervalue, either direct in their persons or by reflection in their kindred, their friends, their nation, their profession, or their name.

Hereby it is manifest that during the time men live without a common power to keep them all in awe, they are in that condition which is called war; and such a war as is of every man against every man. For war consisteth not in battle only, or the act of fighting, but in a tract of time, wherein the will to contend by battle is sufficiently known; and therefore the notion of time is to be considered in the nature of war, as it is in the nature of weather. For as the nature of foul weather lieth not in a shower or two of rain, but in an inclination thereto of many days together: so the nature of war consisteth not in actual fighting, but in the known disposition thereto during all the time there is no assurance to the contrary. All other time is peace.

THE INCOMMODITIES OF SUCH A WAR

Whatsoever therefore is consequent to a time of war, where every man is enemy to every man, the same consequent to the time wherein men live without other security than what their own strength and their own invention shall furnish them withal. In such condition there is no place for industry, because the fruit thereof is uncertain: and consequently no culture of the earth; no navigation, nor use of the commodities that may be imported by sea; no commodious building; no instruments of moving and removing such things as require much force; no knowledge of the face of the earth; no account of time; no arts; no letters; no society; and which is worst of all, continual fear, and danger of violent death; and the life of man, solitary, poor, nasty, brutish, and short.

It may seem strange to some man that has not well weighed these things that Nature should thus dissociate and render men apt to invade and destroy one another: and he may therefore, not trusting to this inference, made from the passions, desire perhaps to have the same confirmed by experience. Let him therefore consider with himself: when taking a journey, he arms himself and seeks to go well accompanied; when going to sleep, he locks his doors; when even in his house he locks his chests; and this when he knows there be laws and public officers, armed, to revenge all injuries shall be done him; what opinion he has of his fellow subjects, when he rides armed; of his fellow citizens, when he locks his doors; and of his children, and servants, when he locks his chests. Does he not there as much accuse mankind by his actions as I do by my words? But neither of us accuse man's nature in it. The desires, and other passions of man, are in themselves no sin. No more are the actions that proceed from those passions till they know a law that forbids them; which till laws be made they cannot know, nor can any law be made till they have agreed upon the person that shall make it.

It may peradventure be thought there was never such a time nor condition of war as this; and I believe it was never generally so, over all the world: but there are many places where they live so now. For the savage people in many places of America, except the government of small families, the concord whereof dependeth on natural lust, have no government at all, and live at this day in that brutish manner, as I said before. Howsoever, it may be perceived what manner of life there would be, where there were no common power to fear, by the manner of life which men that have formerly lived under a peaceful government use to degenerate into a civil war.

But though there had never been any time wherein particular men were in a condition of war one against another, yet in all times kings and persons of sovereign authority, because of their independency, are in continual jealousies, and in the state and posture of gladiators, having their weapons pointing, and their eyes fixed on one another; that is, their forts, garrisons, and guns upon the frontiers of their kingdoms, and continual spies upon their neighbours, which is a posture of war. But because they uphold thereby the industry of their subjects, there does not follow from it that misery which accompanies the liberty of particular men.

IN SUCH A WAR, NOTHING IS UNJUST

To this war of every man against every man, this also is consequent; that nothing can be unjust. The notions of right and wrong, justice and injustice, have there no place. Where there is no common power, there is no law; where no law, no injustice. Force and fraud are in war the two cardinal virtues. Justice and injustice are none of the faculties neither of the body nor mind. If they were, they might be in a man that were alone in the world, as well as his senses and passions. They are qualities that relate to men in society, not in solitude. It is consequent also to the same condition that there be no propriety, no dominion, no mine and thine distinct; but only that to be every man's that he can get, and for so long as he can keep it. And thus much for the ill condition which man by mere nature is actually placed in; though with a possibility to come out of it, consisting partly in the passions, partly in his reason.

THE PASSIONS THAT INCLINE MEN TO PEACE

The passions that incline men to peace are: fear of death; desire of such things as are necessary to commodious living; and a hope by their industry to obtain them. And reason suggesteth convenient articles of peace upon which men may be drawn to agreement. These articles are they which otherwise are called the laws of nature, whereof I shall speak more particularly in the two following chapters.

PART II, CHAPTER XIX

OF THE SEVERAL KINDS OF COMMONWEALTH BY INSTITUTION, AND OF SUCCESSION TO THE SOVEREIGN POWER

The difference of Commonwealths consisteth in the difference of the sovereign, or the person representative of all and every one of the multitude. And because the sovereignty is either in one man, or in an assembly of more than one; and into that assembly either every man hath right to enter, or not every one, but certain men distinguished from the rest; it is manifest there can be but three kinds of Commonwealth. For the representative must needs be one man, or more; and if more, then it is the assembly of all, or but of a part. When the representative is one man, then is the Commonwealth a monarchy; when an assembly of all that will come together, then it is a democracy, or popular Commonwealth; when an assembly of a part only, then it is called an aristocracy. Other kind of Commonwealth there can be none: for either one, or more, or all, must have the sovereign power (which I have shown to be indivisible) entire.

There be other names of government in the histories and books of policy; as tyranny and oligarchy; but they are not the names of other forms of government, but of the same forms misliked. For they that are discontented under monarchy call it tyranny; and they that are displeased with aristocracy call it oligarchy: so also, they which find themselves grieved under a democracy call it anarchy, which signifies want of government; and yet I think no man believes that want of government is any new kind of government: nor by the same reason ought they to believe that the government is of one kind when they like it, and another when they mislike it or are oppressed by the governors.

It is manifest that men who are in absolute liberty may, if they please, give authority to one man to represent them every one, as well as give such authority to any assembly of men whatsoever; and consequently may subject themselves, if they think good, to a monarch as absolutely as to other representative. Therefore, where there is already erected a sovereign power, there can be no other representative of the same people, but only to certain particular ends, by the sovereign limited. For that were to erect two sovereigns; and every man to have his person represented by two actors that, by opposing one another, must needs divide that power, which (if men will live in peace) is indivisible; and thereby reduce the multitude into the condition of war, contrary to the end for which all sovereignty is instituted. And therefore as it is absurd to think that a sovereign assembly, inviting the people of their dominion to send up their deputies with power to make known their advice or desires should therefore hold such deputies, rather than themselves, for the absolute representative of the people; so it is absurd also to think the same in a monarchy. And I know not how this so manifest a truth should of late be so little observed: that in a monarchy he that had the sovereignty from a descent of six hundred years was alone called sovereign, had the title of Majesty from every one of his subjects, and was unquestionably taken by them for their king, was notwithstanding never considered as their representative; that name without contradiction passing for the title of those men which at his command were sent up by the people to carry their petitions and give him, if he permitted it, their advice. Which may serve as an admonition for those that are the true and absolute representative of a people, to instruct men in the nature of that office, and to take heed how they admit of any other general representation upon any occasion whatsoever, if they mean to discharge the trust committed to them.

The difference between these three kinds of Commonwealth consisteth, not in the difference of power, but in the difference of convenience or aptitude to produce the peace and security of the people; for which end they were instituted. And to compare monarchy with the other two, we may observe: first, that whosoever beareth the person of the people, or is one of that assembly that bears it, beareth also his own natural person. And though he be careful in his politic person to procure the common interest, yet he is more, or no less, careful to procure the private good of himself, his family, kindred and friends; and for the most part, if the public interest chance to cross the private, he prefers the private: for the passions of men are commonly more potent than their reason. From whence it follows that where the public and private interest are most closely united, there is the public most advanced. Now in monarchy the private interest is the same with the public. The riches, power, and honour of a monarch arise only from the riches, strength, and reputation of his subjects. For no king can be rich, nor glorious, nor secure, whose subjects are either poor, or contemptible, or too weak through want, or dissension, to maintain a war against their enemies; whereas in a democracy, or aristocracy, the public prosperity confers not so much to the private fortune of one that is corrupt, or ambitious, as doth many times a perfidious advice, a treacherous action, or a civil war.

Secondly, that a monarch receiveth counsel of whom, when, and where he pleaseth; and consequently may hear the opinion of men versed in the matter about which he deliberates, of what rank or quality soever, and as long before the time of action and with as much secrecy as he will. But when a sovereign assembly has need of counsel, none are admitted but such as have a right thereto from the beginning; which for the most part are of those who have been versed more in the acquisition of wealth than of knowledge, and are to give their advice in long discourses which may, and do commonly, excite men to action, but not govern them in it. For the understanding is by the flame of the passions never enlightened, but dazzled: nor is there any place or time wherein an assembly can receive counsel secrecy, because of their own multitude.

Thirdly, that the resolutions of a monarch are subject to no other inconstancy than that of human nature; but in assemblies, besides that of nature, there ariseth an inconstancy from the number. For the absence of a few that would have the resolution, once taken, continue firm (which may happen by security, negligence, or private impediments), or the diligent appearance of a few of the contrary opinion, undoes today all that was concluded yesterday.

Fourthly, that a monarch cannot disagree with himself, out of envy or interest; but an assembly may; and that to such a height as may produce a civil war.

Fifthly, that in monarchy there is this inconvenience; that any subject, by the power of one man, for the enriching of a favourite or flatterer, may be deprived of all he possesseth; which I confess is a great and inevitable inconvenience. But the same may as well happen where the sovereign power is in an assembly: for their power is the same; and they are as subject to evil counsel, and to be seduced by orators, as a monarch by flatterers; and becoming one another's flatterers, serve one another's covetousness and ambition by turns. And whereas the favourites of monarchs are few, and they have none else to advance but their own kindred; the favourites of an assembly are many, and the kindred much more numerous than of any monarch. Besides, there is no favourite of a monarch which cannot as well succour his friends as hurt his enemies: but orators, that is to say, favourites of sovereign assemblies, though they have great power to hurt, have little to save. For to accuse requires less eloquence (such is man's nature) than to excuse; and condemnation, than absolution, more resembles justice.

Sixthly, that it is an inconvenience in monarchy that the sovereignty may descend upon an infant, or one that cannot discern between good and evil: and consisteth in this, that the use of his power must be in the hand of another man, or of some assembly of men, which are to govern by his right and in his name as curators and protectors of his person and authority. But to say there is inconvenience in putting the use of the sovereign power into the hand of a man, or an assembly of men, is to say that all government is more inconvenient than confusion and civil war. And therefore all the danger that can be pretended must arise from the contention of those that, for an office of so great honour and profit, may become competitors. To make it appear that this inconvenience proceedeth not from that form of government we call monarchy, we are to consider that the precedent monarch hath appointed who shall have the tuition of his infant successor, either expressly by testament, or tacitly by not controlling the custom in that case received: and then such inconvenience, if it happen, is to be attributed, not to the monarchy, but to the ambition and injustice of the subjects, which in all kinds of government, where the people are not well instructed in their duty and the rights of sovereignty, is the same. Or else the precedent monarch hath not at all taken order for such tuition; and then the law of nature hath provided this sufficient rule, that the tuition shall be in him that hath by nature most interest in the preservation of the authority of the infant, and to whom least benefit can accrue by his death or diminution. For seeing every man by nature seeketh his own benefit and promotion, to put an infant into the power of those that can promote themselves by his destruction or damage is not tuition, but treachery. So that sufficient provision being taken against all just quarrel about the government under a child, if any contention arise to the disturbance of the public peace, it is not to be attributed to the form of monarchy, but to the ambition of subjects and ignorance of their duty. On the other side, there is no great Commonwealth, the sovereignty whereof is in a great assembly, which is not, as to consultations of peace, and war, and making of laws, in the same condition as if the government were in a child. For as a child wants the judgment to dissent from counsel given him, and is thereby necessitated to take the advice of them, or him, to whom he is committed; so an assembly wanteth the liberty to dissent from the counsel of the major part, be it good or bad. And as a child has need of a tutor, or protector, to preserve his person and authority; so also in great Commonwealths the sovereign assembly, in all great dangers and troubles, have need of *custodes libertatis*; that is, of dictators, or protectors of their authority; which are as much as temporary monarchs to whom for a time they may commit the entire exercise of their power; and have, at the end of that time, been oftener deprived thereof than infant kings by their protectors, regents, or any other tutors.

JOHN LOCKE, SECOND TREATISE OF GOVERNMENT & A LETTER CONCERNING TOLERATION

INTRODUCTION

If anyone is considered to be the philosophical figurehead of early liberalism, it is John Locke (1632-1704). Locke's work, and the work of those who followed in his footsteps, is for this reason of the first importance to the Western world even today, since we also march (or believe we march) under the banner of liberalism. To really understand Locke, then, is to understand something of ourselves. Likewise, it is through exploring what in Locke we find unacceptable, or simply unfathomable, that we can begin to learn how far the current era is from liberalism in its traditional forms, and how many of the political attitudes that we are taught to believe today come from quite different origins altogether.

Locke was the son of a Puritan who fought for Parliament in the English Civil War. Going up to Oxford in the time of Cromwell, he studied medicine, which brought him into contact with Lord Shaftesbury, the radical peer, when Shaftesbury needed surgery for an abscess of the liver. Shaftesbury became Locke's patron and converted him to liberalism. When Shaftesbury briefly occupied the role of Lord Chancellor, Locke followed him into government as secretary to the Board of Trade. Determined, however, to prevent King Charles II's openly Roman Catholic brother, the Duke of York (later King James II), from ascending the throne, Shaftesbury promoted the 'exclusion bill' that, rejected by the House of Lords, led to him falling out of favour with Charles and fleeing to Holland, taking Locke with him. When James II came to power he proceeded to promote Roman Catholics to positions of authority in the kingdom, which gave rise to mounting opposition. On the invitation of a group of English nobles, William of Orange, a nephew of James who had married James' daughter, Mary, arrived in England with an army, and James fled. The Parliament convened by William declared that James had abdicated, decided that Mary should be Queen and William rule alongside her, and passed a Declaration of Right (restated in statutory form in the Bill of Rights). This 'Glorious Revolution' of 1688 allowed Locke to return to England and take up his post again at the Board of Trade. This was the period in which he published the works for which he is now best known, all of which appeared in quick succession: *An Essay Concerning Human Understanding* (1689), the *Two Treatises of Civil Government* (1689), and *A Letter Concerning Toleration* (1689). He died on 28 October 1704. But his ideas would live on—most notably in the achievements of the Founding Fathers of the United States of America.

Locke's political philosophy, like that of Hobbes, rests on his concept of the 'state of nature'. Locke's 'state of nature', however, has very little in common with Hobbes' perpetual war of all against all. In his *Second Treatise of Government* he defines the 'state of nature' as the 'state all men are naturally in, and that is, a state of perfect freedom to order their actions, and dispose of their possessions and persons, as they think fit, within the bounds of the law of nature, without asking leave, or depending upon the will of any other man.' Such 'perfect freedom' to act without obtaining anyone else's consent is a state of *liberty*, but it is not a state of *licence*. The state of nature is constituted by men living together without a common superior on earth and with no authority to judge between them, but living nevertheless 'according to reason'; while man in the state of nature is free to act independently of other men, he nevertheless remains subject to the 'law of nature'.

In fact, it is precisely through the exercise of reason that we are able to identify the natural law and its precepts. 'The state of nature has a law of nature to govern it, which obliges every one,' says Locke, 'and reason, which is that law, teaches all mankind, who will but consult it, that being all equal and independent, no one ought to harm another in his life, health, liberty, or possessions.' Locke's reasoning process and the outlines of his law of nature are, broadly speaking, as follows. The starting point is that we are born free to dispose of our persons and possessions as we see fit, independently of other men. We are also, Locke added, born in a state of equality, where we all have the same faculties and advantages of nature and where all power and jurisdiction is reciprocal. Since we are, however, created beings, and therefore the property of our creator, the law of nature requires us to preserve ourselves; moreover, except when our own preservation is at stake, we ought as far as we can to preserve the rest of mankind, and 'may not, unless it be to do justice on an offender, take away, or impair the life, or what tends to the preservation of the life, the liberty, health, limb, or goods of another.'

The state of nature nevertheless gives rise to inconveniences. The principal difficulty, of course, is that in the state of nature each man is judge in his own cause. As a result, men come together to form governments to administer settled law and provide judges to adjudicate impartially upon it. They do this by way of a 'social contract', through which the people constitute themselves as a people and put themselves under a government. Crucially—and this is where Locke's account differs fundamentally from that of Hobbes—the government is a party to the contract: it is bound by its terms and can justly be resisted if it fails to abide by them.

It is no surprise that Locke is widely considered to be the founding father of political liberalism and, indeed, there is much in Locke that remains widely accepted today. We share with him the view that government's legitimacy originates in the people. We share with him the view that there are natural laws which underpin the best of our man-made laws and serve as inspiration for making those man-made laws better. And we generally agree that men are equal, at least in their political rights, and that we should not impair the lives, liberties, and property of others, except in effecting punishment according to the law.

What is less often acknowledged is just how far we have come from

Lockean first principles. In some respects this is palpable to anyone who applies their mind not only to what is said but also to what is presumed: Locke's support for democracy and majority rule, for example, was premised upon the assumption—one that was widely held until the nineteenth century—that women and men without property would be excluded from the franchise, for reasons that Locke would have thought obvious but which appear for the most part unfathomable to us today. In other respects, however, the differences are subtle and manifold, albeit no less profound. Where Locke had argued that the government is not entitled to take from any man any part of his property without his consent, and indeed that the very point of government is the preservation of men's property, we must remember that in his era there was no income tax, no inheritance tax, and no purchase or value-added tax. Locke would, no doubt, have looked askance on the onerous tax burden borne by working men and women in modern Western democracies—levied in order to advance a whole range of social projects that have little or nothing to do with protecting life, liberty, or property. Locke would have been equally perturbed, one would imagine, by the restrictions imposed on our liberties by new and invasive forms of social control, from surveillance and censorship to secret courts and speech crimes. We are discomfited by certain of Locke's blind spots; he would have been equally discomfited by many of ours.

Locke's work remains, nevertheless, of the greatest significance today, not least by virtue of his having identified where the parameters of liberty must lie. What is crucial is the distinction he draws between liberty and licence. Liberty is the right to dispose of oneself and one's possessions without interference; licence, on the other hand, means stepping outside the laws of nature by engaging in activities that 'take away, or impair the life, or what tends to the preservation of the life, the liberty, health, limb, or goods of another' beyond what may be strictly necessary in the pursuit of justice or self-preservation. In this view, we are entitled to our lives and property, but we are not entitled to impair (or engage in activities that tend to impair) the lives, health, or property of others. It can readily be seen that this in practice grants the most valuable of rights—the right to live free from interference—while at the same time imposing the most stringent of responsibilities in our treatment of others.

Relatedly, while a state ought to practise tolerance, it ought not to do so naively or recklessly. The state is not obliged to tolerate opinions contrary to human society or contrary to the rules which are necessary to the preservation of civil society: this would rule out anarchism and revolutionary socialism. The state is not obliged to tolerate those who arrogate to themselves or their group, albeit secretly, some peculiar power or privilege, by holding that they do not need to keep promises to heretics or that dominion of all things belongs only to themselves; nor is the state obliged to tolerate those who challenge civil and political authority on the basis or pretence of religion. The state is not obliged to tolerate those who are themselves intolerant. It is not obliged to tolerate those who owe loyalty to a foreign sovereign. And it is not obliged to tolerate atheists.

Locke's greatest value, for the modern man, is that he reminds us, as citizens, of our native authority—that governments are entitled to rule by virtue of the consent on the people and in accordance with the terms of the social contract under which they take office. When a ruling cabal violates that contract it declares war on its people which entitles that people to take steps reconstitute the government. This takes the form of a revolution that is also a renovation: the purpose is to return government to its proper position so that it may exercise its powers within the proper bounds; it is not intended that revolution be instigated merely to advance particular social and political agendas. But it is revolution all the same, and there may come a time when it is not only justified, but also necessary.

Second Treatise of Government

Chapter II

OF THE STATE OF NATURE

Sect. 4. To understand political power right, and derive it from its original, we must consider what state all men are naturally in, and that is a state of perfect freedom to order their actions, and dispose of their possessions and persons, as they think fit, within the bounds of the law of nature, without asking leave, or depending upon the will of any other man.

A state also of equality, wherein all the power and jurisdiction is reciprocal, no one having more than another; there being nothing more evident, than that creatures of the same species and rank, promiscuously born to all the same advantages of nature, and the use of the same faculties, should also be equal one amongst another without subordination or subjection, unless the lord and master of them all should, by any manifest declaration of his will, set one above another, and confer on him, by an evident and clear appointment, an undoubted right to dominion and sovereignty.

Sect. 5. This equality of men by nature, the judicious Hooker looks upon as so evident in itself, and beyond all question, that he makes it the foundation of that obligation to mutual love amongst men on which he builds the duties they owe one another, and from whence he derives the great maxims of justice and charity. His words are:

The like natural inducement hath brought men to know that it is no less their duty, to love others than themselves; for seeing those things which are equal, must needs all have one measure; if I cannot but wish to receive good, even as much at every man's hands, as any man can wish unto his own soul, how should I look to have any part of my desire herein satisfied, unless myself be careful to satisfy the like desire, which is undoubtedly in other men, being of one and the same nature? To have any thing offered them repugnant to this desire, must needs in all respects grieve them as much as me; so that if I do harm, I must look to suffer, there being no reason that others should shew greater measure of love to me, than they have by me shewed unto them: my desire therefore to be loved of my equals in nature as much as possible may be, imposeth upon me a natural duty of bearing to them-ward fully the like affection; from which relation of equality between ourselves and them that are as ourselves, what several rules and canons natural reason hath drawn, for direction of life, no man is ignorant, Eccl. Pol. Lib. 1.

Sect. 6. But though this be a state of liberty, yet it is not a state of licence: though man in that state have an uncontrollable liberty to dispose of his person or possessions, yet he has not liberty to destroy himself, or so much as any creature in his possession, but where some nobler use than its bare preservation calls for it. The state of nature has a law of nature to govern it, which obliges every one; and reason, which is that law, teaches all mankind, who will but consult it, that being all equal and independent, no one ought to harm another in his life, health, liberty, or possessions: for men being all the workmanship of one omnipotent, and infinitely wise maker; all the servants of one sovereign master, sent into the world by his order, and about his business; they are his property, whose workmanship they are, made to last during his, not one another's pleasure; and being furnished with like faculties, sharing all in one community of nature, there cannot be supposed any such subordination among us that may authorise us to destroy one another, as if we were made for one another's uses, as the inferior ranks of creatures are for our's. Everyone, as he is bound to preserve himself, and not to quit his station wilfully, so by the like reason, when his own preservation comes not in competition, ought he, as much as he can, to preserve the rest of mankind, and may not, unless it be to do justice on an offender, take away, or impair the life, or what tends to the preservation of the life, the liberty, health, limb, or goods of another. ...

A LETTER CONCERNING TOLERATION

...But some may ask: 'What if the magistrate should enjoin anything by his authority that appears unlawful to the conscience of a private person?' I answer that, if government be faithfully administered and the counsels of the magistrates be indeed directed to the public good, this will seldom happen. But if, perhaps, it do so fall out, I say, that such a private person is to abstain from the action that he judges unlawful, and he is to undergo the punishment which it is not unlawful for him to bear. For the private judgment of any person concerning a law enacted in political matters, for the public good, does not take away the obligation of that law, nor deserve a dispensation. But if the law, indeed, be concerning things that lie not within the verge of the magistrate's authority (as, for example, that the people, or any party amongst them, should be compelled to embrace a strange religion, and join in the worship and ceremonies of another church), men are not in these cases obliged by that law, against their consciences. For the political society is instituted for no other end, but only to secure every man's possession of the things of this life. The care of each man's soul and of the things of heaven, which neither does belong to the commonwealth nor can be subjected to it, is left entirely to every man's self. Thus the safeguard of men's lives and of the things that belong unto this life is the business of the commonwealth; and the preserving of those things unto their owners is the duty of the magistrate. And therefore the magistrate cannot take away these worldly things from this man or party and give them to that; nor change propriety amongst fellow subjects (no not even by a law), for a cause that has no relation to the end of civil government, I mean for their religion, which whether it be true or false does no prejudice to the worldly concerns of their fellow subjects, which are the things that only belong unto the care of the commonwealth.

But what if the magistrate believe such a law as this to be for the public good? I answer: As the private judgment of any particular person, if erroneous, does not exempt him from the obligation of law, so the private judgment (as I may call it) of the magistrate does not give him any new right of imposing laws upon his subjects, which neither was in the constitution of the government granted him, nor ever was in the power of the people to grant, much less if he make it his business to enrich and advance his followers and fellow sectaries with the spoils of others. But what if the magistrate believe that he has a right to make such laws and that they are for the public good, and his subjects believe the contrary? Who shall be judge between them? I answer: God alone. For there is no judge upon earth between the supreme magistrate and the people. God, I say, is the only judge in this case, who will retribute unto every one at the last day according to his deserts; that is, according to his sincerity and uprightness in endeavouring to promote piety, and the public weal, and peace of mankind. But what shall be done in the meanwhile? I answer: The principal and chief care of every one ought to be of his own soul first, and, in the next place, of the public peace; though yet there are very few will think it is peace there, where they see all laid waste.

There are two sorts of contests amongst men, the one managed by law, the other by force; and these are of that nature that where the one ends, the other always begins. But it is not my business to inquire into the power of the magistrate in the different constitutions of nations. I only know what usually happens where controversies arise without a judge to determine them. You will say, then, the magistrate being the stronger will have his will and carry his point. Without doubt; but the question is not here concerning the doubtfulness of the event, but the rule of right.

But to come to particulars. I say, first, no opinions contrary to human society, or to those moral rules which are necessary to the preservation of civil society, are to be tolerated by the magistrate. But of these, indeed, examples in any church are rare. For no sect can easily arrive to such a degree of madness as that it should think fit to teach, for doctrines of religion, such things as manifestly undermine the foundations of society and are, therefore, condemned by the judgment of all mankind; because their own interest, peace, reputation, everything would be thereby endangered.

Another more secret evil, but more dangerous to the commonwealth, is when men arrogate to themselves, and to those of their own sect, some peculiar prerogative covered over with a specious show of deceitful words, but in effect opposite to the civil right of the community. For example: we cannot find any sect that teaches, expressly and openly, that men are not obliged to keep their promise; that princes may be dethroned by those that differ from them in religion; or that the dominion of all things belongs only to themselves. For these things, proposed thus nakedly and plainly, would soon draw on them the eye and hand of the magistrate and awaken all the care of the commonwealth to a watchfulness against the spreading of so dangerous an evil. But, nevertheless, we find those that say the same things in other words. What else do they mean who teach that faith is not to be kept with heretics? Their meaning, forsooth, is that the privilege of breaking faith belongs unto themselves; for they declare all that are not of their communion to be heretics, or at least may declare them so whensoever they think fit. What can be the meaning of their asserting that kings excommunicated forfeit their crowns and kingdoms? It is evident that they thereby arrogate unto themselves the power of deposing kings, because they challenge the power of excommunication, as the peculiar right of their hierarchy. That dominion is founded in grace is also an assertion by which those that maintain it do plainly lay claim to the possession of all things. For they are not so wanting to themselves as not to believe, or at least as not to profess themselves to be the truly pious and faithful. These, therefore, and the like, who attribute unto the faithful, religious, and orthodox, that is, in plain terms, unto themselves, any peculiar privilege or power above other mortals, in civil concernments; or who upon pretence of religion do challenge any manner of authority over such as are not associated with them in their ecclesiastical communion, I say these have no right to be tolerated by the magistrate; as neither those that will not own and teach the duty of tolerating all men in matters of mere religion. For what do all these and the like doctrines signify, but that they may and are ready upon any occasion to seize the government and possess themselves of the estates and fortunes of their fellow subjects; and that they only ask leave to be tolerated by the magistrate so long until they find themselves strong enough to effect it?

Again: that church can have no right to be tolerated by the magistrate which is constituted upon such a bottom that all those who enter into it do thereby ipso facto deliver themselves up to the protection and service of another prince. For by this means the magistrate would give way to the settling of a foreign jurisdiction in his own country and suffer his own people to be listed, as it were, for soldiers against his own government. Nor does the frivolous and fallacious distinction between the court and the church afford any remedy to this inconvenience; especially when both the one and the other are equally subject to the absolute authority of the same person, who has not only power to persuade the members of his church to whatsoever he lists, either as purely religious, or in order thereunto, but can also enjoin it them on pain of eternal fire. It is ridiculous for anyone to profess himself to be a Mahometan only in his religion, but in everything else a faithful subject to a Christian magistrate, whilst at the same time he acknowledges himself bound to yield blind obedience to the Mufti of Constantinople, who himself is entirely obedient to the Ottoman emperor and frames the feigned oracles of that religion according to his pleasure. But this Mahometan living amongst Christians would yet more apparently renounce their government if he acknowledged the same person to be head of his church who is the supreme magistrate in the state.

Lastly, those are not at all to be tolerated who deny the being of a God. Promises, covenants, and oaths, which are the bonds of human society, can have no hold upon an atheist. The taking away of God, though but even in thought, dissolves all; besides also, those that by their atheism undermine and destroy all religion can have no pretence of religion whereupon to challenge the privilege of a toleration. As for other practical opinions, though not absolutely free from all error, if they do not tend to establish domination over others, or civil impunity to the church in which they are taught, there can be no reason why they should not be tolerated. ...

JEAN-JACQUES ROUSSEAU, DISCOURSE ON INEQUALITY & THE SOCIAL CONTRACT

Introduction

'Man is born free; and everywhere he is in chains.' So begins the first book of Rousseau's *The Social Contract* (1762). Many people think that this is a call to arms on behalf of radicals and revolutionaries. The real position is considerably more complicated than that: the freedom to which Rousseau refers is the freedom of the original savage—a freedom to which we are unable to return; the 'chains' are those of man enslaved to wants and desires that cannot be satisfied independently and condemn him to depend upon others. The answer to the conundrum is neither to seek to return to our original freedom nor to accept indefinitely our subjection. Instead we must forge a higher liberty constituted by self-rule through participation in the state: for, says Rousseau, 'the mere impulse of appetite is slavery, while obedience to a law which we prescribe to ourselves is liberty.' This is to be 'forced to be free'. It is Rousseau's greatest gift: a radical politics that addresses not only the political but also the psychological and spiritual roots of our subjection.

Rousseau (1712-78) in his personal life was, admittedly, a dilettante and self-confessed rogue. He was born in Geneva—a state notionally democratic, governed by its adult male citizens, although in fact dominated by a small number of wealthy families exercising power through a twenty-five member council called the *petit conseil* (or 'little council'). Rousseau's father was a watchmaker, and poor, although sufficiently well educated to be able to introduce his son to Plutarch's *Lives of the Noble Greeks and Romans*; his mother, however, died very shortly after his birth. At the age of twelve, Rousseau left school to be apprenticed to various trades, none of which suited, before fleeing several years later to Savoy (a historical territory now shared among France, Italy, and Switzerland), leaving Geneva for good. Rousseau's career, if it can be called that, was a hodgepodge: he was at different times a servant, a secretary, and a tutor; he briefly attended a seminary with the intention of entering the priesthood; and at one time he even occupied the post of secretary to the French ambassador to Venice. His personal life was no less erratic: a lover of aristocratic women, including Madam de Warens—Rousseau called her 'maman' and shared her favours with the steward of her house—he nevertheless took up with a laundress by the name of Thérèse le Vasseur, with whom he had five children (all given up to a foundling hospital), and with whom he lived for the rest of his life. In spite of these vicissitudes, Rousseau's philosophical output was striking and influential, and included his prize-winning essay on the arts and sciences for the Academy of Dijon (1750) and his *Discourse on Inequality* (1754), as well as his incendiary treatises on education and politics, *Emile* and *The Social Contract* (both of which appeared in 1762). Fame, however, came at a price. *Emile*, which set forth the principles of natural theology, enraged the religious orthodoxy. *The Social Contract* was perceived to be still more provocative: it triggered outright political hostility as a result of its advocacy of democracy and denial of the divine right of kings. The French government responded by ordering Rousseau's arrest, forcing him to flee France; the Council of Geneva, in turn, ordered the two books to be burnt and for Rousseau to be arrested if he entered the territory. Obtaining temporary refuge in Prussia, he was ultimately driven out again, fleeing to England, where he resided until his paranoid delusions convinced him that David Hume, who had invited him over in the first place, was plotting against his life. Mentally ill and no longer in a position to trouble anyone, he spent the final years of his life back in France, where he died in poverty in 1778.

The central feature of Rousseau's work is his philosophy of man. For Rousseau, man in his savage state is *whole*. True, says Rousseau, savage man is disadvantaged in many respects compared to civilized man: if you allow civilized man time to gather together his tools and his machines, he will defeat the savage man, in any contest between the two, with great ease. But set them together naked and unarmed, and it is a different matter: 'you will soon see the advantage of having all our forces constantly at our disposal, of being always prepared for every event, and of carrying one's self, as it were, perpetually whole and entire about one.' Rousseau is at pains to stress that the differences between savage man and civilized man go to the root of his being: as horses, cats, and bulls have greater stature, are more robust, and have vigour, strength, and courage when they are allowed to run free but lose these advantages when domesticated, so the 'effeminate' way of life in civilized societies enervates man's strength and courage and makes him grow weak, timid, and servile. Savage man, on the other hand, lives wholly in the present and his desires and fears are limited to those that arise from the animal state; the only goods he recognizes are 'food, a female, and sleep', and the only evils he fears are pain and hunger. He stands in no need of his fellow creatures nor has any desire to hurt them. Everyone is his own master: there is no dominion and submission, not because all are equal, but because all are independent.

In the state of nature such inequalities as nature imposes upon us—differences in wit, beauty, strength, skill, merit, and talent—don't make a great deal of difference. It is when men come together in society that such qualities, as capable of commanding respect from others, become valuable, which incentivizes men to try to present themselves other than they really are. It is also when men come into society that they begin to conceive of the notion of property as something distinct from and extending beyond the land and cattle over which solitary primitive man is able to exert possession. From this moment on, estates multiply until a point is reached when they border one upon another with the consequence that men can only aggrandise themselves at the expense of others; meanwhile, the propertyless 'supernumeraries' find that they have 'become poor without sustaining any loss' because 'while they saw everything about them change, they remained the same'.

Rousseau's recognition of the fundamental difficulty facing

mankind in society is his most profoundly philosophic insight: for he appreciates, in full agreement with the great spiritual leaders of mankind, that we are brought into our greatest subjection by our very own wants and desires. In consequence of this multitude of wants and desires, men in society are made subject not only to all nature but also, more especially, to one another. This is a subjection that is felt by all: the rich need services and the poor the assistance of others. Human life, therefore, becomes an endless effort to get others sufficiently interested to satisfy these wants and desires. We become imperious and cruel to frighten some into compliance; we are also made artful and sly in order to make others see their apparent advantage in promoting our own. Increasingly, the ambition to raise fortunes arises not so much from real want, but from a desire to surpass our fellow men. We are filled with a 'vile propensity to injure one another' and a secret jealousy which is all the more dangerous when it 'puts on the mask of benevolence to carry its point with greater security'.

It is through the body politic that man rises above the difficulties and degradations that human society would otherwise subject him to. The body politic, explains Rousseau in *The Social Contract* (1762), is founded upon a 'social contract' which effects 'the total alienation of each associate, together with all his rights, to the whole community'. This alienation is total and no rights are reserved, for if they were, there would be no common superior to determine disputes and the state of nature would persist; and, in giving himself to all, each associate gives himself to nobody, as each gains an equivalent right over the others as he surrenders to them. From the union of the individual contracting parties there arises a public person—the 'body politic' or republic—which acts under the supreme direction of a 'general will' to which the parties have surrendered their persons and their powers. Rousseau's view differs starkly from that of Locke in one important respect: the body politic, whether in its active capacity as sovereign or passive capacity as state, is not a party to the contract; it is, rather, *constituted* by that contract. It cannot have any interests contrary to those of its members. 'The sovereign,' says Rousseau, 'merely by virtue of what it is, is always what it should be.'

It is the great insight of Rousseau that our basic freedoms come into being as a result of our incorporation in the body politic. Liberty, of course, has always been at the heart of his philosophy: 'To renounce liberty is to renounce being a man,' he says, 'to surrender the rights of humanity and even its duties.' Civil and moral liberty, though, is obtained precisely through subjecting ourselves to the law, because obedience to a law that we ourselves prescribe *is* liberty, so that we become truly masters of ourselves, where we might otherwise be slaves to impulse and appetite. The exchange is a good one: civil liberty and proprietorship of all we possess in place of natural liberty and unlimited right to everything we try to gain and succeed in getting. It is true that we will not be entitled to extract private benefits at public cost by asserting rights that benefit ourselves to the detriment of the body politic. But should we be allowed to do so, the body politic would soon become unviable, and we would all be thrust back into unregulated mutual dependence with all that this would entail. It is in this respect that we must be 'forced to be free'.

Rousseau has much to offer the modern man. His sociological and psychological insight is profound: it is through our many wants and desires that we grow dependent on others, and it is through our dependence on others that we are brought into subjection and rendered susceptible to the myriad of ills that plague our social existence. But it Rousseau's political remedy that is truly important: we must find our freedom, he insists, not by fleeing from social existence but by intensifying our engagement with the polity and thereby realizing the heightened emancipation that comes from obedience to laws that we have had a part in making. Rousseau's republicanism is the very opposite of the totalitarianism that takes the form of a narrow political establishment or nomenklatura lording it over the politically inert masses. It is a call to reconstitute ourselves as political beings who are citizens every bit much as subjects—men in the truest, most dignified, and most self-realized state.

A DISCOURSE ON THE ORIGIN OF INEQUALITY

...Behold then all human faculties developed, memory and imagination in full play, egoism interested, reason active, and the mind almost at the highest point of its perfection. Behold all the natural qualities in action, the rank and condition of every man assigned him; not merely his share of property and his power to serve or injure others, but also his wit, beauty, strength or skill, merit or talents; and these being the only qualities capable of commanding respect, it soon became necessary to possess or to affect them.

It now became the interest of men to appear what they really were not. To be and to seem became two totally different things; and from this distinction sprang insolent pomp and cheating trickery, with all the numerous vices that go in their train. On the other hand, free and independent as men were before, they were now, in consequence of a multiplicity of new wants, brought into subjection, as it were, to all nature, and particularly to one another; and each became in some degree a slave even in becoming the master of other men: if rich, they stood in need of the services of others; if poor, of their assistance; and even a middle condition did not enable them to do without one another. Man must now, therefore, have been perpetually employed in getting others to interest themselves in his lot, and in making them, apparently at least, if not really, find their advantage in promoting his own. Thus he must have been sly and artful in his behaviour to some, and imperious and cruel to others; being under a kind of necessity to ill-use all the persons of whom he stood in need, when he could not frighten them into compliance, and did not judge it his interest to be useful to them. Insatiable ambition, the thirst of raising their respective fortunes, not so much from real want as from the desire to surpass others, inspired all men with a vile propensity to injure one another, and with a secret jealousy, which is the more dangerous, as it puts on the mask of benevolence to carry its point with greater security. In a word, there arose rivalry and competition on the one hand, and conflicting interests on the other, together with a secret desire on both of profiting at the expense of others. All these evils were the first effects of property, and the inseparable attendants of growing inequality.

Before the invention of signs to represent riches, wealth could hardly consist in anything but lands and cattle, the only real possessions men can have. But, when inheritances so increased in number and extent as to occupy the whole of the land, and to border on one another, one man could aggrandise himself only at the expense of another; at the same time the supernumeraries, who had been too weak or too indolent to make such acquisitions, and had grown poor without sustaining any loss, because, while they saw everything change around them, they remained still the same, were obliged to receive their subsistence, or steal it, from the rich; and this soon bred, according to their different characters, dominion and slavery, or violence and rapine. The wealthy, on their part, had no sooner begun to taste the pleasure of command, than they disdained all others, and, using their old slaves to acquire new, thought of nothing but subduing and enslaving their neighbours; like ravenous wolves, which, having once tasted human flesh, despise every other food and thenceforth seek only men to devour.

Thus, as the most powerful or the most miserable considered their might or misery as a kind of right to the possessions of others, equivalent, in their opinion, to that of property, the destruction of equality was attended by the most terrible disorders. Usurpations by the rich, robbery by the poor, and the unbridled passions of both, suppressed the cries of natural compassion and the still feeble voice of justice, and filled men with avarice, ambition, and vice. Between the title of the strongest and that of the first occupier, there arose perpetual conflicts, which never ended but in battles and bloodshed. The newborn state of society thus gave rise to a horrible state of war; men thus harassed and depraved were no longer capable of retracing their steps or renouncing the fatal acquisitions they had made, but, labouring by the abuse of the faculties which do them honour, merely to their own confusion, brought themselves to the brink of ruin.

> *Attonitus novitate mali, divesque miserque,*
> *Effugere optat opes; et quæ modo voverat odit.*[1]

It is impossible that men should not at length have reflected on so wretched a situation, and on the calamities that overwhelmed them. The rich, in particular, must have felt how much they suffered by a constant state of war, of which they bore all the expense; and in which, though all risked their lives, they alone risked their property. Besides, however speciously they might disguise their usurpations, they knew that they were founded on precarious and false titles; so that, if others took from them by force what they themselves had gained by force,

---

1. 'Shocked by the novelty of the evil, both rich and wretched,/ He flees his wealth, and hates what he once prayed for.' From Ovid, *Metamorphoses* 11.127-28, describing Midas after being granted his wish that everything be turned to gold.

they would have no reason to complain. Even those who had been enriched by their own industry could hardly base their proprietorship on better claims. It was in vain to repeat, 'I built this well; I gained this spot by my industry.' Who gave you your standing, it might be answered, and what right have you to demand payment of us for doing what we never asked you to do? Do you not know that numbers of your fellow creatures are starving, for want of what you have too much of? You ought to have had the express and universal consent of mankind before appropriating more of the common subsistence than you needed for your own maintenance. Destitute of valid reasons to justify and sufficient strength to defend himself, able to crush individuals with ease, but easily crushed himself by a troop of bandits, one against all, and incapable, on account of mutual jealousy, of joining with his equals against numerous enemies united by the common hope of plunder, the rich man, thus urged by necessity, conceived at length the profoundest plan that ever entered the mind of man: this was to employ in his favour the forces of those who attacked him, to make allies of his adversaries, to inspire them with different maxims, and to give them other institutions as favourable to himself as the law of nature was unfavourable.

With this view, after having represented to his neighbours the horror of a situation which armed every man against the rest, and made their possessions as burdensome to them as their wants, and in which no safety could be expected either in riches or in poverty, he readily devised plausible arguments to make them close with his design. 'Let us join,' said he, 'to guard the weak from oppression, to restrain the ambitious, and secure to every man the possession of what belongs to him: let us institute rules of justice and peace, to which all without exception may be obliged to conform; rules that may in some measure make amends for the caprices of fortune, by subjecting equally the powerful and the weak to the observance of reciprocal obligations. Let us, in a word, instead of turning our forces against ourselves, collect them in a supreme power which may govern us by wise laws, protect and defend all the members of the association, repulse their common enemies, and maintain eternal harmony among us.'

Far fewer words to this purpose would have been enough to impose on men so barbarous and easily seduced; especially as they had too many disputes among themselves to do without arbitrators, and too much ambition and avarice to go long without masters. All ran headlong to their chains, in hopes of securing their liberty; for they had just wit enough to perceive the advantages of political institutions, without experience enough to enable them to foresee the dangers. The most capable of foreseeing the dangers were the very persons who expected to benefit by them; and even the most prudent judged it not inexpedient to sacrifice one part of their freedom to ensure the rest; as a wounded man has his arm cut off to save the rest of his body.

Such was, or may well have been, the origin of society and law, which bound new fetters on the poor, and gave new powers to the rich; which irretrievably destroyed natural liberty, eternally fixed the law of property and inequality, converted clever usurpation into unalterable right, and, for the advantage of a few ambitious individuals, subjected all mankind to perpetual labour, slavery, and wretchedness. It is easy to see how the establishment of one community made that of all the rest necessary, and how, in order to make head against united forces, the rest of mankind had to unite in turn. Societies soon multiplied and spread over the face of the earth, till hardly a corner of the world was left in which a man could escape the yoke, and withdraw his head from beneath the sword which he saw perpetually hanging over him by a thread. Civil right having thus become the common rule among the members of each community, the law of nature maintained its place only between different communities, where, under the name of the right of nations, it was qualified by certain tacit conventions, in order to make commerce practicable, and serve as a substitute for natural compassion, which lost, when applied to societies, almost all the influence it had over individuals, and survived no longer except in some great cosmopolitan spirits, who, breaking down the imaginary barriers that separate different peoples, follow the example of our Sovereign Creator, and include the whole human race in their benevolence. ...

THE SOCIAL CONTRACT

BOOK I

I mean to inquire if, in the civil order, there can be any sure and legitimate rule of administration, men being taken as they are and laws as they might be. In this inquiry I shall endeavour always to unite what right sanctions with what is prescribed by interest, in order that justice and utility may in no case be divided. I enter upon my task without proving the importance of the subject. I shall be asked if I am a prince or a legislator, to write on politics. I answer that I am neither, and that is why I do so. If I were a prince or a legislator, I should not waste time in saying what wants doing; I should do it, or hold my peace. As I was born a citizen of a free state, and a member of the sovereign, I feel that, however feeble the influence my voice can have on public affairs, the right of voting on them makes it my duty to study them; and I am happy, when I reflect upon governments, to find my inquiries always furnish me with new reasons for loving that of my own country.

I. SUBJECT OF THE FIRST BOOK

Man is born free; and everywhere he is in chains. One thinks himself the master of others, and still remains a greater slave than they. How did this change come about? I do not know. What can make it legitimate? That question I think I can answer.

If I took into account only force, and the effects derived from it, I should say: 'As long as people are compelled to obey, and they obey, it does well; as soon as they can shake off the yoke, and they shake it off, it does still better; for, regaining their liberty by the same right as took it away, either it is justified in resuming it, or there was no justification for those who took it away.' But the social order is a sacred right which is the basis of all other rights. Nevertheless, this right does not come from nature, and must therefore be founded on conventions. Before coming to that, I have to prove what I have just asserted.

2. THE FIRST SOCIETIES

The most ancient of all societies, and the only one that is natural, is the family; and even so, the children remain attached to the father only so long as they need him for their preservation. As soon as this need ceases, the natural bond is dissolved. The children, released from the obedience they owed to the father, and the father, released from the care he owed his children, return equally to independence. If they remain united, they continue so no longer naturally, but voluntarily; and the family itself is then maintained only by convention.

This common liberty results from the nature of man. His first law is to provide for his own preservation, his first cares are those which he owes to himself; and, as soon as he reaches years of discretion, he is the sole judge of the proper means of preserving himself, and consequently becomes his own master. The family then may be called the first model of political societies: the ruler corresponds to the father, and the people to the children; and all, being born free and equal, alienate their liberty only for their own advantage. The whole difference is that, in the family, the love of the father for his children repays him for the care he takes of them, while, in the state, the pleasure of commanding takes the place of the love which the chief cannot have for the peoples under him. Grotius denies that all human power is established in favour of the governed, and quotes slavery as an example. His usual method of reasoning is constantly to establish right by fact.[2] It would be possible to employ a more logical method, but none could be more favourable to tyrants.

It is then, according to Grotius, doubtful whether the human race belongs to a hundred men, or that hundred men to the human race; and, throughout his book, he seems to incline to the former alternative, which is also the view of Hobbes. On this showing, the human species is divided into so many herds of cattle, each with its ruler, who keeps guard over them for the purpose of devouring them.

As a shepherd is of a nature superior to that of his flock, the shepherds of men, i.e. their rulers, are of a nature superior to that of the peoples under them. Thus, Philo tells us, the Emperor Caligula reasoned, concluding equally well either that kings were gods, or that men were beasts.

The reasoning of Caligula agrees with that of Hobbes and Grotius.

---

2. 'Learned inquiries into public right are often only the history of past abuses; and troubling to study them too deeply is a profitless infatuation' (*Essay on the Interests of France in Relation to its Neighbours*, by the Marquis d'Argenson). This is exactly what Grotius has done.

Aristotle, before any of them, had said that men are by no means equal naturally, but that some are born for slavery, and others for dominion.

Aristotle was right; but he took the effect for the cause. Nothing can be more certain than that every man born in slavery is born for slavery. Slaves lose everything in their chains, even the desire of escaping from them: they love their servitude, as the comrades of Ulysses loved their brutish condition.[3] If then there are slaves by nature, it is because there have been slaves against nature. Force made the first slaves, and their cowardice perpetuated the condition.

I have said nothing of King Adam, or Emperor Noah, father of the three great monarchs who shared out the universe, like the children of Saturn, whom some scholars have recognised in them. I trust to getting due thanks for my moderation; for, being a direct descendant of one of these princes, perhaps of the eldest branch, how do I know that a verification of titles might not leave me the legitimate king of the human race? In any case, there can be no doubt that Adam was sovereign of the world, as Robinson Crusoe was of his island, as long as he was its only inhabitant; and this empire had the advantage that the monarch, safe on his throne, had no rebellions, wars, or conspirators to fear.

3. THE RIGHT OF THE STRONGEST

The strongest is never strong enough to be always the master, unless he transforms strength into right, and obedience into duty. Hence the right of the strongest, which, though to all seeming meant ironically, is really laid down as a fundamental principle. But are we never to have an explanation of this phrase? Force is a physical power, and I fail to see what moral effect it can have. To yield to force is an act of necessity, not of will—at the most, an act of prudence. In what sense can it be a duty?

Suppose for a moment that this so-called 'right' exists. I maintain that the sole result is a mass of inexplicable nonsense. For, if force creates right, the effect changes with the cause: every force that is greater than the first succeeds to its right. As soon as it is possible to disobey with impunity, disobedience is legitimate; and, the strongest being always in the right, the only thing that matters is to act so as to become the strongest. But what kind of right is that which perishes

3. See a short treatise of Plutarch's entitled *That Animals Reason*.

when force fails? If we must obey perforce, there is no need to obey
because we ought; and if we are not forced to obey, we are under no
obligation to do so. Clearly, the word 'right' adds nothing to force: in
this connection, it means absolutely nothing.

Obey the powers that be. If this means yield to force, it is a good
precept, but superfluous: I can answer for its never being violated. All
power comes from God, I admit; but so does all sickness: does that
mean that we are forbidden to call in the doctor? A brigand surprises
me at the edge of a wood: must I not merely surrender my purse on
compulsion; but, even if I could withhold it, am I in conscience bound
to give it up? For certainly the pistol he holds is also a power. Let us
then admit that force does not create right, and that we are obliged to
obey only legitimate powers. In that case, my original question recurs.

4. SLAVERY

Since no man has a natural authority over his fellow, and force creates
no right, we must conclude that conventions form the basis of all
legitimate authority among men.

If an individual, says Grotius, can alienate his liberty and make
himself the slave of a master, why could not a whole people do the
same and make itself subject to a king? There are in this passage plenty
of ambiguous words which would need explaining; but let us confine
ourselves to the word alienate. To alienate is to give or to sell. Now, a
man who becomes the slave of another does not give himself; he sells
himself, at the least for his subsistence: but for what does a people
sell itself? A king is so far from furnishing his subjects with their
subsistence that he gets his own only from them; and, according to
Rabelais, kings do not live on nothing. Do subjects then give their
persons on condition that the king takes their goods also? I fail to see
what they have left to preserve. It will be said that the despot assures
his subjects civil tranquility. Granted; but what do they gain, if the
wars his ambition brings down upon them, his insatiable avidity, and
the vexatious conduct of his ministers press harder on them than their
own dissensions would have done? What do they gain, if the very
tranquility they enjoy is one of their miseries? Tranquility is found also
in dungeons; but is that enough to make them desirable places to live

103

in? The Greeks imprisoned in the cave of the Cyclops lived there very tranquilly, while they were awaiting their turn to be devoured.

To say that a man gives himself gratuitously is to say what is absurd and inconceivable; such an act is null and illegitimate, from the mere fact that he who does it is out of his mind. To say the same of a whole people is to suppose a people of madmen; and madness creates no right.

Even if each man could alienate himself, he could not alienate his children: they are born men and free; their liberty belongs to them, and no one but they has the right to dispose of it. Before they come to years of discretion, the father can, in their name, lay down conditions for their preservation and well-being, but he cannot give them irrevocably and without conditions: such a gift is contrary to the ends of nature, and exceeds the rights of paternity. It would therefore be necessary, in order to legitimise an arbitrary government, that in every generation the people should be in a position to accept or reject it; but, were this so, the government would be no longer arbitrary.

To renounce liberty is to renounce being a man, to surrender the rights of humanity and even its duties. For him who renounces everything no indemnity is possible. Such a renunciation is incompatible with man's nature; to remove all liberty from his will is to remove all morality from his acts. Finally, it is an empty and contradictory convention that sets up, on the one side, absolute authority, and, on the other, unlimited obedience. Is it not clear that we can be under no obligation to a person from whom we have the right to exact everything? Does not this condition alone, in the absence of equivalence or exchange, in itself involve the nullity of the act? For what right can my slave have against me, when all that he has belongs to me, and, his right being mine, this right of mine against myself is a phrase devoid of meaning?

Grotius and the rest find in war another origin for the so-called right of slavery. The victor having, as they hold, the right of killing the vanquished, the latter can buy back his life at the price of his liberty; and this convention is the more legitimate because it is to the advantage of both parties.

But it is clear that this supposed right to kill the conquered is by no means deducible from the state of war. Men, from the mere fact that, while they are living in their primitive independence, they have no mutual relations stable enough to constitute either the state of peace or the state of war, cannot be naturally enemies. War is constituted by a relation between things, and not between persons; and, as the state of war cannot arise out of simple personal relations, but only out of real relations, private war, or war of man with man, can exist neither in the state of nature, where there is no constant property, nor in the social state, where everything is under the authority of the laws.

Individual combats, duels and encounters, are acts which cannot constitute a state; while the private wars, authorised by the establishments of Louis IX, King of France, and suspended by the Peace of God, are abuses of feudalism, in itself an absurd system if ever there was one, and contrary to the principles of natural right and to all good polity.

War then is a relation, not between man and man, but between state and state, and individuals are enemies only accidentally, not as men, nor even as citizens,[4] but as soldiers; not as members of their country, but as its defenders. Finally, each state can have for enemies only other states, and not men; for between things disparate in nature there can be no real relation.

Furthermore, this principle is in conformity with the established rules of all times and the constant practice of all civilized peoples. Declarations of war are intimations less to powers than to their subjects. The foreigner, whether king, individual, or people, who robs, kills or detains the subjects, without declaring war on the prince, is not an enemy, but a brigand. Even in real war, a just prince, while laying hands, in the enemy's country, on all that belongs to the public, respects the lives and goods of individuals: he respects rights on which his own are founded. The object of the war being the destruction of the hostile state, the other side has a right to kill its defenders, while they are bearing arms; but as soon as they lay them down and

---

4. The Romans, who understood and respected the right of war more than any other nation on earth, carried their scruples on this head so far that a citizen was not allowed to serve as a volunteer without engaging himself expressly against the enemy, and against such and such an enemy by name. A legion in which the younger Cato was seeing his first service under Popilius having been reconstructed, the elder Cato wrote to Popilius that if he wished his son to continue serving under him, he must administer to him a new military oath, because, the first having been annulled, he was no longer able to bear arms against the enemy. The same Cato wrote to his son telling him to take great care not to go into battle before taking this new oath. I know that the siege of Clusium and other isolated events can be quoted against me; but I am citing laws and customs. The Romans are the people that least often transgressed its laws; and no other people has had such good ones.

surrender, they cease to be enemies or instruments of the enemy, and become once more merely men, whose life no one has any right to take. Sometimes it is possible to kill the state without killing a single one of its members; and war gives no right which is not necessary to the gaining of its object. These principles are not those of Grotius: they are not based on the authority of poets, but derived from the nature of reality and based on reason.

The right of conquest has no foundation other than the right of the strongest. If war does not give the conqueror the right to massacre the conquered peoples, the right to enslave them cannot be based upon a right which does not exist. No one has a right to kill an enemy except when he cannot make him a slave, and the right to enslave him cannot therefore be derived from the right to kill him. It is accordingly an unfair exchange to make him buy at the price of his liberty his life, over which the victor holds no right.

Is it not clear that there is a vicious circle in founding the right of life and death on the right of slavery, and the right of slavery on the right of life and death?

Even if we assume this terrible right to kill everybody, I maintain that a slave made in war, or a conquered people, is under no obligation to a master, except to obey him as far as he is compelled to do so. By taking an equivalent for his life, the victor has not done him a favour; instead of killing him without profit, he has killed him usefully. So far then is he from acquiring over him any authority in addition to that of force, that the state of war continues to subsist between them: their mutual relation is the effect of it, and the usage of the right of war does not imply a treaty of peace. A convention has indeed been made; but this convention, so far from destroying the state of war, presupposes its continuance.

So, from whatever aspect we regard the question, the right of slavery is null and void, not only as being illegitimate, but also because it is absurd and meaningless. The words slave and right contradict each other, and are mutually exclusive. It will always be equally foolish for a man to say to a man or to a people: 'I make with you a convention wholly at your expense and wholly to my advantage; I shall keep it as long as I like, and you will keep it as long as I like.'

Even if I granted all that I have been refuting, the friends of despotism would be no better off. There will always be a great difference between subduing a multitude and ruling a society. Even if scattered individuals were successively enslaved by one man, however numerous they might be, I still see no more than a master and his slaves, and certainly not a people and its ruler; I see what may be termed an aggregation, but not an association; there is as yet neither public good nor body politic. The man in question, even if he has enslaved half the world, is still only an individual; his interest, apart from that of others, is still a purely private interest. If this same man comes to die, his empire, after him, remains scattered and without unity, as an oak falls and dissolves into a heap of ashes when the fire has consumed it.

A people, says Grotius, can give itself to a king. Then, according to Grotius, a people is a people before it gives itself. The gift is itself a civil act, and implies public deliberation. It would be better, before examining the act by which a people gives itself to a king, to examine that by which it has become a people; for this act, being necessarily prior to the other, is the true foundation of society.

Indeed, if there were no prior convention, where, unless the election were unanimous, would be the obligation on the minority to submit to the choice of the majority? How have a hundred men who wish for a master the right to vote on behalf of ten who do not? The law of majority voting is itself something established by convention, and presupposes unanimity, on one occasion at least.

6. THE SOCIAL CONTRACT

I suppose men to have reached the point at which the obstacles in the way of their preservation in the state of nature show their power of resistance to be greater than the resources at the disposal of each individual for his maintenance in that state. That primitive condition can then subsist no longer; and the human race would perish unless it changed its manner of existence. But, as men cannot engender new forces, but only unite and direct existing ones, they have no other means of preserving themselves than the formation, by aggregation, of a sum of forces great enough to overcome the resistance. These they have to bring into play by means of a single motive power, and cause to act in concert.

This sum of forces can arise only where several persons come together: but, as the force and liberty of each man are the chief instruments of his self-preservation, how can he pledge them without harming his own interests, and neglecting the care he owes to himself? This difficulty, in its bearing on my present subject, may be stated in the following terms: 'The problem is to find a form of association which will defend and protect with the whole common force the person and goods of each associate, and in which each, while uniting himself with all, may still obey himself alone, and remain as free as before.' This is the fundamental problem of which the 'social contract' provides the solution.

The clauses of this contract are so determined by the nature of the act that the slightest modification would make them vain and ineffective; so that, although they have perhaps never been formally set forth, they are everywhere the same and everywhere tacitly admitted and recognised, until, on the violation of the social compact, each regains his original rights and resumes his natural liberty, while losing the conventional liberty in favour of which he renounced it.

These clauses, properly understood, may be reduced to one—the total alienation of each associate, together with all his rights, to the whole community; for, in the first place, as each gives himself absolutely, the conditions are the same for all; and, this being so, no one has any interest in making them burdensome to others.

Moreover, the alienation being without reserve, the union is as perfect as it can be, and no associate has anything more to demand: for, if the individuals retained certain rights, as there would be no common superior to decide between them and the public, each, being on one point his own judge, would ask to be so on all; the state of nature would thus continue, and the association would necessarily become inoperative or tyrannical.

Finally, each man, in giving himself to all, gives himself to nobody; and as there is no associate over whom he does not acquire the same right as he yields others over himself, he gains an equivalent for everything he loses, and an increase of force for the preservation of what he has.

If then we discard from the social compact what is not of its essence, we shall find that it reduces itself to the following terms: 'Each of us puts his person and all his power in common under the supreme direction of the general will, and, in our corporate capacity, we receive each member as an indivisible part of the whole.'

At once, in place of the individual personality of each contracting party, this act of association creates a moral and collective body, composed of as many members as the assembly contains votes, and receiving from this act its unity, its common identity, its life and its will. This public person, so formed by the union of all other persons, formerly took the name of city,[5] and now takes that of republic or body politic; it is called by its members state when passive, sovereign when active, and power when compared with others like itself. Those who are associated in it take collectively the name of people, and severally are called citizens, as sharing in the sovereign power, and subjects, as being under the laws of the state. But these terms are often confused and taken one for another: it is enough to know how to distinguish them when they are being used with precision.

7. THE SOVEREIGN

This formula shows us that the act of association comprises a mutual undertaking between the public and the individuals, and that each individual, in making a contract, as we may say, with himself, is bound in a double capacity; as a member of the sovereign he is bound to the individuals, and as a member of the state to the sovereign. But the maxim of civil right, that no one is bound by undertakings made to himself, does not apply in this case; for there is a great difference between incurring an obligation to yourself and incurring one to a whole of which you form a part.

---

5. The real meaning of this word has been almost wholly lost in modern times; most people mistake a town for a city, and a townsman for a citizen. They do not know that houses make a town, but citizens a city. The same mistake long ago cost the Carthaginians dear. I have never read of the title of citizens being given to the subjects of any prince, not even the ancient Macedonians or the English of today, though they are nearer liberty than anyone else. The French alone everywhere familiarly adopt the name of citizens, because, as can be seen from their dictionaries, they have no idea of its meaning; otherwise they would be guilty in usurping it of the crime of lèse majesté: among them, the name expresses a virtue, and not a right. When Bodin spoke of our citizens and townsmen, he fell into a bad blunder in taking the one class for the other. M. d'Alembert has avoided the error, and, in his article on Geneva, has clearly distinguished the four orders of men (or even five, counting mere foreigners) who dwell in our town, of which two only compose the Republic. No other French writer, to my knowledge, has understood the real meaning of the word citizen.

Attention must further be called to the fact that public deliberation, while competent to bind all the subjects to the sovereign, because of the two different capacities in which each of them may be regarded, cannot, for the opposite reason, bind the sovereign to itself; and that it is consequently against the nature of the body politic for the sovereign to impose on itself a law which it cannot infringe. Being able to regard itself in only one capacity, it is in the position of an individual who makes a contract with himself; and this makes it clear that there neither is nor can be any kind of fundamental law binding on the body of the people—not even the social contract itself. This does not mean that the body politic cannot enter into undertakings with others, provided the contract is not infringed by them; for in relation to what is external to it, it becomes a simple being, an individual.

But the body politic or the sovereign, drawing its being wholly from the sanctity of the contract, can never bind itself, even to an outsider, to do anything derogatory to the original act, for instance, to alienate any part of itself, or to submit to another sovereign. Violation of the act by which it exists would be self-annihilation; and that which is itself nothing can create nothing. As soon as this multitude is so united in one body, it is impossible to offend against one of the members without attacking the body, and still more to offend against the body without the members resenting it. Duty and interest therefore equally oblige the two contracting parties to give each other help; and the same men should seek to combine, in their double capacity, all the advantages dependent upon that capacity.

Again, the sovereign, being formed wholly of the individuals who compose it, neither has nor can have any interest contrary to theirs; and consequently the sovereign power need give no guarantee to its subjects, because it is impossible for the body to wish to hurt all its members. We shall also see later on that it cannot hurt any in particular. The sovereign, merely by virtue of what it is, is always what it should be.

This, however, is not the case with the relation of the subjects to the sovereign, which, despite the common interest, would have no security that they would fulfil their undertakings, unless it found means to assure itself of their fidelity.

In fact, each individual, as a man, may have a particular will contrary or dissimilar to the general will which he has as a citizen. His particular interest may speak to him quite differently from the common interest: his absolute and naturally independent existence may make him look upon what he owes to the common cause as a gratuitous contribution, the loss of which will do less harm to others than the payment of it is burdensome to himself; and, regarding the moral person which constitutes the state as a *persona ficta*,[6] because not a man, he may wish to enjoy the rights of citizenship without being ready to fulfil the duties of a subject. The continuance of such an injustice could not but prove the undoing of the body politic.

In order then that the social compact may not be an empty formula, it tacitly includes the undertaking, which alone can give force to the rest, that whoever refuses to obey the general will shall be compelled to do so by the whole body. This means nothing less than that he will be forced to be free; for this is the condition which, by giving each citizen to his country, secures him against all personal dependence. In this lies the key to the working of the political machine; this alone legitimises civil undertakings, which, without it, would be absurd, tyrannical, and liable to the most frightful abuses.

8. THE CIVIL STATE

The passage from the state of nature to the civil state produces a very remarkable change in man, by substituting justice for instinct in his conduct, and giving his actions the morality they had formerly lacked. Then only, when the voice of duty takes the place of physical impulses and right of appetite, does man, who so far had considered only himself, find that he is forced to act on different principles, and to consult his reason before listening to his inclinations. Although, in this state, he deprives himself of some advantages which he got from nature, he gains in return others so great, his faculties are so stimulated and developed, his ideas so extended, his feelings so ennobled, and his whole soul so uplifted, that, did not the abuses of this new condition often degrade him below that which he left, he would be bound to bless continually the happy moment which took him from it forever, and, instead of a stupid and unimaginative animal, made him an intelligent being and a man.

Let us draw up the whole account in terms easily commensurable.

---

6. A fictitious person created under the law.

What man loses by the social contract is his natural liberty and an unlimited right to everything he tries to get and succeeds in getting; what he gains is civil liberty and the proprietorship of all he possesses. If we are to avoid mistake in weighing one against the other, we must clearly distinguish natural liberty, which is bounded only by the strength of the individual, from civil liberty, which is limited by the general will; and possession, which is merely the effect of force or the right of the first occupier, from property, which can be founded only on a positive title. We might, over and above all this, add, to what man acquires in the civil state, moral liberty, which alone makes him truly master of himself; for the mere impulse of appetite is slavery, while obedience to a law which we prescribe to ourselves is liberty. But I have already said too much on this head, and the philosophical meaning of the word liberty does not now concern us.

9. REAL PROPERTY

Each member of the community gives himself to it, at the moment of its foundation, just as he is, with all the resources at his command, including the goods he possesses. This act does not make possession, in changing hands, change its nature, and become property in the hands of the sovereign; but, as the forces of the city are incomparably greater than those of an individual, public possession is also, in fact, stronger and more irrevocable, without being any more legitimate, at any rate from the point of view of foreigners. For the state, in relation to its members, is master of all their goods by the social contract, which, within the state, is the basis of all rights; but, in relation to other powers, it is so only by the right of the first occupier, which it holds from its members.

The right of the first occupier, though more real than the right of the strongest, becomes a real right only when the right of property has already been established. Every man has naturally a right to everything he needs; but the positive act which makes him proprietor of one thing excludes him from everything else. Having his share, he ought to keep to it, and can have no further right against the community. This is why the right of the first occupier, which in the state of nature is so weak, claims the respect of every man in civil society. In this right we are respecting not so much what belongs to another as what does not belong to ourselves. In general, to establish the right of the first occupier over a plot of ground, the following conditions are necessary: first, the land must not yet be inhabited; secondly, a man must occupy only the amount he needs for his subsistence; and, in the third place, possession must be taken, not by an empty ceremony, but by labour and cultivation, the only sign of proprietorship that should be respected by others, in default of a legal title.

In granting the right of first occupancy to necessity and labour, are we not really stretching it as far as it can go? Is it possible to leave such a right unlimited? Is it to be enough to set foot on a plot of common ground, in order to be able to call yourself at once the master of it? Is it to be enough that a man has the strength to expel others for a moment, in order to establish his right to prevent them from ever returning? How can a man or a people seize an immense territory and keep it from the rest of the world except by a punishable usurpation, since all others are being robbed, by such an act, of the place of habitation and the means of subsistence which nature gave them in common? When Nunez Balboa, standing on the seashore, took possession of the South Seas and the whole of South America in the name of the crown of Castile, was that enough to dispossess all their actual inhabitants, and to shut out from them all the princes of the world? On such a showing, these ceremonies are idly multiplied, and the Catholic King need only take possession all at once, from his apartment, of the whole universe, merely making a subsequent reservation about what was already in the possession of other princes.

We can imagine how the lands of individuals, where they were contiguous and came to be united, became the public territory, and how the right of sovereignty, extending from the subjects over the lands they held, became at once real and personal. The possessors were thus made more dependent, and the forces at their command used to guarantee their fidelity. The advantage of this does not seem to have been felt by ancient monarchs, who called themselves Kings of the Persians, Scythians, or Macedonians, and seemed to regard themselves more as rulers of men than as masters of a country. Those of the present day more cleverly call themselves Kings of France, Spain, England, etc.: thus holding the land, they are quite confident of holding the inhabitants.

The peculiar fact about this alienation is that, in taking over the goods of individuals, the community, so far from despoiling them, only assures them legitimate possession, and changes usurpation into a true right and enjoyment into proprietorship. Thus the possessors, being regarded as depositaries of the public good, and having their rights respected by all the members of the state and maintained against foreign aggression by all its forces, have, by a cession which benefits both the public and still more themselves, acquired, so to speak, all that they gave up. This paradox may easily be explained by the distinction between the rights which the sovereign and the proprietor have over the same estate, as we shall see later on.

It may also happen that men begin to unite one with another before they possess anything, and that, subsequently occupying a tract of country which is enough for all, they enjoy it in common, or share it out among themselves, either equally or according to a scale fixed by the sovereign. However the acquisition be made, the right which each individual has to his own estate is always subordinate to the right which the community has over all: without this, there would be neither stability in the social tie, nor real force in the exercise of sovereignty.

I shall end this chapter and this book by remarking on a fact on which the whole social system should rest: i.e. that, instead of destroying natural inequality, the fundamental compact substitutes, for such physical inequality as nature may have set up between men, an equality that is moral and legitimate, and that men, who may be unequal in strength or intelligence, become every one equal by convention and legal right.[7]

---

7. Under bad governments, this equality is only apparent and illusory: it serves only to keep the pauper in his poverty and the rich man in the position he has usurped. In fact, laws are always of use to those who possess and harmful to those who have nothing: from which it follows that the social state is advantageous to men only when all have something and none too much.

7

EDMUND BURKE, REFLECTIONS ON THE REVOLUTION IN FRANCE

INTRODUCTION

Chinese premier Zhou Enlai, when asked in 1972 about the historical impact of the French Revolution (1789-1799), is famously said to have replied that it was 'too early to tell'. It is not wholly clear whether Zhou had fully understood which 'revolution' was, in fact, being referred to. But the fact that the anecdote has taken hold of the popular imagination itself reveals something widely understood, if only intuitively, by people at large: that we all live now, to a greater or lesser degree, in the shadow of that momentous event. The French Revolution was indeed in many respects the defining moment in the long march towards the modern 'soft-totalitarian' regimes that dominate the West at this moment in history. Its uniqueness stems from the fact that it marked the passing of an old order (the *ancien régime* of feudal traditions supporting absolutist monarchy) and the arrival of new ways of thinking, ruling, despoiling, and killing.

Since the French Revolution is the foundational event of political modernity, there is little that could be more instructive than to learn of its principal characteristics from its foremost contemporary critic,

Edmund Burke, a man who is also widely considered to be the father of modern conservatism.

Edmund Burke (1730-1797) was both political theorist and practical politician. An Irishman by birth, Burke was was born in Dublin and studied at Trinity College, before moving to London where, still a young man, he became part of Dr Johnson's circle. Burke's political career was established in 1765 when he became private secretary to Charles, Marquess of Rockingham, who was then Prime Minister of Great Britain, and took a seat in the House of Commons as Member of Parliament for Wendover. He came to public attention in the mid-1770s when, in the context of the rebellion that was brewing in the American colonies, he made an impassioned plea for tolerance towards the colonists who, in his view, were 'descendants of Englishmen...devoted to liberty, but to liberty according to English ideas and on English principles'; he was also an advocate of parliamentary democracy as a form of representative government in which the representative was not a delegate, tasked merely with giving effect to his constituents' instructions, but someone who owed his constituents the benefit of his independent judgment and enlightened conscience. It was, however, Jacobinism and the French Revolution that—once he had recognized the threat that they constituted—most powerfully engaged Burke's efforts. By the time Burke died in 1797, the French revolutionary armies were victorious over virtually the whole of Europe. Whether his political philosophy, or the conservative tradition inspired by it, has been sufficiently robust to counter its legacy will be a question for historians of the future.

The historical outline of the Revolution is simple enough. King Louis XVI, seeking to impose a land tax, in 1789 reconvened the Estates General (*les états généraux*)—an assembly representing France's clergy, nobility and middle class. The non-aristocratic 'Third Estate', in disagreement with the procedures for examining credentials of deputies, however, soon abandoned the name of the Estates General, and adopted for itself instead the title of National Assembly; this was followed by popular revolt in Paris, the storming of the Bastille, and agrarian revolt in the countryside; all of which led inexorably to the execution of the King, along with his wife Marie-Antoinette, and a bloody ten-month Reign of Terror (*la Terreur*), during which thousands of suspected enemies of the revolution were sent to the guillotine. In one sense, it was a terrible failure: the outcome of all this mayhem and bloodshed was the *coup d'état* of a young and successful general by the name of Napoleon Bonaparte who established himself as 'first consul' and *de facto* dictator. But in one sense, at least, the revolutionaries had achieved their goals: the old order was dead, and there would be no going back.

The French Revolution brought the 'rights of man' to the fore. On 4 August 1789, the Assembly adopted the 'Declaration of the Rights of Man and of the Citizen' (*Déclaration des droits de l'homme et du citoyen*). The document did not simply *enact* rights; it purported to *recognize* them as pre-existing under the auspices of a 'Supreme Being'. Any society that did not guarantee these rights was not simply imperfect but (in the words of the Declaration) had no constitution at all. It declared that man was born free and equal—and that social distinctions could only be tolerated when founded upon the common good. It conferred (or 'recognized') the rights to liberty, property, safety, and resistance against oppression; it also required the establishment of a 'public force' and a 'common contribution' to be 'equally distributed between all the citizens, according to their ability to pay'. In retrospect, it is evident that the Declaration prefigured the arrival of the state in its recognizably modern form: it provided that such a state would provide us with liberty of a kind (we had a right to that) and equality of a kind (we had a right to that too), although it was seemingly blind to the potential contradictions between these two rights. It was much less blind to the fact that it would need to be handsomely funded and well armed in case we were to step out of line: one of the first things it did was to bring war to the rest of Europe in the dream of spreading the fruits of the revolution.

The Revolution heralded the arrival of a new kind of political practice adapted to a more democratic era. Political players needed above all, from this point on, to find ways of working with (or more commonly *upon*) the masses. They learned to do this by way of social pressure and public commitments: the earliest revolutionaries' green ribbon (cockade)—intended originally as a symbol of spring, hope, and liberty—became so prevalent that it was soon dangerous to be seen outdoors without one. They did it by way of misinformation and fake news: despite its status as the symbol of an oppressive regime, it is now known that the Bastille rarely held more than ten prisoners, including, in the spring of 1789, four forgers, a Count whose family had arranged for him to be imprisoned for incest, and a mentally disturbed Irishman who believed himself to be, alternately, Julius Caesar and God. And they did it by making use of hoax events and political shills as when, for example, a crowd of market-women marching upon Versailles was infiltrated by men dressed as women (all in the pay of the Duc d'Orléans and other agitators) to demand the acceptance of their political demands.[1]

The main thrust of Burke's political thinking, in the revolutionary context, is that we ought to view our rights as an *inheritance*—the 'rights of Englishmen inherited from their forefathers' in Burke's words—rather than as abstract principles in the revolutionary form of 'rights of man'. This approach in no way rules out the possibility of justified resistance to arbitrary rule: Burke explicitly, and approvingly, points back to England's own 'Glorious Revolution' of 1688, when William of Orange was invited to ascend the throne upon James II's supposed abdication, and on this occasion the Declaration of Right expressly referred to the 'ancient rights and liberties' and 'true ancient and indubitable rights and liberties of the people of this kingdom'. Resistance, for Burke, can be fully and properly justified by calling upon the native tradition of rights in an act of national revival and reinvigoration; it is not rights per se, but the overturning of the native tradition and its replacement with alien and abstract principles, that he deprecates.

Burke's political thinking was based not on any nostalgia or antiquarianism but rather on his uniquely *organic* view of the world. What motivated his philosophy was a spirit of analogy: the British political system coincided with the order of the universe, in the sense that it was the 'kind of existence possessed by a permanent body with temporary parts', journeying through 'a varied tenor of perpetual decay, fall, renovation, and progression'. Within it, the principles of conservation and transmission meet with the principle of improvement, and the advantages that can be obtained through the process of gradual renovation and reform can be locked in for posterity.

There's a lot that Burke throws out in the *Reflections* that remains

1. Christopher Hibbert, *The Days of the French Revolution* (London: Harper Perennial, 1981), 66, 72, 97.

of the greatest relevance today. Burke was experienced enough in the ways of the world to grasp that the revolutionary firebrands who wanted to bring down their betters would not be willing to subject themselves to the same levelling or equalisation ('those who attempt to level never equalise'); he was likewise clear that men naively overestimate what share they will have in the property of the wealthy once that property is redistributed, and that, in any event, those who lead them in revolution never intend to make such a distribution. Burke was cognisant of the demoralization programme that the French revolutionary party had effected against the people: in order to justify the overturning of the established order, the French had to be encouraged to view themselves as 'lowborn servile wretches until the emancipating year of 1789', and this act of psychological warfare had 'slain the mind' of the country. He hinted darkly at conspiratorial forces guiding revolutionary activity from behind the curtain, and he drew attention to the 'compulsory paper money' that was to be made available to facilitate 'plunder by devaluation'. He anticipated that if this generation of revolutionaries had been small-town lawyers and curates, the next generation would constitute a still less impressive new 'nobility' of craftsmen ('artificers'), peasants ('clowns'), and money men.

In the final analysis, though, it is Burke's conception of our rights and liberties that is most important today. Burke provides a sober-minded and critical view of rights and their origins: he sees that natural rights—insofar as the term is meaningful at all—are those we have in nature, and yet when each man has a right to all things (as in the state of nature) he has a right to nothing. Government is our way of providing for our human *wants*—not for the 'rights' that in the state of nature had left us so hopeless—and the most basic want is, of course, that other men be restrained so that we may be free to enjoy our lives, liberties, and property. The way that we manage all of the various wants of mankind is a matter of convention and not natural rights; it is a process of achieving balances between varieties of good, compromises between good and evil, and sometimes also balances and compromises between evil and evil. None of this is easy: causation is not always immediately apparent, so that granting certain persons a particular 'right' now may have devastating consequences for the well-being of many others further down the line; restraining the desire for satisfaction of our wants today may, conversely, promote the realization of our 'rights' further out in the future. This is a view that the simplistic abstract rights asserted by the French revolutionaries, and the similar ones promoted by 'human rights' advocates around the world today, cannot, it seems, fully comprehend.

<hr />

REFLECTIONS ON THE REVOLUTION IN FRANCE

[OUR LIBERTIES AS AN INHERITANCE]

...Our oldest reformation is that of Magna Carta. You will see that Sir Edward Coke, that great oracle of our law, and indeed all the great men who follow him, to Blackstone, are industrious to prove the pedigree of our liberties. They endeavour to prove that the ancient charter, the Magna Carta of King John, was connected with another positive charter from Henry the First, and that both the one and the other were nothing more than a reaffirmance of the still more ancient standing law of the kingdom. In the matter of fact, for the greater part, these authors appear to be in the right; perhaps not always: but if the lawyers mistake in some particulars, it proves my position still the more strongly; because it demonstrates the powerful prepossession towards antiquity with which the minds of all our lawyers and legislators, and of all the people whom they wish to influence, have been always filled, and the stationary policy of this kingdom in considering their most sacred rights and franchises as an *inheritance*.

In the famous law of the 3rd[2] of Charles the First, called the *Petition of Right*, the Parliament says to the king, 'Your subjects have *inherited* this freedom': claiming their franchises, not on abstract principles, 'as the rights of men', but as the rights of Englishmen, and as a patrimony derived from their forefathers. Selden, and the other profoundly learned men who drew this Petition of Right, were as well acquainted, at least, with all the general theories concerning the 'rights of men' as any of the discoursers in our pulpits or on your tribune: full as well as Dr Price, or as the Abbé Sièyes. But, for reasons worthy of that practical wisdom which superseded their theoretic science, they

2. The third Parliament.

preferred this positive, recorded, *hereditary* title to all which can be dear to the man and the citizen to that vague, speculative right which exposed their sure inheritance to be scrambled for and torn to pieces by every wild, litigious spirit.

The same policy pervades all the laws which have since been made for the preservation of our liberties. In the 1st[3] of William and Mary, in the famous statute called the Declaration of Right, the two Houses utter not a syllable of 'a right to frame a government for themselves'. You will see that their whole care was to secure the religion, laws, and liberties that had been long possessed, and had been lately endangered. 'Taking into their most serious consideration the *best* means for making such an establishment that their religion, laws, and liberties might not be in danger of being again subverted,' they auspicate all their proceedings by stating as some of those *best* means, 'in the *first place*,' to do 'as their *ancestors in like cases have usually* done for vindicating their *ancient* rights and liberties, to *declare*,' and then they pray the king and queen, 'that it may be *declared* and enacted that *all and singular* the rights and liberties *asserted and declared* are the true *ancient* and indubitable rights and liberties of the people of this kingdom.'

You will observe, that, from Magna Carta to the Declaration of Right, it has been the uniform policy of our constitution to claim and assert our liberties as an *entailed inheritance* derived to us from our forefathers, and to be transmitted to our posterity as an estate specially belonging to the people of this kingdom, without any reference whatever to any other more general or prior right. By this means our constitution preserves a unity in so great a diversity of its parts. We have an inheritable crown, an inheritable peerage, and a House of Commons and a people inheriting privileges, franchises, and liberties from a long line of ancestors.

This policy appears to me to be the result of profound reflection—or rather the happy effect of following nature, which is wisdom without reflection, and above it. A spirit of innovation is generally the result of a selfish temper and confined views. People will not look forward to posterity, who never look backward to their ancestors. Besides, the people of England well know that the idea of inheritance furnishes a

---

3. The first Parliament.

sure principle of conservation, and a sure principle of transmission, without at all excluding a principle of improvement. It leaves acquisition free; but it secures what it acquires. Whatever advantages are obtained by a state proceeding on these maxims are locked fast as in a sort of family settlement, grasped as in a kind of mortmain forever. By a constitutional policy working after the pattern of nature, we receive, we hold, we transmit our government and our privileges, in the same manner in which we enjoy and transmit our property and our lives. The institutions of policy, the goods of fortune, the gifts of Providence, are handed down to us, and from us, in the same course and order. Our political system is placed in a just correspondence and symmetry with the order of the world, and with the mode of existence decreed to a permanent body composed of transitory parts, wherein, by the disposition of a stupendous wisdom, moulding together the great mysterious incorporation of the human race, the whole, at one time, is never old or middle-aged or young, but, in a condition of unchangeable constancy, moves on through the varied tenor of perpetual decay, fall, renovation, and progression. Thus, by preserving the method of nature in the conduct of the state, in what we improve we are never wholly new, in what we retain we are never wholly obsolete. By adhering in this manner and on those principles to our forefathers, we are guided, not by the superstition of antiquarians, but by the spirit of philosophic analogy. In this choice of inheritance we have given to our frame of polity the image of a relation in blood: binding up the constitution of our country with our dearest domestic ties; adopting our fundamental laws into the bosom of our family affections; keeping inseparable, and cherishing with the warmth of all their combined and mutually reflected charities, our state, our hearths, our sepulchres, and our altars.

Through the same plan of a conformity to nature in our artificial institutions, and by calling in the aid of her unerring and powerful instincts to fortify the fallible and feeble contrivances of our reason, we have derived several other, and those no small benefits, from considering our liberties in the light of an inheritance. Always acting as if in the presence of canonized forefathers, the spirit of freedom, leading in itself to misrule and excess, is tempered with an awful gravity. This idea of a liberal descent inspires us with a sense of habitual native dignity, which prevents that upstart insolence almost inevitably adhering to and disgracing those who are the first acquirers of any distinction. By this means our liberty becomes a noble freedom. It carries an imposing and majestic aspect. It has a pedigree and illustrating ancestors. It has its bearings and its ensigns armorial. It has its gallery of portraits, its monumental inscriptions, its records, evidences, and titles. We procure reverence to our civil institutions on the principle upon which nature teaches us to revere individual men: on account of their age, and on account of those from whom they are descended. All your sophisters cannot produce anything better adapted to preserve a rational and manly freedom than the course that we have pursued, who have chosen our nature rather than our speculations, our breasts rather than our inventions, for the great conservatories and magazines of our rights and privileges.

[DIGNITY OF THE NATION]

When men of rank sacrifice all ideas of dignity to an ambition without a distinct object, and work with low instruments and for low ends, the whole composition becomes low and base. Does not something like this now appear in France? Does it not produce something ignoble and inglorious: a kind of meanness in all the prevalent policy; a tendency in all that is done to lower along with individuals all the dignity and importance of the state? Other revolutions have been conducted by persons who, whilst they attempted or affected changes in the commonwealth, sanctified their ambition by advancing the dignity of the people whose peace they troubled. They had long views. They aimed at the rule, not at the destruction of their country. They were men of great civil and great military talents, and if the terror, the ornament of their age. They were not like Jew brokers contending with each other who could best remedy with fraudulent circulation and depreciated paper the wretchedness and ruin brought on their country by their degenerate councils. The compliment made to one of the great bad men of the old stamp (Cromwell) by his kinsman, a favourite poet of that time, shows what it was he proposed, and what indeed to a great degree he accomplished in the success of his ambition:

Still as you rise, the state, exalted too,
Finds no distemper whilst 't is changed by you;

Changed like the world's great scene, when without noise
The rising sun night's vulgar lights destroys.

These disturbers were not so much like men usurping power as asserting their natural place in society. Their rising was to illuminate and beautify the world. Their conquest over their competitors was by outshining them. The hand that, like a destroying angel, smote the country, communicated to it the force and energy under which it suffered. I do not say (God forbid!), I do not say that the virtues of such men were to be taken as a balance to their crimes; but they were some corrective to their effects. Such was, as I said, our Cromwell. Such were your whole race of Guises, Condés, and Colignys. Such the Richelieus, who in more quiet times acted in the spirit of a civil war. Such, as better men, and in a less dubious cause, were your Henry the Fourth, and your Sully, though nursed in civil confusions, and not wholly without some of their taint. It is a thing to be wondered at, to see how very soon France, when she had a moment to respire, recovered and emerged from the longest and most dreadful civil war that ever was known in any nation. Why? Because, among all their massacres, they had not slain the *mind* in their country. A conscious dignity, a noble pride, a generous sense of glory and emulation, was not extinguished. On the contrary, it was kindled and inflamed. The organs also of the state, however shattered, existed. All the prizes of honour and virtue, all the rewards, all the distinctions, remained. But your present confusion, like a palsy, has attacked the fountain of life itself. Every person in your country, in a situation to be actuated by a principle of honour, is disgraced and degraded, and can entertain no sensation of life, except in a mortified and humiliated indignation. But this generation will quickly pass away. The next generation of the nobility will resemble the artificers and clowns, and money-jobbers, usurers, and Jews, who will be always their fellows, sometimes their masters. Believe me, sir, those who attempt to level never equalize. In all societies consisting of various descriptions of citizens, some description must be uppermost. The levellers, therefore, only change and pervert the natural order of things: they load the edifice of society by setting up in the air what the solidity of the structure requires to be on the ground. The associations of tailors and carpenters of which the republic (of Paris, for instance) is composed cannot be equal to the situation into which by the worst of usurpations—a usurpation on the prerogatives of nature—you attempt to force them.

The Chancellor of France, at the opening of the States, said, in a tone of oratorial flourish, that all occupations were honourable. If he meant only that no honest employment was disgraceful, he would not have gone beyond the truth. But in asserting that anything is honourable, we imply some distinction in its favour. The occupation of a hairdresser, or of a working tallow chandler,[4] cannot be a matter of honour to any person—to say nothing of a number of other more servile employments. Such descriptions of men ought not to suffer oppression from the state; but the state suffers oppression if such as they, either individually or collectively, are permitted to rule. In this you think you are combating prejudice, but you are at war with nature.

I do not, my dear sir, conceive you to be of that sophistical, captious spirit, or of that uncandid dullness, as to require, for every general observation or sentiment, an explicit detail of the correctives and exceptions which reason will presume to be included in all the general propositions which come from reasonable men. You do not imagine that I wish to confine power, authority, and distinction to blood and names and titles. No, sir. There is no qualification for government but virtue and wisdom, actual or presumptive. Wherever they are actually found, they have, in whatever state, condition, profession, or trade, the passport of Heaven to human place and honour. Woe to the country which would madly and impiously reject the service of the talents and virtues, civil, military, or religious, that are given to grace and to serve it; and would condemn to obscurity everything formed to diffuse lustre and glory around a state! Woe to that country, too, that, passing into the opposite extreme, considers a low education, a mean, contracted view of things, a sordid, mercenary occupation, as a preferable title to command! Everything ought to be open—but not indifferently to every man. No rotation, no appointment by lot, no mode of election operating in the spirit of sortition[5] or rotation, can be generally good in a government conversant in extensive objects; because they have no tendency, direct or indirect, to select the man with a view to the duty, or to accommodate the one to the other. I do not hesitate to say that the road to eminence and power, from obscure condition, ought

4. Candlemaker.
5. Election by lot.

not to be made too easy, nor a thing too much of course. If rare merit be the rarest of all rare things, it ought to pass through some sort of probation. The temple of honour ought to be seated on an eminence. If it be opened through virtue, let it be remembered, too, that virtue is never tried but by some difficulty and some struggle.

Nothing is a due and adequate representation of a state that does not represent its ability, as well as its property. But as ability is a vigorous and active principle, and as property is sluggish, inert, and timid, it never can be safe from the invasions of ability, unless it be, out of all proportion, predominant in the representation. It must be represented, too, in great masses of accumulation, or it is not rightly protected. The characteristic essence of property, formed out of the combined principles of its acquisition and conservation, is to be *unequal*. The great masses, therefore, which excite envy, and tempt rapacity, must be put out of the possibility of danger. Then they form a natural rampart about the lesser properties in all their gradations. The same quantity of property which is by the natural course of things divided among many has not the same operation. Its defensive power is weakened as it is diffused. In this diffusion each man's portion is less than what, in the eagerness of his desires, he may flatter himself to obtain by dissipating the accumulations of others. The plunder of the few would, indeed, give but a share inconceivably small in the distribution to the many. But the many are not capable of making this calculation; and those who lead them to rapine never intend this distribution.

The power of perpetuating our property in our families is one of the most valuable and interesting circumstances belonging to it, and that which tends the most to the perpetuation of society itself. It makes our weakness subservient to our virtue; it grafts benevolence even upon avarice. The possessors of family wealth, and of the distinction which attends hereditary possession, as most concerned in it, are the natural securities for this transmission. With us the House of Peers[6] is formed upon this principle. It is wholly composed of hereditary property and hereditary distinction, and made, therefore, the third of the legislature, and, in the last event, the sole judge of all property in all its subdivisions. The House of Commons, too, though not necessarily, yet in fact is always so composed in the far greater part. Let those large

6. The House of Lords.

proprietors be what they will (and they have their chance of being amongst the best), they are, at the very worst, the ballast in the vessel of the commonwealth. For though hereditary wealth, and the rank which goes with it, are too much idolized by creeping sycophants, and the blind, abject admirers of power, they are too rashly slighted in shallow speculations of the petulant, assuming, short-sighted coxcombs of philosophy. Some decent, regulated preeminence, some preference (not exclusive appropriation) given to birth, is neither unnatural, nor unjust, nor impolitic.

[THE *REAL* RIGHTS OF MEN]

It is no wonder, therefore, that, with these ideas of everything in their constitution and government at home, either in church or state, as illegitimate and usurped, or at best as a vain mockery, they look abroad with an eager and passionate enthusiasm. Whilst they are possessed by these notions, it is vain to talk to them of the practice of their ancestors, the fundamental laws of their country, the fixed form of a constitution whose merits are confirmed by the solid test of long experience and an increasing public strength and national prosperity. They despise experience as the wisdom of unlettered men; and as for the rest, they have wrought underground a mine that will blow up, at one grand explosion, all examples of antiquity, all precedents, charters, and acts of parliament. They have 'the rights of men'. Against these there can be no prescription; against these no argument is binding; these admit no temperament and no compromise: anything withheld from their full demand is so much of fraud and injustice. Against these their rights of men let no government look for security in the length of its continuance, or in the justice and lenity of its administration. The objections of these speculatists, if its forms do not quadrate with their theories, are as valid against such an old and beneficent government as against the most violent tyranny or the greenest usurpation. They are always at issue with governments, not on a question of abuse, but a question of competency and a question of title. I have nothing to say to the clumsy subtilty of their political metaphysics. Let them be their amusement in the schools.

Illa se jactet in aula
Æolus, et clauso ventorum carcere regnet.

But let them not break prison to burst like a levanter,[7] to sweep the earth with their hurricane, and to break up the fountains of the great deep to overwhelm us!

Far am I from denying in theory, full as far is my heart from withholding in practice (if I were of power to give or to withhold) the *real* rights of men. In denying their false claims of right, I do not mean to injure those which are real, and are such as their pretended rights would totally destroy. If civil society be made for the advantage of man, all the advantages for which it is made become his right. It is an institution of beneficence; and law itself is only beneficence acting by a rule. Men have a right to live by that rule; they have a right to justice, as between their fellows, whether their fellows are in politic function or in ordinary occupation. They have a right to the fruits of their industry, and to the means of making their industry fruitful. They have a right to the acquisitions of their parents, to the nourishment and improvement of their offspring, to instruction in life and to consolation in death. Whatever each man can separately do, without trespassing upon others, he has a right to do for himself; and he has a right to a fair portion of all which society, with all its combinations of skill and force, can do in his favour. In this partnership all men have equal rights; but not to equal things. He that has but five shillings in the partnership has as good a right to it as he that has five hundred pounds has to his larger proportion; but he has not a right to an equal dividend in the product of the joint stock. And as to the share of power, authority, and direction which each individual ought to have in the management of the state, that I must deny to be amongst the direct original rights of man in civil society; for I have in my contemplation the civil social man, and no other. It is a thing to be settled by convention.

If civil society be the offspring of convention, that convention must be its law. That convention must limit and modify all the descriptions of constitution which are formed under it. Every sort of legislative, judicial, or executory power are its creatures. They can have no being in any other state of things; and how can any man claim, under the conventions of civil society, rights which do not so much as suppose its existence—rights which are absolutely repugnant to it? One of the first motives to civil society, and which becomes one of its fundamental

7. A strong easterly wind in the Mediterranean area.

rules, is, *that no man should be judge in his own cause*. By this each person has at once divested himself of the first fundamental right of uncovenanted man, that is, to judge for himself, and to assert his own cause. He abdicates all right to be his own governor. He inclusively, in a great measure, abandons the right of self-defence, the first law of nature. Men cannot enjoy the rights of an uncivil and of a civil state together. That he may obtain justice, he gives up his right of determining what it is in points the most essential to him. That he may secure some liberty, he makes a surrender in trust of the whole of it.

Government is not made in virtue of natural rights, which may and do exist in total independence of it—and exist in much greater clearness, and in a much greater degree of abstract perfection: but their abstract perfection is their practical defect. By having a right to everything they want everything. Government is a contrivance of human wisdom to provide for human *wants*. Men have a right that these wants should be provided for by this wisdom. Among these wants is to be reckoned the want, out of civil society, of a sufficient restraint upon their passions. Society requires not only that the passions of individuals should be subjected, but that even in the mass and body, as well as in the individuals, the inclinations of men should frequently be thwarted, their will controlled, and their passions brought into subjection. This can only be done *by a power out of themselves*, and not, in the exercise of its function, subject to that will and to those passions which it is its office to bridle and subdue. In this sense the restraints on men, as well as their liberties, are to be reckoned among their rights. But as the liberties and the restrictions vary with times and circumstances, and admit of infinite modifications, they cannot be settled upon any abstract rule; and nothing is so foolish as to discuss them upon that principle.

The moment you abate anything from the full rights of men each to govern himself, and suffer any artificial, positive limitation upon those rights, from that moment the whole organization of government becomes a consideration of convenience. This it is which makes the constitution of a state, and the due distribution of its powers, a matter of the most delicate and complicated skill. It requires a deep knowledge of human nature and human necessities, and of the things which facilitate or obstruct the various ends which are to be pursued by the mechanism of civil institutions. The state is to have recruits to its strength and remedies to its distempers. What is the use of discussing a man's abstract right to food or medicine? The question is upon the method of procuring and administering them. In that deliberation I shall always advise to call in the aid of the farmer and the physician, rather than the professor of metaphysics.

The science of constructing a commonwealth, or renovating it, or reforming it, is, like every other experimental science, not to be taught *a priori*. Nor is it a short experience that can instruct us in that practical science; because the real effects of moral causes are not always immediate, but that which in the first instance is prejudicial may be excellent in its remoter operation, and its excellence may arise even from the ill effects it produces in the beginning. The reverse also happens; and very plausible schemes, with very pleasing commencements, have often shameful and lamentable conclusions. In states there are often some obscure and almost latent causes, things which appear at first view of little moment, on which a very great part of its prosperity or adversity may most essentially depend. The science of government being, therefore, so practical in itself, and intended for such practical purposes, a matter which requires experience, and even more experience than any person can gain in his whole life, however sagacious and observing he may be, it is with infinite caution that any man ought to venture upon pulling down an edifice which has answered in any tolerable degree for ages the common purposes of society, or on building it up again without having models and patterns of approved utility before his eyes.

These metaphysic rights entering into common life, like rays of light which pierce into a dense medium, are, by the laws of Nature, refracted from their straight line. Indeed, in the gross and complicated mass of human passions and concerns, the primitive rights of men undergo such a variety of refractions and reflections that it becomes absurd to talk of them as if they continued in the simplicity of their original direction. The nature of man is intricate; the objects of society are of the greatest possible complexity: and therefore no simple disposition or direction of power can be suitable either to man's nature or to the quality of his affairs. When I hear the simplicity of contrivance aimed at and boasted of in any new political constitutions, I am at no loss to decide that the artificers are grossly ignorant of their trade or totally negligent of their duty. The simple governments are fundamentally defective, to say no worse of them. If you were to contemplate society in but one point of view, all these simple modes of polity are infinitely captivating. In effect each would answer its single end much more perfectly than the more complex is able to attain all its complex purposes. But it is better that the whole, should be imperfectly and anomalously answered than that while some parts are provided for with great exactness, others might be totally neglected, or perhaps materially injured, by the over-care of a favourite member.

The pretended rights of these theorists are all extremes; and in proportion as they are metaphysically true, they are morally and politically false. The rights of men are in a sort of *middle*, incapable of definition, but not impossible to be discerned. The rights of men in governments are their advantages; and these are often in balances between differences of good—in compromises sometimes between good and evil, and sometimes between evil and evil. Political reason is a computing principle: adding, subtracting, multiplying, and dividing, morally, and not metaphysically or mathematically, true moral denominations.

By these theorists the right of the people is almost always sophistically confounded with their power. The body of the community, whenever it can come to act, can meet with no effectual resistance; but till power and right are the same, the whole body of them has no right inconsistent with virtue, and the first of all virtues, prudence. Men have no right to what is not reasonable, and to what is not for their benefit; for though a pleasant writer said, '*Liceat perire poetis*',[8] when one of them, in cold blood, is said to have leaped into the flames of a volcanic revolution, '*ardentem frigidus Ætnam insiluit*',[9] I consider such a frolic rather as an unjustifiable poetic license than as one of the franchises of Parnassus; and whether he were poet, or divine, or politician, that chose to exercise this kind of right, I think that more wise, because more charitable, thoughts would urge me rather to save the man than to preserve his brazen slippers as the monuments of his folly.

8. 'Let poets have the right to perish as they please.'
9. 'He [Empedocles] leapt in cold blood into burning Etna': Horace, *Ars Poetica*, 465 f.

But the age of chivalry is gone. That of sophisters, economists, and calculators has succeeded; and the glory of Europe is extinguished forever. Never, never more, shall we behold that generous loyalty to rank and sex, that proud submission, that dignified obedience, that subordination of the heart, which kept alive, even in servitude itself, the spirit of an exalted freedom! The unbought grace of life, the cheap defence of nations, the nurse of manly sentiment and heroic enterprise, is gone! It is gone, that sensibility of principle, that chastity of honour, which felt a stain like a wound, which inspired courage whilst it mitigated ferocity, which ennobled whatever it touched, and under which vice itself lost half its evil by losing all its grossness!

This mixed system of opinion and sentiment had its origin in the ancient chivalry; and the principle, though varied in its appearance by the varying state of human affairs, subsisted and influenced through a long succession of generations, even to the time we live in. If it should ever be totally extinguished, the loss, I fear, will be great. It is this which has given its character to modern Europe. It is this which has distinguished it under all its forms of government, and distinguished it to its advantage, from the states of Asia, and possibly from those states which flourished in the most brilliant periods of the antique world. It was this, which, without confounding ranks, had produced a noble equality, and handed it down through all the gradations of social life. It was this opinion which mitigated kings into companions, and raised private men to be fellows with kings. Without force or opposition, it subdued the fierceness of pride and power; it obliged sovereigns to submit to the soft collar of social esteem, compelled stern authority to submit to elegance, and gave a domination, vanquisher of laws, to be subdued by manners.

But now all is to be changed. All the pleasing illusions which made power gentle and obedience liberal, which harmonized the different shades of life, and which by a bland assimilation incorporated into politics the sentiments which beautify and soften private society, are to be dissolved by this new conquering empire of light and reason. All the decent drapery of life is to be rudely torn off. All the superadded ideas, furnished from the wardrobe of a moral imagination, which the heart owns and the understanding ratifies, as necessary to cover the defects of our naked, shivering nature, and to raise it to dignity in our own estimation, are to be exploded, as a ridiculous, absurd, and antiquated fashion.

On this scheme of things, a king is but a man, a queen is but a woman, a woman is but an animal—and an animal not of the highest order. All homage paid to the sex in general as such, and without distinct views, is to be regarded as romance and folly. Regicide, and parricide, and sacrilege, are but fictions of superstition, corrupting jurisprudence by destroying its simplicity. The murder of a king, or a queen, or a bishop, or a father, are only common homicide—and if the people are by any chance or in any way gainers by it, a sort of homicide much the most pardonable, and into which we ought not to make too severe a scrutiny.

On the scheme of this barbarous philosophy, which is the offspring of cold hearts and muddy understandings and which is as void of solid wisdom as it is destitute of all taste and elegance, laws are to be supported only by their own terrors, and by the concern which each individual may find in them from his own private speculations, or can spare to them from his own private interests. In the groves of *their* academy, at the end of every vista, you see nothing but the gallows. Nothing is left which engages the affections on the part of the commonwealth. On the principles of this mechanic philosophy, our institutions can never be embodied, if I may use the expression, in persons, so as to create in us love, veneration, admiration, or attachment. But that sort of reason which banishes the affections is incapable of filling their place. These public affections, combined with manners, are required sometimes as supplements, sometimes as correctives, always as aids to law. The precept given by a wise man, as well as a great critic, for the construction of poems, is equally true as to states: '*Non satis est pulchra esse poemata, dulcia sunto.*'[10] There ought to be a system of manners in every nation which a well-formed mind would be disposed to relish. To make us love our country, our country ought to be lovely.

But power, of some kind or other, will survive the shock in which manners and opinions perish; and it will find other and worse means for its support. The usurpation, which, in order to subvert ancient institutions, has destroyed ancient principles, will hold power by arts

10. 'It is not enough for poems to be beautiful; they must also be sweet, and divert the mind of the listener.'

similar to those by which it has acquired it. When the old feudal and chivalrous spirit of *fealty*, which, by freeing kings from fear, freed both kings and subjects from the precautions of tyranny, shall be extinct in the minds of men, plots and assassinations will be anticipated by preventive murder and preventive confiscation, and that long roll of grim and bloody maxims which form the political code of all power not standing on its own honour and the honour of those who are to obey it. Kings will be tyrants from policy, when subjects are rebels from principle.

When ancient opinions and rules of life are taken away, the loss cannot possibly be estimated. From that moment we have no compass to govern us, nor can we know distinctly to what port we steer. Europe, undoubtedly, taken in a mass, was in a flourishing condition the day on which your revolution was completed. How much of that prosperous state was owing to the spirit of our old manners and opinions is not easy to say; but as such causes cannot be indifferent in their operation, we must presume that, on the whole, their operation was beneficial.

We are but too apt to consider things in the state in which we find them, without sufficiently adverting to the causes by which they have been produced, and possibly may be upheld. Nothing is more certain than that our manners, our civilization, and all the good things which are connected with manners and with, civilization, have, in this European world of ours, depended for ages upon two principles, and were, indeed, the result of both combined: I mean the spirit of a gentleman, and the spirit of religion. The nobility and the clergy, the one by profession, and the other by patronage, kept learning in existence, even in the midst of arms and confusions, and whilst governments were rather in their causes than formed. Learning paid back what it received to nobility and to priesthood, and paid it with usury, by enlarging their ideas, and by furnishing their minds. Happy, if they had all continued to know their indissoluble union, and their proper place! Happy, if learning, not debauched by ambition, had been satisfied to continue the instructor, and not aspired to be the master! Along with its natural protectors and guardians, learning will be cast into the mire and trodden down under the hoofs of a swinish multitude.

If, as I suspect, modern letters owe more than they are always willing to own to ancient manners, so do other interests which we value full as much as they are worth. Even commerce, and trade, and manufacture, the gods of our economical politicians, are themselves perhaps but creatures, are themselves but effects, which, as first causes, we choose to worship. They certainly grew under the same shade in which learning flourished. They, too, may decay with their natural protecting principles. With you, for the present at least, they all threaten to disappear together. Where trade and manufactures are wanting to a people, and the spirit of nobility and religion remains, sentiment supplies, and not always ill supplies, their place; but if commerce and the arts should be lost in an experiment to try how well a state may stand without these old fundamental principles, what sort of a thing must be a nation of gross, stupid, ferocious, and at the same time poor and sordid barbarians, destitute of religion, honour, or manly pride, possessing nothing at present, and hoping for nothing hereafter?

I wish you may not be going fast, and by the shortest cut, to that horrible and disgustful situation. Already there appears a poverty of conception, a coarseness and vulgarity, in all the proceedings of the Assembly and of all their instructors. Their liberty is not liberal. Their science is presumptuous ignorance. Their humanity is savage and brutal.

8

JEREMY BENTHAM, ANARCHICAL FALLACIES

INTRODUCTION

What are we to make of the fact that the man said to be one of the key figures in the emergence of modern liberalism thought that the principal dogma of liberalism's current instantiation—namely, the proposition that our political and legal order is subject to higher-order 'natural' or human rights—was no more than 'nonsense on stilts'?

Jeremy Bentham (1748-1832) was a philosopher, jurist, economist and—by the standards of his own day—radical. A child prodigy, he began to study Latin at the age of three, was sent to Oxford University at the age of twelve, and took his bachelor's degree there three years later. Bentham advocated for individual and economic freedoms, freedom of expression, separation of church and state, female suffrage, sexual liberty, and abolition of the death penalty. He was immensely prolific and a lifelong bachelor. As per his instructions, on Bentham's death his body was dissected, embalmed, dressed and placed in a chair, and now resides in a cabinet in a corridor of the main building of University College London.

Bentham's great work, *An Introduction to the Principles of Morals and Legislation* (1789), lays out the philosophy of utilitarianism for which he is best known today. Mankind, he said, is governed by two sovereign motives—pleasure and pain. We ought, therefore, to secure as much of the former at the cost of the least of the latter, and it was through what has become known as the 'felicific calculus' that we are to measure the pleasure or pain associated with an act and hence its 'utility'. The object of all legislation must be 'the greatest happiness of the greatest number'.

Utilitarianism is of great value for the modern man in at least two respects. In the first place, it is a wholly rational approach to ethics and politics: it does not need to call upon the existence of an otherworldly realm or otherworldly entities to establish its moral code, nor does it require us to accept as a matter of faith the existence of rights that transcend all practical considerations. Of no less significance is the fact that it requires us to consider the interests of the community as a whole, rather than merely the demands of individuals or special interest groups, when establishing moral rules and expectations or setting social, political, or economic policy.

Bentham has, it is true, often been credited with providing the philosophical foundations for liberal social reform. Hovering in the shadows of his philosophy, however, can already be detected the spectres of both totalitarianism and vulgarism. As has often been observed, the greatest happiness principle can be readily deployed to justify exploitation by the majority of minorities: it is arguable, for example, that the pleasure obtained by the majority in silencing radical or unpopular ideas might, in aggregate, exceed the pain felt by the minority whose ideas are shut down. At the same time, the greatest happiness principle in its Benthamite form tends towards the vulgarisation of society in that it overlooks the *quality* of pleasures that are to be entered in the felicific calculus: there is no particular reason to prefer pleasures obtained by conversation, study, or sport, for example, over pleasures obtained through watching cartoons or late-night talk shows. It is also distinctly possible that policies that are perceived to bring happiness to existing persons might lead to long-term degradation of civilizational values or the environment affecting generations to come.

In fact, one need look no further than Bentham's own writings to see something of the dark underbelly of utilitarianism. Consider, for example, the chapter entitled 'Of Slavery' in Part 3 of Bentham's *Principles of the Civil Code* (1843). Here he openly and frankly works through the logic of the utilitarian philosophy as applied to the institution of slavery. He proceeds on the self-evident basis that slavery is agreeable to the masters and accepts that it must be disagreeable to the slaves. He argues, however, that once slavery is established, it becomes the condition and destiny of the greatest number: 'A master counts his slaves as his flocks, by hundreds, by thousands, by tens of thousands.' Since the benefit is on the side of the single slaveowner as against the disadvantage faced by the multitude of slaves, therefore, the outcome of the felicific calculus will plainly be in favour of abolition, and this conclusion is supported by economic productivity losses that Bentham attributes to slavery. The unsettling aspect of Bentham's argument, however, is that there is no reference to the intrinsic value of liberty and the unenslaved state; the philosophy does not *inherently* come out as opposed to the institution of slavery. Indeed, it is plain from Bentham's argument that slavery could be justified by the felicific calculus if a large number of masters outnumbered a relatively small contingent of slaves.

Bentham's razor-sharp mind was perhaps most triumphantly applied to a matter that remains of the utmost significance today—the question of natural rights. Human rights today may offer us a warm fuzzy feeling of doing good and signalling virtue; for Bentham, observing the bloody horrors of the Revolution in France and the Reign of Terror, there was a chain of causation leading directly from what he called the 'terrorist language' of 'imprescriptible rights' all the way to the guillotine. His *Anarchical Fallacies* (written between 1791 and 1795, although not published until 1816) is a powerful attack on both the concept of natural rights as well as its concrete realization in the Declaration of the Rights of Man and Citizen of 1789 (as reprinted in 1791) of the French National Assembly.

The central philosophical difficulty with the idea of 'natural rights', explains Bentham, is that rights are created by law, through the command of the sovereign, which means that they cannot exist prior to, or separately from, government. The very notion of 'natural rights', in fact, relies on the fallacy of 'begging the question': it is no answer to the question of how such 'rights' arise to assert that they arise from 'nature'. Bentham accepts, it must be admitted, that equivalent benefits could be conferred by a government legislating for such. These benefits would not, however, be 'rights' in any meaningful sense, and they could always be altered or dispensed with by further legislation.

The concept of 'natural rights' is not, though, merely a logical fallacy; it is also a subversive threat which gives rise to the anarchical consequences suggested by the title of Bentham's essay. This is because, explains Bentham, all such 'natural rights' are of necessity extra-legal, and must, therefore, be asserted as a challenge to the existing legal order. Moreover, since such rights must, by definition, be anterior to law, they cannot be regulated or repealed by law. Worse yet, if they are truly 'natural', they must be applicable universally and forever; so while vis-à-vis the existing legal order 'natural rights' are 'anarchical', the new order which they purport to establish is totalitarian in nature and admits of no exceptions. 'In us is the perfection of virtue and wisdom: in all mankind besides, the extremity of wickedness and folly,' mocks Bentham of the posturing of natural rights advocates. 'All nations—all future ages—shall be, for they are predestined to be, our slaves.'

How, then, are we more rationally to approach the question of 'rights'? We should establish such 'rights' (which are not really rights at all) as are advantageous to society, suggests Bentham, and maintain them so long as (and no longer than) they remain, on the whole, advantageous to society; when, on the whole, any 'right' is no longer advantageous to society, it should be abolished. Whether or not a 'right' is advantageous must be looked at in the specific context in which it is proposed to be established or abolished. And all proposed 'rights' must be specifically and precisely described—not 'jumbled with an undistinguishable heap of others, under any such vague general terms as property, liberty, and the like'.

Bentham's 'Critical Examination' is a lot of fun. He pokes fun at the arrant illogicality of his target and runs rings around the lesser wits who had the impudence to erect a political order on such shaky foundations. His language is rambunctious and ebullient: all this stuff about rights, he tells us, is 'shallow and reckless vanity', 'a perpetual vein of nonsense, flowing from a perpetual abuse of words', and, most famously, 'nonsense on stilts'. Through a combination of mockery and incisive philosophical analysis he explodes the great shibboleths of the modern political order. To the proposition that all men are born and remain free, he answers: 'No, not a single man: not a single man that ever was, or is, or will be.' To the suggestion that all men are equal in rights, he has this to say: 'The apprentice, then, is equal in rights to his master; he has as much liberty with relation to the master, as the master has with relation to him; he has as much right to command and to punish him; he is as much owner and master of the master's house, as the master himself.' The reader is tempted to borrow Bentham's own language in agreement and exclaim together with him: *Absurd and miserable nonsense!*

Bentham would, no doubt, have been thoroughly dismayed to know that abstract rights of the same basic type as he excoriated in the French Declaration of 1789 are now deeply embedded in the consciousness of Western man, and his legal order, as unquestionable *a priori* truths. Indeed, it may be no accident, given that our political order is founded on what Bentham called this 'terrorist' material, that the conceptual difficulties with 'natural' or 'human rights' are not more widely talked about. This renders his 'Critical Examination' all the more important and, viewed correctly, potentially incendiary. These are ideas whose time has—after a difficult two centuries—perhaps finally come.

A CRITICAL EXAMINATION OF THE DECLARATION OF RIGHTS

PRELIMINARY OBSERVATIONS

The Declaration of Rights—I mean the paper published under that name by the French National Assembly in 1791—assumes for its subject matter a field of disquisition as unbounded in point of extent as it is important in its nature. But the more ample the extent given to any proposition or string of propositions, the more difficult it is to keep the import of it confined without deviation within the bounds of truth and reason. If in the smallest corners of the field it ranges over, it fail of coinciding with the line of rigid rectitude, no sooner is the aberration pointed out, than (inasmuch as there is no medium between truth and falsehood) its pretensions to the appellation of a truism are gone, and whoever looks upon it must recognise it to be false and erroneous—and if, as here, political conduct be the theme, so far as the error extends and fails of being detected, pernicious.

In a work of such extreme importance with a view to practice, and which throughout keeps practice so closely and immediately and professedly in view, a single error may be attended with the most fatal consequences. The more extensive the propositions, the more consummate will be the knowledge, the more exquisite the skill, indispensably requisite to confine them in all points within the pale of truth. The most consummate ability in the whole nation could not have been too much for the task—one may venture to say, it would not have been equal to it. But that, in the sanctioning of each proposition, the most consummate ability should happen to be vested in the heads of the sorry majority in whose hands the plenitude of power happened on that same occasion to be vested, is an event against which the chances are almost as infinity to one.

Here, then, is a radical and all-pervading error—the attempting to give to a work on such a subject the sanction of government; especially of such a government—a government composed of members so numerous, so unequal in talent, as well as discordant in inclinations and affections. Had it been the work of a single hand, and that a private one, and in that character given to the world, every good effect would have been produced by it that could be produced by it when published as the work of government, without any of the bad effects which in case of the smallest error must result from it when given as the work of government.

The revolution, which threw the government into the hands of the penners and adopters of this declaration, having been the effect of insurrection, the grand object evidently is to justify the cause. But by justifying it, they invite it: in justifying past insurrection, they plant and cultivate a propensity to perpetual insurrection in time future; they sow the seeds of anarchy broad-cast: in justifying the demolition of existing authorities, they undermine all future ones, their own consequently in the number. Shallow and reckless vanity! They imitate in their conduct the author of that fabled law, according to which the assassination of the prince upon the throne gave to the assassin a title to succeed him. 'People, behold your rights! If a single article of them be violated, insurrection is not your right only, but the most sacred of your duties.' Such is the constant language, for such is the professed object of this source and model of all laws—this self-consecrated oracle of all nations.

The more abstract—that is, the more extensive the proposition is, the more liable is it to involve a fallacy. Of fallacies, one of the most natural modifications is that which is called begging the question—the abuse of making the abstract proposition resorted to for proof, a lever for introducing, in the company of other propositions that are nothing to the purpose, the very proposition which is admitted to stand in need of proof.

Is the provision in question fit in point of expediency to be passed into a law for the government of the French nation? That, *mutatis mutandis*, would have been the question put in England: that was the proper question to have been put in relation to each provision it was proposed should enter into the composition of the body of French laws. Instead of that, as often as the utility of a provision appeared (by reason of the wideness of its extent, for instance) of a doubtful nature, the way taken to clear the doubt was to assert it to be a provision fit to be made law for all men—for all Frenchmen—and for all Englishmen, for example, into the bargain. This medium of proof was the more alluring, inasmuch as to the advantage of removing opposition, was added the pleasure, the sort of titillation so exquisite to the nerve of vanity in a French heart—the satisfaction, to use a homely, but not the less apposite proverb, of teaching grandmothers to suck eggs. Hark! Ye citizens of the other side of the water! Can you tell us what rights you have belonging to you? No, that you can't. It's we that understand rights: not our own only, but yours into the bargain; while you—poor simple souls!—know nothing about the matter.

Hasty generalization, the great stumbling block of intellectual vanity! Hasty generalization, the rock that even genius itself is so apt to split upon! Hasty generalization, the bane of prudence and of science!

In the British Houses of Parliament, more especially in the most efficient house for business, there prevails a well-known jealousy of, and repugnance to, the voting of abstract propositions. This jealousy is not less general than reasonable. A jealousy of abstract propositions is an aversion to whatever is beside the purpose—an aversion to impertinence.

The great enemies of public peace are the selfish and dissocial passions—necessary as they are—the one to the very existence of each individual, the other to his security. On the part of these affections, a deficiency in point of strength is never to be apprehended: all that is to be apprehended in respect of them, is to be apprehended on the side of their excess. Society is held together only by the sacrifices that men can be induced to make of the gratifications they demand: to obtain these sacrifices is the great difficulty, the great task of government. What has been the object, the perpetual and palpable object, of this declaration of pretended rights? To add as much force as possible to these passions, already but too strong—to burst the cords that hold them in—to say to the selfish passions, there—everywhere—is your prey!—to the angry passions, there—everywhere—is your enemy.

Such is the morality of this celebrated manifesto, rendered famous by the same qualities that gave celebrity to the incendiary of the Ephesian temple.

The logic of it is of a piece with its morality: a perpetual vein of nonsense, flowing from a perpetual abuse of words—words having a variety of meanings, where words with single meanings were equally at hand—the same words used in a variety of meanings in the same page—words used in meanings not their own, where proper words were equally at hand—words and propositions of the most unbounded signification, turned loose without any of those exceptions or modifications which are so necessary on every occasion to reduce their import within the compass, not only of right reason, but even of the design in hand, of whatever nature it may be—the same inaccuracy, the same inattention in the penning of this cluster of truths on which the fate of nations was to hang, as if it had been an oriental tale, or an allegory for a magazine—stale epigrams, instead of necessary distinctions—figurative expressions preferred to simple ones—sentimental conceits, as trite as they are unmeaning, preferred to apt and precise expressions—frippery ornament preferred to the majestic simplicity of good sound sense—and the acts of the senate loaded and disfigured by the tinsel of the playhouse.

In a play or a novel, an improper word is but a word; and the impropriety, whether noticed or not, is attended with no consequences. In a body of laws—especially of laws given as constitutional and fundamental ones—an improper word may be a national calamity—and civil war may be the consequence of it. Out of one foolish word may start a thousand daggers.

Imputations like these may appear general and declamatory—and rightly so, if they stood alone: but they will be justified even to satiety by the details that follow. Scarcely an article, which in rummaging it, will not be found a true Pandora's box.

In running over the several articles, I shall on the occasion of each article point out, in the first place, the errors it contains in theory; and then, in the second place, the mischiefs it is pregnant with in practice.

The criticism is verbal—true, but what else can it be? Words—words without a meaning, or with a meaning too flatly false to be maintained by anybody, are the stuff it is made of. Look to the letter, you find nonsense—look beyond the letter, you find nothing.

Men are born and remain free and equal in respect of rights. Social distinctions cannot be founded but upon common utility.

In this article are contained, grammatically speaking, two distinct sentences. The first is full of error, the other of ambiguity.

In the first are contained four distinguishable propositions, all of them false—all of them notoriously and undeniably false:

1. That all men are born free.

2. That all men remain free.

3. That all men are born equal in rights.

4. That all men remain (i.e. remain forever, for the proposition is indefinite and unlimited) equal in rights.

All men are born free? All men remain free? No, not a single man: not a single man that ever was, or is, or will be. All men, on the contrary, are born in subjection, and the most absolute subjection—the subjection of a helpless child to the parents on whom he depends every moment for his existence. In this subjection every man is born—in this subjection he continues for years—for a great number of years—and the existence of the individual and of the species depends upon his so doing.

What is the state of things to which the supposed existence of these supposed rights is meant to bear reference—a state of things prior to the existence of government, or a state of things subsequent to the existence of government? If to a state prior to the existence of government, what would the existence of such rights as these be to the purpose, even if it were true, in any country where there is such a thing as government? If to a state of things subsequent to the formation of government—it in a country where there is a government, in what single instance—in the instance of what single government, is it true?

145

Setting aside the case of parent and child, let any man name that single government under which any such equality is recognised.

All men born free? Absurd and miserable nonsense! When the great complaint—a complaint made perhaps by the very same people at the same time—is that so many men are born slaves. Oh! but when we acknowledge them to be born slaves, we refer to the laws in being; which laws being void, as being contrary to those laws of nature which are the efficient causes of those rights of man that we are declaring, the men in question are free in one sense, though slaves in another; slaves, and free, at the same time: free in respect of the laws of nature—slaves in respect of the pretended human laws, which, though called laws, are no laws at all, as being contrary to the laws of nature. For such is the difference—the great and perpetual difference, betwixt the good subject, the rational censor of the laws, and the anarchist—between the moderate man and the man of violence. The rational censor, acknowledging the existence of the law he disapproves, proposes the repeal of it: the anarchist, setting up his will and fancy for a law before which all mankind are called upon to bow down at the first word—the anarchist, trampling on truth and decency, denies the validity of the law in question, denies the existence of it in the character of a law, and calls upon all mankind to rise up in a mass, and resist the execution of it.

Whatever is, is, was the maxim of Descartes, who looked upon it as so sure, as well as so instructive a truth, that everything else which goes by the name of truth might be deduced from it. The philosophical vortex-maker—who, however mistaken in his philosophy and his logic, was harmless enough at least—the manufacturer of identical propositions and celestial vortices—little thought how soon a part of his own countrymen, fraught with pretensions as empty as his own, and as mischievous as his were innocent, would contest with him even this his favourite and fundamental maxim, by which everything else was to be brought to light. Whatever is, is not—is the maxim of the anarchist, as often as anything comes across him in the shape of a law which he happens not to like.

'Cruel is the judge,' says Lord Bacon, 'who, in order to enable himself to torture men, applies torture to the law.' Still more cruel is the anarchist, who, for the purpose of effecting the subversion of the

146

laws themselves, as well as the massacre of the legislators, tortures not only the words of the law, but the very vitals of the language.

All men are born equal in rights. The rights of the heir of the most indigent family equal to the rights of the heir of the most wealthy? In what case is this true? I say nothing of hereditary dignities and powers. Inequalities such as these being proscribed under and by the French government in France are consequently proscribed by that government under every other government, and consequently have no existence anywhere. For the total subjection of every other government to French government is a fundamental principle in the law of universal independence—the French law. Yet neither was this true at the time of issuing this Declaration of Rights, nor was it meant to be so afterwards. The 13th article, which we shall come to in its place, proceeds on the contrary supposition: for, considering its other attributes, inconsistency could not be wanting to the list. It can scarcely be more hostile to all other laws than it is at variance with itself.

All men (i.e. all human creatures of both sexes) remain equal in rights. All men, meaning doubtless all human creatures. The apprentice, then, is equal in rights to his master; he has as much liberty with relation to the master, as the master has with relation to him; he has as much right to command and to punish him; he is as much owner and master of the master's house, as the master himself. The case is the same as between ward and guardian. So again as between wife and husband. The madman has as good a right to confine anybody else, as anybody else has to confine him. The idiot has as much right to govern everybody, as anybody can have to govern him. The physician and the nurse, when called in by the next friend of a sick man seized with a delirium, have no more right to prevent his throwing himself out of the window, than he has to throw them out of it. All this is plainly and incontestably included in this article of the Declaration of Rights: in the very words of it, and in the meaning—if it have any meaning. Was this the meaning of the authors of it—or did they mean to admit this explanation as to some of the instances, and to explain the article away as to the rest? Not being idiots, nor lunatics, nor under a delirium, they would explain it away with regard to the madman, and the man under a delirium. Considering that a child may become an orphan as soon as it has seen the light, and that in that case, if not subject to government, it must perish, they would explain it away, I think, and contradict themselves, in the case of guardian and ward. In the case of master and apprentice, I would not take upon me to decide: it may have been their meaning to proscribe that relation altogether—at least, this may have been the case as soon as the repugnancy between that institution and this oracle was pointed out; for the professed object and destination of it is to be the standard of truth and falsehood, of right and wrong, in everything that relates to government. But to this standard, and to this article of it, the subjection of the apprentice to the master is flatly and diametrically repugnant. If it do not proscribe and exclude this inequality, it proscribes none: if it do not do this mischief, it does nothing. ...

ARTICLE II

The end in view of every political association is the preservation of the natural and imprescriptible rights of man. These rights are liberty, property, security, and resistance to oppression.

Sentence 1. The end in view of every political association is the preservation of the natural and imprescriptible rights of man.

More confusion—more nonsense—and the nonsense, as usual, dangerous nonsense. The words can scarcely be said to have a meaning: but if they have, or rather if they had a meaning, these would be the propositions either asserted or implied:

1. That there are such things as rights anterior to the establishment of governments: for natural, as applied to rights, if it mean anything, is meant to stand in opposition to legal—to such rights as are acknowledged to owe their existence to government, and are consequently posterior in their date to the establishment of government.

2. That these rights cannot be abrogated by government: for cannot is implied in the form of the word imprescriptible, and the sense it wears when so applied, is the cut-throat sense above explained.

3. That the governments that exist derive their origin from formal associations, or what are now called conventions: associations entered into by a partnership contract, with all the members for partners—entered into at a day prefixed, for a predetermined purpose, the formation of a new government where there was none before (for as to formal meetings holden under the control of an existing

148

government, they are evidently out of question here) in which it seems again to be implied in the way of inference, though a necessary and an unavoidable inference, that all governments (that is, self-called governments, knots of persons exercising the powers of government) that have had any other origin than an association of the above description, are illegal, that is, no governments at all; resistance to them, and subversion of them, lawful and commendable; and so on.

Such are the notions implied in this first part of the article. How stands the truth of things? That there are no such things as natural rights—no such things as rights anterior to the establishment of government—no such things as natural rights opposed to, in contradistinction to, legal: that the expression is merely figurative; that when used, in the moment you attempt to give it a literal meaning it leads to error, and to that sort of error that leads to mischief—to the extremity of mischief.

We know what it is for men to live without government—and living without government, to live without rights: we know what it is for men to live without government, for we see instances of such a way of life—we see it in many savage nations, or rather races of mankind; for instance, among the savages of New South Wales, whose way of living is so well known to us: no habit of obedience, and thence no government—no government, and thence no laws—no laws, and thence no such things as rights—no security—no property: liberty, as against regular control, the control of laws and government—perfect; but as against all irregular control, the mandates of stronger individuals, none. In this state, at a time earlier than the commencement of history—in this same state, judging from analogy, we, the inhabitants of the part of the globe we call Europe, were; no government, consequently no rights; no rights, consequently no property—no legal security—no legal liberty: security not more than belongs to beasts—forecast and sense of insecurity keener—consequently in point of happiness below the level of the brutal race.

In proportion to the want of happiness resulting from the want of rights, a reason exists for wishing that there were such things as rights. But reasons for wishing there were such things as rights, are not rights: a reason for wishing that a certain right were established, is not that right—want is not supply—hunger is not bread.

That which has no existence cannot be destroyed—that which cannot be destroyed cannot require anything to preserve it from destruction. Natural rights is simple nonsense: natural and imprescriptible rights, rhetorical nonsense—nonsense upon stilts. But this rhetorical nonsense ends in the old strain of mischievous nonsense: for immediately a list of these pretended natural rights is given, and those are so expressed as to present to view legal rights. And of these rights, whatever they are, there is not, it seems, any one of which any government can, upon any occasion whatever, abrogate the smallest particle.

So much for terrorist language. What is the language of reason and plain sense upon this same subject? That in proportion as it is right or proper, i.e. advantageous to the society in question, that this or that right—a right to this or that effect—should be established and maintained, in that same proportion it is wrong that it should be abrogated: but that as there is no right which ought not to be maintained so long as it is upon the whole advantageous to the society that it should be maintained, so there is no right which, when the abolition of it is advantageous to society, should not be abolished. To know whether it would be more for the advantage of society that this or that right should be maintained or abolished, the time at which the question about maintaining or abolishing is proposed must be given, and the circumstances under which it is proposed to maintain or abolish it; the right itself must be specifically described, not jumbled with an undistinguishable heap of others, under any such vague general terms as property, liberty, and the like.

One thing, in the midst of all this confusion, is but too plain. They know not of what they are talking under the name of natural rights, and yet they would have them imprescriptible—proof against all the power of the laws—pregnant with occasions summoning the members of the community to rise up in resistance against the laws. What, then, was their object in declaring the existence of imprescriptible rights, and without specifying a single one by any such mark as it could be known by? This and no other—to excite and keep up a spirit of resistance to all laws—a spirit of insurrection against all governments—against the governments of all other nations instantly—against the government of their own nation—against the government they themselves were pretending to establish—even that, as soon as their own reign should be at an end. In us is the perfection of virtue and wisdom: in all mankind besides, the extremity of wickedness and folly. Our will shall consequently reign without control, and forever: reign now we are living—reign after we are dead.

All nations—all future ages—shall be, for they are predestined to be, our slaves.

Future governments will not have honesty enough to be trusted with the determination of what rights shall be maintained, what abrogated—what laws kept in force, what repealed. Future subjects (I should say future citizens, for French government does not admit of subjects) will not have wit enough to be trusted with the choice whether to submit to the determination of the government of their time, or to resist it. Governments, citizens—all to the end of time—all must be kept in chains.

Such are their maxims—such their premises—for it is by such premises only that the doctrine of imprescriptible rights and unrepealable laws can be supported.

What is the real source of these imprescriptible rights—these unrepealable laws? Power turned blind by looking from its own height: self-conceit and tyranny exalted into insanity. No man was to have any other man for a servant, yet all men were forever to be their slaves. Making laws with imposture in their mouths, under pretence of declaring them—giving for laws anything that came uppermost, and these unrepealable ones, on pretence of finding them ready made. Made by what? Not by a God—they allow of none; but by their goddess, Nature.

The origination of governments from a contract is a pure fiction, or in other words, a falsehood. It never has been known to be true in any instance; the allegation of it does mischief, by involving the subject in error and confusion, and is neither necessary nor useful to any good purpose.

All governments that we have any account of have been gradually established by habit, after having been formed by force; unless in the instance of governments formed by individuals who have been emancipated, or have emancipated themselves, from governments already formed, the governments under which they were born—a rare case, and from which nothing follows with regard to the rest. What signifies it how governments are formed? Is it the less proper—the less conducive to the happiness of society—that the happiness of society should be the one object kept in view by the members of the government in all their measures? Is it the less the interest of men to be happy—less to be wished that they may be so—less the moral duty of their governors to make them so, as far as they can, at Mogadore than at Philadelphia?

Whence is it, but from government, that contracts derive their binding force? Contracts came from government, not government from contracts. It is from the habit of enforcing contracts, and seeing them enforced, that governments are chiefly indebted for whatever disposition they have to observe them.

Sentence 2. These rights are liberty, property, security, and resistance to oppression.

Observe the extent of these pretended rights, each of them belonging to every man, and all of them without bounds. Unbounded liberty; that is, amongst other things, the liberty of doing or not doing on every occasion whatever each man pleases. Unbounded property; that is, the right of doing with everything around him (with everything at least, if not with every person) whatsoever he pleases; communicating that right to anybody, and withholding it from anybody. Unbounded security; that is, security for such his liberty, for such his property, and for his person, against every defalcation that can be called for on any account in respect of any of them. Unbounded resistance to oppression; that is, unbounded exercise of the faculty of guarding himself against whatever unpleasant circumstance may present itself to his imagination or his passions under that name. Nature, say some of the interpreters of the pretended law of nature—nature gave to each man a right to everything; which is, in effect, but another way of saying—nature has given no such right to anybody; for in regard to most rights, it is as true that what is every man's right is no man's right, as that what is every man's business is no man's business. Nature gave—gave to every man a right to everything—be it so—true; and hence the necessity of human government and human laws, to give to every man his own right, without which no right whatsoever would amount to anything. Nature gave every man a right to everything before the existence of laws, and in default of laws. This nominal universality and real nonentity of right, set up provisionally by nature in default of laws, the French oracle lays hold of, and perpetuates it under the law and in spite of laws. These anarchical rights which nature had set out with, democratic art attempts to rivet down, and declares indefeasible.

Unbounded liberty—I must still say unbounded liberty—for though the next article but one returns to the charge, and gives such a definition of liberty as seems intended to set bounds to it, yet in effect the limitation amounts to nothing; and when, as here, no warning is given of any exception in the texture of the general rule, every exception which turns up is, not a confirmation but a contradiction of the rule—liberty, without any pre-announced or intelligible bounds; and as to the other rights, they remain unbounded to the end: rights of man composed of a system of contradictions and impossibilities.

In vain would it be said, that though no bounds are here assigned to any of these rights, yet it is to be understood as taken for granted, and tacitly admitted and assumed, that they are to have bounds; viz. such bounds as it is understood will be set them by the laws. Vain, I say, would be this apology; for the supposition would be contradictory to the express declaration of the article itself, and would defeat the very object which the whole declaration has in view. It would be self-contradictory, because these rights are, in the same breath in which their existence is declared, declared to be imprescriptible; and imprescriptible, or, as we in England should say, indefeasible, means nothing unless it exclude the interference of the laws.

It would be not only inconsistent with itself, but inconsistent with the declared and sole object of the declaration, if it did not exclude the interference of the laws. It is against the laws themselves, and the laws only, that this declaration is levelled. It is for the hands of the legislator and all legislators, and none but legislators, that the shackles it provides are intended—it is against the apprehended encroachments of legislators that the rights in question, the liberty and property, and so forth, are intended to be made secure—it is to such encroachments, and damages, and dangers, that whatever security it professes to give has respect. Precious security for unbounded rights against legislators, if the extent of those rights in every direction were purposely left to depend upon the will and pleasure of those very legislators!

Nonsensical or nugatory, and in both cases mischievous: such is the alternative.

So much for all these pretended indefeasible rights in the lump: their inconsistency with each other, as well as the inconsistency of them in the character of indefeasible rights with the existence of government and all peaceable society, will appear still more plainly when we examine them one by one.

1. Liberty, then, is imprescriptible—incapable of being taken away—out of the power of any government ever to take away: liberty—that is, every branch of liberty—every individual exercise of liberty; for no line is drawn—no distinction—no exception made. What these instructors as well as governors of mankind appear not to know is that all rights are made at the expense of liberty—all laws by which rights are created or confirmed. No right without a correspondent obligation. Liberty, as against the coercion of the law, may, it is true, be given by the simple removal of the obligation by which that coercion was applied—by the simple repeal of the coercing law. But as against the coercion applicable by individual to individual, no liberty can be given to one man but in proportion as it is taken from another. All coercive laws, therefore (that is, all laws but constitutional laws, and laws repealing or modifying coercive laws) and in particular all laws creative of liberty, are, as far as they go, abrogative of liberty. Not here and there a law only—not this or that possible law, but almost all laws, are therefore repugnant to these natural and imprescriptible rights: consequently null and void, calling for resistance and insurrection, and so on, as before.

Laws creative of rights of property are also struck at by the same anathema. How is property given? By restraining liberty; that is, by taking it away so far as is necessary for the purpose. How is your house made yours? By debarring every one else from the liberty of entering it without your leave.

2. Property. Property stands second on the list—proprietary rights are in the number of the natural and imprescriptible rights of man—of the rights which a man is not indebted for to the laws, and which cannot be taken from him by the laws. Men—that is, every man (for a general expression given without exception is a universal one) has a right to property, to proprietary rights, a right which cannot be taken away from him by the laws. To proprietary rights. Good: but in relation to what subject? For as to proprietary rights—without a subject to which they are referable—without a subject in or in relation to which they can be exercised—they will hardly be of much value, they will

hardly be worth taking care of, with so much solemnity. In vain would all the laws in the world have ascertained that I have a right to something. If this be all they have done for me—if there be no specific subject in relation to which my proprietary rights are established, I must either take what I want without right, or starve. As there is no such subject specified with relation to each man, or to any man (indeed how could there be?) the necessary inference (taking the passage literally) is that every man has all manner of proprietary rights with relation to every subject of property without exception: in a word, that every man has a right to everything. Unfortunately, in most matters of property, what is every man's right is no man's right; so that the effect of this part of the oracle, if observed, would be, not to establish property, but to extinguish it—to render it impossible ever to be revived: and this is one of the rights declared to be imprescriptible.

It will probably be acknowledged, that according to this construction, the clause in question is equally ruinous and absurd—and hence the inference may be, that this was not the construction—this was not the meaning in view. But by the same rule, every possible construction which the words employed can admit of might be proved not to have been the meaning in view: nor is this clause a whit more absurd or ruinous than all that goes before it, and a great deal of what comes after it. And, in short, if this be not the meaning of it, what is? Give it a sense—give it any sense whatever—it is mischievous: to save it from that imputation, there is but one course to take, which is to acknowledge it to be nonsense.

Thus much would be clear, if anything were clear in it, that according to this clause, whatever proprietary rights, whatever property a man once has, no matter how, being imprescriptible, can never be taken away from him by any law: or of what use or meaning is the clause? So that the moment it is acknowledged in relation to any article, that such article is my property, no matter how or when it became so, that moment it is acknowledged that it can never be taken away from me: therefore, for example, all laws and all judgments, whereby anything is taken away from me without my free consent—all taxes, for example, and all fines—are void, and, as such, call for resistance and insurrection, and so forth, as before.

3. Security. Security stands the third on the list of these natural and imprescriptible rights which laws did not give, and which laws

are not in any degree to be suffered to take away. Under the head of security, liberty might have been included, so likewise property: since security for liberty, or the enjoyment of liberty, may be spoken of as a branch of security—security for property, or the enjoyment of proprietary rights, as another. Security for person is the branch that seems here to have been understood: security for each man's person, as against all those hurtful or disagreeable impressions (exclusive of those which consist in the mere disturbance of the enjoyment of liberty) by which a man is affected in his person; loss of life—loss of limbs—loss of the use of limbs—wounds, bruises, and the like. All laws are null and void, then, which on any account or in any manner seek to expose the person of any man to any risk—which appoint capital or other corporal punishment—which expose a man to personal hazard in the service of the military power against foreign enemies, or in that of the judicial power against delinquents—all laws which, to preserve the country from pestilence, authorize the immediate execution of a suspected person, in the event of his transgressing certain bounds.

4. Resistance to oppression. Fourth and last in the list of natural and imprescriptible rights, resistance to oppression—meaning, I suppose, the right to resist oppression. What is oppression? Power misapplied to the prejudice of some individual. What is it that a man has in view when he speaks of oppression? Some exertion of power which he looks upon as misapplied to the prejudice of some individual—to the producing on the part of such individual some suffering, to which (whether as forbidden by the laws or otherwise) we conceive he ought not to have been subjected. But against everything that can come under the name of oppression, provision has been already made, in the manner we have seen, by the recognition of the three preceding rights; since no oppression can fall upon a man which is not an infringement of his rights in relation to liberty, rights in relation to property, or rights in relation to security, as above described. Where, then, is the difference—to what purpose this fourth clause after the three first? To this purpose: the mischief they seek to prevent, the rights they seek to establish, are the same; the difference lies in the nature of the remedy endeavoured to be applied. To prevent the mischief in question, the endeavour of the three former clauses is to tie the hand of the legislator and his subordinates, by the fear of nullity, and the remote apprehension of general resistance and insurrection. The aim

of this fourth clause is to raise the hand of the individual concerned to prevent the apprehended infraction of his rights at the moment when he looks upon it as about to take place.

Whenever you are about to be oppressed, you have a right to resist oppression: whenever you conceive yourself to be oppressed, conceive yourself to have a right to make resistance, and act accordingly. In proportion as a law of any kind—any act of power, supreme or subordinate, legislative, administrative, or judicial, is unpleasant to a man, especially if, in consideration of such its unpleasantness, his opinion is, that such act of power ought not to have been exercised, he of course looks upon it as oppression: as often as anything of this sort happens to a man—as often as anything happens to a man to inflame his passions—this article, for fear his passions should not be sufficiently inflamed of themselves, sets itself to work to blow the flame, and urges him to resistance. Submit not to any decree or other act of power of the justice of which you are not yourself perfectly convinced. If a constable call upon you to serve in the militia, shoot the constable and not the enemy—if the commander of a press-gang trouble you, push him into the sea—if a bailiff, throw him out of the window. If a judge sentence you to be imprisoned or put to death, have a dagger ready, and take a stroke first at the judge.

ARTICLE IV

Liberty consists in being able to do that which is not hurtful to another, and therefore the exercise of the natural rights of each man has no other bounds than those which insure to the other members of the society the enjoyment of the same rights. These bounds cannot be determined but by the law.

In this article, three propositions are included:

Proposition 1. Liberty consists in being able to do that which is not hurtful to another. What! In that, and nothing else? Is not the liberty of doing mischief liberty? If not, what is it? And what word is there for it in the language, or in any language by which it can be spoken of? How childish, how repugnant to the ends of language, is this perversion of language! To attempt to confine a word in common and perpetual use, to an import to which nobody ever confined it before, or will continue to confine it! And so I am never to know whether I am at

157

liberty or not to do or to omit doing one act, till I see whether or no there is anybody that may be hurt by it—till I see the whole extent of all its consequences? Liberty! What liberty? As against what power? As against coercion from what source? As against coercion issuing from the law? Then to know whether the law have left me at liberty in any respect in relation to any act, I am to consult not the words of the law, but my own conception of what would be the consequences of the act. If among these consequences there be a single one by which anybody would be hurt, then, whatever the law says to me about it, I am not at liberty to do it. I am an officer of justice, appointed to superintend the execution of punishments ordered by justice: if I am ordered to cause a thief to be whipped, to know whether I am at liberty to cause the sentence to be executed, I must know whether whipping would hurt the thief; if it would, then I am not at liberty to whip the thief—to inflict the punishment which it is my duty to inflict.

Proposition 2. And therefore the exercise of the natural rights of each man has no other bounds than those which insure to the other members of the society the enjoyment of those same rights. Has no other bounds? Where is it that it has no other bounds? In what nation—under what government? If under any government, then the state of legislation under that government is in a state of absolute perfection. If there be no such government, then, by a confession necessarily implied, there is no nation upon earth in which this definition is conformable to the truth.

Proposition 3. These bounds cannot be determined but by the law. More contradiction, more confusion. What then? This liberty, this right, which is one of four rights that existed before laws, and will exist in spite of all that laws can do, owes all the boundaries it has, all the extent it has, to the laws. Till you know what the laws say to it, you do not know what there is of it, nor what account to give of it: and yet it existed, and that in full force and vigour, before there were any such things as laws; and so will continue to exist, and that forever, in spite of anything which laws can do to it. Still the same inaptitude of expressions—still the same confusion of that which it is supposed is, with that which it is conceived ought to be.

What says plain truth upon this subject? What is the sense most approaching to this nonsense?

The liberty which the law ought to allow of, and leave in

existence—leave uncoerced, unremoved—is the liberty which concerns those acts only, by which, if exercised, no damage would be done to the community upon the whole; that is, either no damage at all, or none but what promises to be compensated by at least equal benefit.

Accordingly, the exercise of the rights allowed to and conferred upon each individual, ought to have no other bounds set to it by the law than those which are necessary to enable it to maintain every other individual in the possession and exercise of such rights as it is consistent with the greatest good of the community that he should be allowed. The marking out of these bounds ought not to be left to anybody but the legislator acting as such—that is, to him or them who are acknowledged to be in possession of the sovereign power: that is, it ought not to be left to the occasional and arbitrary declaration of any individual, whatever share he may possess of subordinate authority.

The word *autrui*—another, is so loose—making no distinction between the community and individuals—as, according to the most natural construction, to deprive succeeding legislators of all power of repressing, by punishment or otherwise, any acts by which no individual sufferers are to be found; and to deprive them beyond a doubt of all power of affording protection to any man, woman, or child, against his or her own weakness, ignorance, or imprudence.

ARTICLE X

No-one ought to be molested for his opinions, even in matters of religion, provided that the manifestation of them does not disturb the public order established by the law.

Liberty of publication with regard to opinions, under certain exceptions, is a liberty which it would be highly proper and fit to establish, but which would receive but a very precarious establishment from an article thus worded. Disturb the public order? What does that mean? Louis XIV need not have hesitated about receiving an article thus worded into his code. The public order of things in this behalf, was an order in virtue of which the exercise of every religion but the Catholic, according to his edition of it, was proscribed. A law is enacted, forbidding men to express a particular opinion, or set of opinions, relative to a particular point in religion: forbidding men to express any of those opinions in the expression of which the Lutheran doctrine, for example, or the Calvinistic doctrine, or the Church of England doctrine consists—in a prohibition to this effect, consists the public order established by the law. Spite of this, a man manifests an opinion of the number of those which thus stand prohibited as belonging to the religion thus proscribed. The act by which this opinion is manifested, is it not an act of disturbance with relation to the public order thus established? Extraordinary indeed must be the assurance of him who could take upon him to answer in the negative.

Thus nugatory, thus flimsy, is this buckler of rights and liberties, in one of the few instances in which any attempt is made to apply it to a good purpose.

What should it have done, then? To this question an answer is scarcely within the province of this paper: the proposition with which I set out is not that the Declaration of Rights should have been worded differently, but that nothing under any such name, or with any such design, should have been attempted.

A word or two, however, may be given as a work of supererogation: that opinions of all sorts might be manifested without fear of punishment; that no publication should be deemed to subject a man to punishment on account of any opinions it may be found to contain, considered as mere opinions; but at the same time, that the plea of manifesting religious opinions, or the practising certain acts supposed to be enjoined or recommended in virtue of certain religious opinions as proper or necessary to be practised, should not operate as a justification for either exercising, or prompting men to exercise, any act which the legislature, without any view or reference to religion, has already thought fit, or may hereafter think fit, to insert into the catalogue of prohibited acts or offences.

To instance two species of delinquency—one of the most serious, the other of the slightest nature—acts tending to the violent subversion of the government by force—acts tending to the obstruction of the passage in the streets. An opinion that has been supposed by some to belong to the Christian religion is that every form of government but the monarchical is unlawful; an opinion that has been supposed by some to belong to the Christian religion—by some at least of those that adhere to that branch of the Christian religion which is termed the Roman Catholic—is that it is a duty, or at least a

160

merit, to join in processions of a certain description, to be performed on certain occasions.

What, then, is the true sense of the clause in question, in relation to these two cases? What ought to be the conduct of a government that is neither monarchical nor Catholic, with reference to the respective manifestation of these two opinions?

First, as to the opinion relative to the unlawfulness of a government not monarchical. The falsity or erroneousness which the members of such a government could not but attribute in their own minds to such an opinion is a consideration which, according to the spirit and intent of the provision in question, would not be sufficient to authorize their using penal or other coercive measures for the purpose of preventing the manifestation of them. At the same time, should such manifestation either have already had the effect of engaging individuals in any attempt to effect a violent subversion of the government by force, or appear to have produced a near probability of any such attempt—in such case, the engagement to permit the free manifestation of opinions in general, and of religious opinions in particular, is not to be understood to preclude the government from restraining the manifestation of the opinion in question, in every such way as it may deem likely to promote or facilitate any such attempt.

Again, as to the opinion relative to the meritoriousness of certain processions. By the principal part of the provision, government stands precluded from prohibiting publications manifesting an opinion in favour of the obligatoriness or meritoriousness of such processions. By the spirit of the same engagement, they stand precluded from prohibiting the performance of such processions, unless a persuasion of a political inconvenience as resulting from such practice—a persuasion not grounded on any notions of their unlawfulness in a religious view—should come to be entertained: as if, for example, the multitude of the persons joining in the procession, or the crowd of persons flocking to observe them, should fill up the streets to such a degree, or for such a length of time, and at intervals recurring with such frequency, as to be productive of such a degree of obstruction to the free use of the streets for the purposes of business, as in the eye of government should constitute a body of inconvenience worth encountering by a prohibitive law.

It would be a violation of the spirit of this part of the engagement, if the government—not by reason of any view it entertained of the political inconveniences of these processions (for example, as above) but for the purpose of giving an ascendency to religious opinions of an opposite nature (determined, for example, by a Protestant antipathy to Catholic processions)—were to make use of the real or pretended obstruction to the free use of the streets as a pretence for prohibiting such processions.

These examples, while they serve to illustrate the ground and degree and limits of the liberty which it may seem proper, on the score of public tranquillity and peace, to leave to the manifestation of opinions of a religious nature, may serve, at the same time, to render apparent the absurdity and perilousness of every attempt on the part of the government for the time being to tie up the hands of succeeding governments in relation to this or any other spot in the field of legislation. Observe how nice, and incapable of being described beforehand by any particular marks, are the lines which mark the limits of right and wrong in this behalf—which separate the useful from the pernicious—the prudent course from the imprudent!—how dependent upon the temper of the times—upon the events and circumstances of the day!—with how fatal a certainty persecution and tyranny on the one hand, or revolt and civil war on the other, may follow from the slightest deviation from propriety in the drawing of such lines!—and what a curse to any country a legislator may be, who, with the purest intentions, should set about settling the business to all eternity by inflexible and adamantine rules, drawn from the sacred and inviolable and imprescriptible rights of man, and the primeval and everlasting laws of nature!

CONCLUSION

On the subject of the fundamental principles of government, we have seen what execrable trash the choicest talents of the French nation have produced.

On the subject of chemistry, Europe has beheld with admiration, and adopted with unanimity and gratitude, the systematic views of the same nation, supported as they were by a series of decisive experiments and conclusive reasonings.

Chemistry has commonly been reckoned, and not altogether

without reason, among the most abstruse branches of science. In chemistry, we see how high they have soared above the sublimest knowledge of past times; in legislation, how deep they have sunk below the profoundest ignorance—how much inferior has the maturest design that could be furnished by the united powers of the whole nation proved in comparison of the wisdom and felicity of the chance-medley of the British constitution.

Comparatively speaking, a select few applied themselves to the cultivation of chemistry—almost an infinity, in comparison, have applied themselves to the science of legislation.

In the instance of chemistry, the study is acknowledged to come within the province of science: the science is acknowledged to be an abstruse and difficult one, and to require a long course of study on the part of those who have had the previous advantage of a liberal education; whilst the cultivation of it, in such manner as to make improvements in it, requires that a man should make it the great business of his life; and those who have made these improvements have thus applied themselves.

In chemistry there is no room for passion to step in and to confound the understanding—to lead men into error, and to shut their eyes against knowledge: in legislation, the circumstances are opposite, and vastly different.

What, then, shall we say of that system of government of which the professed object is to call upon the untaught and unlettered multitude (whose existence depends upon their devoting their whole time to the acquisition of the means of supporting it) to occupy themselves without ceasing upon all questions of government (legislation and administration included) without exception—important and trivial—the most general and the most particular, but more especially upon the most important and most general—that is, in other words, the most scientific—those that require the greatest measures of science to qualify a man for deciding upon, and in respect of which any want of science and skill are liable to be attended with the most fatal consequences?

What should we have said if, with a view of collecting the surest grounds for the decision of any of the great questions of chemistry, the French Academy of Sciences (if its members had remained unmurdered) had referred such questions to the Primary Assemblies?

If a collection of general propositions, put together with the design that seems to have given birth to this performance—propositions of the most general and extensive import, embracing the whole field of legislation—were capable of being so worded and put together as to be of use, it could only be on the condition of their being deduced in the way of abridgment from an already formed and existing assemblage of less general propositions, constituting the tenor of the body of the laws. But for these more general propositions to have been abstracted from that body of particular ones, that body must have been already in existence: the general and introductory part, though placed first, must have been constructed last—though first in the order of communication, it should have been last in the order of composition. For the framing of the propositions which were to be included, time, knowledge, genius, temper, patience, everything was wanting. Yet the system of propositions which were to include them it was determined to have at any rate. Of time, a small quantity indeed might be made to serve, upon the single and very simple condition of not bestowing a single thought upon the propositions which they were to include; and as to knowledge, genius, temper, and patience, the place of all these trivial requisites was abundantly supplied by effrontery and self-conceit. The business, instead of being performed in the way of abridgment, was performed in the way of anticipation—by a loose conjecture of what the particular propositions in question, were they to be found, might amount to.

What I mean to attack is not the subject or citizen of this or that country—not this or that citizen—not citizen Sieyes or citizen anybody else, but all anti-legal rights of man, all declarations of such rights. What I mean to attack is not the execution of such a design in this or that instance, but the design itself.

It is not that they have failed in their execution of the design by using the same word promiscuously in two or three senses—contradictory and incompatible senses—but in undertaking to execute a design which could not be executed at all without this abuse of words. Let a man distinguish the senses—let him allot, and allot invariably a separate word for each, and he will find it impossible to make up any such declaration at all, without running into such nonsense as must stop the hand even of the maddest of the mad.

Ex uno, disce omnes—from this declaration of rights, learn what all other declarations of rights—of rights asserted as against government in general must ever be—the rights of anarchy—the order of chaos.

It is right I should continue to possess the coat I have upon my back, and so on with regard to everything else I look upon as my property, at least till I choose to part with it.

It is right I should be at liberty to do as I please—it would be better if I might be permitted to add, whether other people were pleased with what it pleased me to do or not. But as that is hopeless, I must be content with such a portion of liberty, though it is the least I can be content with, as consists in the liberty of doing as I please, subject to the exception of not doing harm to other people.

It is right I should be secure against all sorts of harm.

It is right I should be upon a par with everybody else—upon a par at least; and if I can contrive to get a peep over other people's heads, where will be the harm in it?

But if all this is right now, at what time was it ever otherwise? It is now naturally right, and at what future time will it be otherwise? It is then unalterably right for everlasting.

As it is right I should possess all these blessings, I have a right to all of them.

But if I have a right to the coat on my back, I have a right to knock any man down who attempts to take it from me.

For the same reason, if I have a right to be secure against all sorts of harm, I have a right to knock any man down who attempts to harm me.

For the same reason, if I have a right to do whatever I please, subject only to the exception of not doing harm to other people, it follows that, subject only to that exception, I have a right to knock any man down who attempts to prevent my doing anything that I please to do.

For the same reason, if I have a right to be upon a par with everybody else in every respect, it follows that should any man take upon him to raise his house higher than mine, rather than it should continue so, I have a right to pull it down about his ears, and to knock him down if he attempt to hinder me.

Thus easy, thus natural, under the guidance of the selfish and anti-social passions, thus insensible is the transition from the language of utility and peace to the language of mischief. Transition, did I say? What transition? From right to right? The propositions are identical—there is no transition in the case. Certainly, as far as words

CLASSIC POLITICAL PHILOSOPHY FOR THE MODERN MAN

go, scarcely any: no more than if you were to trust your horse with a man for a week or so, and he were to return it blind and lame—it was your horse you trusted to him—it is your horse you have received again—what you had trusted to him, you have received.

It is in England, rather than in France, that the discovery of the rights of man ought naturally to have taken its rise: it is we—we English, that have the better right to it. It is in the English language that the transition is more natural, than perhaps in most others: at any rate, more so than in the French. It is in English, and not in French, that we may change the sense without changing the word, and, like Don Quixote on the enchanted horse, travel as far as the moon, and farther, without ever getting off the saddle. One and the same word, right—right, that most enchanting of words—is sufficient for operating the fascination. The word is ours—that magic word, which, by its single unassisted powers, completes the fascination. In its adjective shape, it is as innocent as a dove: it breathes nothing but morality and peace. It is in this shape that, passing in at the heart, it gets possession of the understanding—it then assumes its substantive shape, and joining itself to a band of suitable associates, sets up the banner of insurrection, anarchy, and lawless violence.

It is right that men should be as near upon a par with one another in every respect as they can be made consistently with general security: here we have it in its adjective form, synonymous with desirable, proper, becoming, consonant to general utility, and the like. I have a right to put myself upon a par with everybody in every respect: here we have it in its substantive sense, forming with the other words a phrase equivalent to this—wherever I find a man who will not let me put myself on a par with him in every respect, it is right, and proper, and becoming, that I should knock him down, if I have a mind to do so, and if that will not do, knock him on the head, and so forth.

The French language is fortunate enough not to possess this mischievous abundance. But a Frenchman will not be kept back from his purpose by a want of words: the want of an adjective composed of the same letters as the substantive right is no loss to him. Is, has, been, ought to be, shall be, can—all are put for one another—all are pressed into the service—all made to answer the same purposes. By this inebriating compound, we have seen all the elements of the understanding confounded, every fibre of the heart inflamed, the lips prepared for every folly, and the hand for every crime.

Our right to this precious discovery, such as it is, of the rights of man, must, I repeat it, have been prior to that of the French. It has been seen how peculiarly rich we are in materials for making it. Right, the substantive right, is the child of law: from real laws come real rights; but from imaginary laws, from laws of nature, fancied and invented by poets, rhetoricians, and dealers in moral and intellectual poisons, come imaginary rights, a bastard brood of monsters, 'gorgons and chimæras dire'. And thus it is that from legal rights, the offspring of law, and friends of peace, come anti-legal rights, the mortal enemies of law, the subverters of government, and the assassins of security.

Will this antidote to French poisons have its effect? Will this preservative for the understanding and the heart against the fascination of sounds find lips to take it? This, in point of speedy or immediate efficacy at least, is almost too much to hope for. Alas! How dependent are opinions upon sound! Who shall break the chains which bind them together? By what force shall the associations between words and ideas be dissolved—associations coeval with the cradle—associations to which every book and every conversation give increased strength? By what authority shall this original vice in the structure of language be corrected? How shall a word which has taken root in the vitals of a language be expelled? By what means shall a word in continual use be deprived of half its signification? The language of plain strong sense is difficult to learn; the language of smooth nonsense is easy and familiar. The one requires a force of attention capable of stemming the tide of usage and example; the other requires nothing but to swim with it.

It is for education to do what can be done; and in education is, though unhappily the slowest, the surest as well as earliest resource. The recognition of the nothingness of the laws of nature and the rights of man that have been grounded on them is a branch of knowledge of as much importance to an Englishman, though a negative one, as the most perfect acquaintance that can be formed with the existing laws of England.

It must be so: Shakespeare, whose plays were filling English hearts with rapture, while the drama of France was not superior to that of

Caffraria[1]—Shakespeare, who had a key to all the passions and all the stores of language, could never have let slip an instrument of delusion of such superior texture. No: it is not possible that the rights of man—the natural, pre-adamitical, ante-legal, and anti-legal rights of man—should have been unknown to, have been unemployed by Shakespeare. How could the Macbeths, the Jaffiers, the Iagos, do without them? They present a cloak for every conspiracy—they hold out a mask for every crime—they are every villain's armoury—every spendthrift's treasury.

But if the English were the first to bring the rights of man into the closet from the stage, it is to the stage and the closet that they have confined them. It was reserved for France—for France in her days of degradation and degeneration—in those days, in comparison of which the worst of her days of fancied tyranny were halcyon ones—to turn debates into tragedies, and the senate into a stage.

The mask is now taken off, and the anarchist may be known by the language which he uses.

He will be found asserting rights and acknowledging them at the same time not to be recognised by government. Using, instead of ought and ought not, the words is or is not—can or can not.

In former times, in the times of Grotius and Puffendorf, these expressions were little more than improprieties in language, prejudicial to the growth of knowledge: at present, since the French Declaration of Rights has adopted them, and the French Revolution displayed their import by a practical comment, the use of them is already a moral crime, and not undeserving of being constituted a legal crime, as hostile to the public peace.

1. Territories along the southeast coast of Africa colonized by the Portuguese and British.

9

ALEXIS DE TOCQUEVILLE, DEMOCRACY IN AMERICA

INTRODUCTION

There is no more insightful analysis of the merits and demerits of democracy—and the equalist philosophies associated with democracy—than that of Alexis de Tocqueville.

Tocqueville (1805-1859) was a French philosopher and statesman famous today for his *Democracy in America* (1835/1840), a monumental two-volume study of the influence of democracy in the United States on intellectual movements, opinions, customs, and political society. Born into an old and distinguished aristocratic family with roots going back to eleventh century Normandy, Tocqueville's parents barely escaped the guillotine during the days of the Terror, and his great-grandfather, Lamoignon-Malesherbes, who had defended Louis XVI at trial, had been guillotined (along with his daughter, son-in-law, and grandchildren) in 1794. After attending the lyceé in Metz, Tocqueville went on to study law at Paris, after which he joined the government legal service before becoming a magistrate. In 1831, however, he obtained permission to study prison conditions in the United States, and, with his friend Gustave de Beaumont, he travelled to America over nine months in 1831 and 1832. Tocqueville recorded his reflections in *Democracy in America*. It was a great success: the first volume, which made him famous, was published in 1835, and the second volume, published five years later, led to his election to the Académie Française. In 1839, Tocqueville was elected to the National Assembly, where he sat on the centre-left, supporting the abolitionist movement and free trade. In 1849, he was made Minister of Foreign Affairs, but the mood soon turned against him, and his political career came to an end with the coup d'état of Louis Bonaparte in 1851. Tocqueville responded by retreating to his castle, the Château de Tocqueville, where he lived the life of a gentleman scholar until his death in 1859 of tuberculosis.

Democracy in America is, viewed from one perspective, a historical and sociological account of the United States as a nation of a unique people evolving together in a unique way. Tocqueville credited the Anglo-Americans, especially those of the New England states, as the primary force driving this evolution. In particular, he recognized the unique context from which those founding peoples came: England, wracked as it had been by centuries of struggle between different religious factions, had learned about freedom the hard way, and its sons and daughters brought to America a political culture that had already incorporated the concept of government by common consent. What makes Tocqueville's account especially valuable, however, is the way in which high-level generalization is informed by deep insight into America's past as lived experience. In 'Two Weeks in the Wilderness', for example, he describes the struggles of the pioneer to clear a ground in the wilderness and begin planting his modest first acre with maize and potatoes, accompanied by his wife who, having exchanged the attractions of society and pleasures of her own house for the isolation of the forests, carries her profound sadness with courage and dignity, while remaining at all times vulnerable to the forest fever that can strike down whole families at time, sixty miles from the nearest doctor, leaving them to 'do as the Indians do'—die or get better. *Democracy in America* is less immediately concerned with the settlers' day-to-day struggles for existence, but it is deeply informed by them nonetheless.

Democracy in America is in many ways prescient: it connects America's foundational past with Toqueville's lived present and the future that he anticipated for the federation as a whole. In the language of his day, Toqueville referred to what he called the 'three races' of America: the incoming European whites, the Native Americans, and the African Americans. The relentless advance of the former is his main focus of attention because it was their democracy that appeared to him to constitute the future—not only for America but also for Europe and beyond. Toqueville's account of the troubled situation of the Native Americans, encircled and retreating ever further to the West, although couched in language that we would find unfamiliar, is sympathetic and poignant: their collective ownership of land, suggested Toqueville, meant that no particular areas would be defended by a single powerful interest; the wild animals on which they depended were being driven ever further back by the advance of industrialization; and while their needs were being increased by the arrival of Europeans, their resources were being thrown into decline. It was slavery, though, that called down Tocqueville's most unforgiving contempt. 'I reserve my execration,' he said, 'for those who, after a thousand years of freedom, brought back slavery into the world once more.' But slavery in America was crueller than it had ever been, because at least slaves in the ancient world, who had often been captured in war, could be educated and might be freed, whereas it had been forbidden in America to teach slaves to read or write—they were intended to be slaves indefinitely, as were their offspring. Cruel as it was to the slave, Tocqueville added that it was also fatal for the master, for slavery robbed free labour of its dignity and value, and it diminished the character of the slaveholder.

Illuminating as it is as the record of a particular society at a particular time, the principal interest of *Democracy in America* is not so much what it says about the United States specifically, as what it says about democracy as a political and social phenomenon. Tocqueville approaches this from two main angles: he combines broad observations about the effect of democracy and equality upon society and personality with a detailed consideration of the particular risks to freedom and well-being that are likely to arise in democratic societies.

Individualism is at the heart of the democratic society. Tocqueville is careful to spell out what he means by this: individualism is not 'egoism', nor is it excessive self-love, but refers instead to the calm and considered feeling that persuades each man to cut himself off from his fellows and withdraw into his own circle of family and friends. Individualism comes to predominate through the growth of social equality, as people acquire enough material resources to satisfy their own needs without having to depend upon others, and begin to imagine that their destinies are entirely in their own hands, forgetting their fellow men, as well as their own ancestors—and even their own descendants. Tocqueville is too sophisticated, however, to think that the individual thereby obtains autonomy and self-mastery: for while each man looks upon each of his fellows with a feeling of pride and superiority, he is at the same time overwhelmed by a powerful awareness of his own insignificance and weakness in the face of the great body of men as a whole. As a result, mass opinion comes to constitute an immense pressure that takes hold of men's souls and inserts into them a multitude of 'ready-made opinions', relieving them (or seeming to relieve them) from the necessity of forming opinions of their own.

In democracies, we are, as Tocqueville says, 'restless in prosperity'. Men pursue prosperity with feverish enthusiasm and are ever brooding over the advantages that they do not possess; they are haunted by a vague dread that constantly torments them lest they should not have chosen the shortest path to success. Life becomes at once 'agitated but monotonous'. It is agitated because the passion for wealth is strong—not because men's souls are smaller or more covetous, but because in times of equality men's cooperation can only be secured by money, which multiplies its value. It is monotonous because precisely in order to obtain such wealth men adopt habits that are orderly and regular, because the general pursuit of money gives all men's passions a 'family resemblance', and because men increasingly discard the opinions and feelings of class, profession, and family to converge upon the essence of man, which is everywhere the same.

Equality leads to a society of many ambitious men with very few lofty ambitions. The tragic paradox, explains Tocqueville, is that while equality opens up a whole new range of possibilities, at the same time it removes the means by which any of them are likely to be realized, for if opportunities are open to all, then every path is one into which many others are also crowding. In order to preserve the principle of equality, all contenders must be subjected to a range of petty preliminary exercises and tests in the process of which 'their youth is wasted and imagination quenched', so that by the time they are in a position to achieve something extraordinary they are likely to have already lost the taste for it. Equality, therefore, presents a boundless field in which are encountered a mass of 'intermediate obstacles'; the permanent struggle between the instinct to progress and the inadequate means to do so wearies the soul.

As to the political trajectory of, and risks associated with, democratic societies, Tocqueville's whole approach is determined by one crucial insight: that while democracy may, at best, give full reign to the forces of both freedom and equality, these by no means necessarily walk hand-in-hand, and in any contest between the two the push for equality will tend to prevail over the preservation of freedom. In eras of equality, explains Tocqueville, each man is relatively insignificant, and since there are few (if any) 'secondary powers' of the type to be found under other systems of government such as aristocracy, we tend to think in terms of a 'sole central power' entitled to interfere in all aspects of our lives. Equality also tends to increase uniformity, and the more uniformity we encounter among men the more obvious—and insupportable—become the small differences between them. Although one of the tendencies begotten by equality is towards political freedoms and independence, then, there is another that conducts 'by a longer, more secret, but more certain road', says Tocqueville, to servitude.

The result is 'soft despotism': the equalist state degrades men, without necessarily causing them tangible harm, through continual interference in all aspects of social and private life. This reduces us to a state of perpetual childhood; it 'robs man of all the uses of himself'. Petty rules compress and enervate us, our spirit is broken by subjection in minor affairs, and we are stripped, tells Tocqueville, of our highest qualities—those selfsame qualities that, ultimately, make us truly human, and make being human truly worthwhile.

Volume II, Book IV: Influence Of Democratic Opinions On Political Society

Chapter I

THAT EQUALITY NATURALLY GIVES MEN A TASTE FOR FREE INSTITUTIONS

I should imperfectly fulfil the purpose of this book if, after having shown what opinions and sentiments are suggested by the principle of equality, I did not point out, ere I conclude, the general influence which these same opinions and sentiments may exercise upon the government of human societies. To succeed in this object I shall frequently have to retrace my steps; but I trust the reader will not refuse to follow me through paths already known to him, which may lead to some new truth.

The principle of equality, which makes men independent of each other, gives them a habit and a taste for following, in their private actions, no other guide but their own will. This complete independence, which they constantly enjoy towards their equals and in the intercourse of private life, tends to make them look upon all authority with a jealous eye, and speedily suggests to them the notion and the love of political freedom. Men living at such times have a natural bias to free institutions. Take any one of them at a venture, and search if you can his most deep-seated instincts; you will find that of all governments he will soonest conceive and most highly value that government whose head he has himself elected, and whose administration he may control. Of all the political effects produced by the equality of conditions, this love of independence is the first to strike the observing, and to alarm the timid; nor can it be said that their alarm is wholly misplaced, for anarchy has a more formidable aspect in democratic countries than elsewhere. As the citizens have no direct influence on each other, as soon as the supreme power of the nation fails, which kept them all in their several stations, it would seem that disorder must instantly reach its utmost pitch, and that, every man drawing aside in a different direction, the fabric of society must at once crumble away.

I am, however, persuaded that anarchy is not the principal evil which democratic ages have to fear, but the least. For the principle of equality begets two tendencies; the one leads men straight to independence, and may suddenly drive them into anarchy; the other conducts them by a longer, more secret, but more certain road, to servitude. Nations readily discern the former tendency, and are prepared to resist it; they are led away by the latter, without perceiving its drift; hence it is peculiarly important to point it out. For myself, I am so far from urging as a reproach to the principle of equality that it renders men untractable, that this very circumstance principally calls forth my approbation. I admire to see how it deposits in the mind and heart of man the dim conception and instinctive love of political independence, thus preparing the remedy for the evil which it engenders; it is on this very account that I am attached to it.

CHAPTER II

THAT THE NOTIONS OF DEMOCRATIC NATIONS ON GOVERNMENT ARE NATURALLY FAVORABLE TO THE CONCENTRATION OF POWER

The notion of secondary powers, placed between the sovereign and his subjects, occurred naturally to the imagination of aristocratic nations, because those communities contained individuals or families raised above the common level, and apparently destined to command by their birth, their education, and their wealth. This same notion is naturally wanting in the minds of men in democratic ages, for converse reasons: it can only be introduced artificially, it can only be kept there with difficulty; whereas they conceive, as it were, without thinking upon the subject, the notion of a sole and central power which governs the whole community by its direct influence. Moreover in politics, as well as in philosophy and in religion, the intellect of democratic nations is peculiarly open to simple and general notions. Complicated systems are repugnant to it, and its favourite conception is that of a great nation composed of citizens all resembling the same pattern, and all governed by a single power.

The very next notion to that of a sole and central power, which presents itself to the minds of men in the ages of equality, is the notion of uniformity of legislation. As every man sees that he differs but little from those about him, he cannot understand why a rule which is applicable to one man should not be equally applicable to all others. Hence the slightest privileges are repugnant to his reason; the faintest dissimilarities in the political institutions of the same people offend him, and uniformity of legislation appears to him to be the first condition of good government. I find, on the contrary, that this same notion of a uniform rule, equally binding on all the members of the community, was almost unknown to the human mind in aristocratic ages; it was either never entertained, or it was rejected. These contrary tendencies of opinion ultimately turn on either side to such blind instincts and such ungovernable habits that they still direct the actions of men, in spite of particular exceptions. Notwithstanding the immense variety of conditions in the Middle Ages, a certain number of persons existed at that period in precisely similar circumstances; but this did not prevent the laws then in force from assigning to each of them distinct duties and different rights. On the contrary, at the present time all the powers of government are exerted to impose the same customs and the same laws on populations which have as yet but few points of resemblance. As the conditions of men become equal amongst a people, individuals seem of less importance, and society of greater dimensions; or rather, every citizen, being assimilated to all the rest, is lost in the crowd, and nothing stands conspicuous but the great and imposing image of the people at large. This naturally gives the men of democratic periods a lofty opinion of the privileges of society, and a very humble notion of the rights of individuals; they are ready to admit that the interests of the former are everything, and those of the latter nothing. They are willing to acknowledge that the power which represents the community has far more information and wisdom than any of the members of that community; and that it is the duty, as well as the right, of that power to guide as well as govern each private citizen.

If we closely scrutinize our contemporaries, and penetrate to the root of their political opinions, we shall detect some of the notions which I have just pointed out, and we shall perhaps be surprised to find so much accordance between men who are so often at variance. The Americans hold that in every state the supreme power ought to emanate from the people; but when once that power is constituted, they can conceive, as it were, no limits to it, and they are ready to admit that it has the right to do whatever it pleases. They have not the slightest notion of peculiar privileges granted to cities, families, or persons: their minds appear never to have foreseen that it might be possible not to apply with strict uniformity the same laws to every part, and to all the inhabitants. These same opinions are more and more diffused in Europe; they even insinuate themselves amongst those nations which most vehemently reject the principle of the sovereignty of the people. Such nations assign a different origin to the supreme power, but they ascribe to that power the same characteristics. Amongst them all, the idea of intermediate powers is weakened and obliterated: the idea of rights inherent in certain individuals is rapidly disappearing from the minds of men; the idea of the omnipotence and sole authority of society at large rises to fill its place. These ideas take root and spread in proportion as social conditions become more equal, and men more alike; they are engendered by equality, and in turn they hasten the progress of equality.

In France, where the revolution of which I am speaking has gone further than in any other European country, these opinions have got complete hold of the public mind. If we listen attentively to the language of the various parties in France, we shall find that there is not one which has not adopted them. Most of these parties censure the conduct of the government, but they all hold that the government ought perpetually to act and interfere in everything that is done. Even those which are most at variance are nevertheless agreed upon this head. The unity, the ubiquity, the omnipotence of the supreme power, and the uniformity of its rules, constitute the principal characteristics of all the political systems which have been put forward in our age. They recur even in the wildest visions of political regeneration: the human mind pursues them in its dreams. If these notions spontaneously arise in the minds of private individuals, they suggest themselves still more forcibly to the minds of princes. Whilst the ancient fabric of European society is altered and dissolved, sovereigns acquire new conceptions of their opportunities and their duties; they learn for the first time that the central power which they represent may and ought to administer by its own agency, and on a uniform plan, all the concerns of the whole community. This opinion, which, I will venture to say, was never conceived before our time by the monarchs of Europe, now sinks deeply into the minds of kings, and abides there amidst all the agitation of more unsettled thoughts.

Our contemporaries are therefore much less divided than is commonly supposed; they are constantly disputing as to the hands in which supremacy is to be vested, but they readily agree upon the duties and the rights of that supremacy. The notion they all form of government is that of a sole, simple, providential, and creative power. All secondary opinions in politics are unsettled; this one remains fixed, invariable, and consistent. It is adopted by statesmen and political philosophers; it is eagerly laid hold of by the multitude; those who govern and those who are governed agree to pursue it with equal ardour: it is the foremost notion of their minds, it seems inborn. It originates therefore in no caprice of the human intellect, but it is a necessary condition of the present state of mankind.

CHAPTER III

THAT THE SENTIMENTS OF DEMOCRATIC NATIONS ACCORD WITH THEIR OPINIONS IN LEADING THEM TO CONCENTRATE POLITICAL POWER

If it be true that, in ages of equality, men readily adopt the notion of a great central power, it cannot be doubted on the other hand that their habits and sentiments predispose them to recognize such a power and to give it their support. This may be demonstrated in a few words, as the greater part of the reasons to which the fact may be attributed have been previously stated. As the men who inhabit democratic countries have no superiors, no inferiors, and no habitual or necessary partners in their undertakings, they readily fall back upon themselves and consider themselves as beings apart. I had occasion to point this out at considerable length in treating of individualism. Hence such men can never, without an effort, tear themselves from their private affairs to engage in public business; their natural bias leads them to abandon the latter to the sole visible and permanent representative of the interests of the community, that is to say, to the state. Not only are they naturally wanting in a taste for public business, but they have frequently no time to attend to it. Private life is so busy in democratic periods, so excited, so full of wishes and of work, that hardly any energy or leisure remains to each individual for public life. I am the last man to contend that these propensities are unconquerable, since my chief object in writing this book has been to combat them. I only maintain that at the present day a secret power is fostering them in the human heart, and that if they are not checked they will wholly overgrow it.

I have also had occasion to show how the increasing love of well-being, and the fluctuating character of property, cause democratic nations to dread all violent disturbance. The love of public tranquility is frequently the only passion which these nations retain, and it becomes more active and powerful amongst them in proportion as all other passions droop and die. This naturally disposes the members of the community constantly to give or to surrender additional rights to the central power, which alone seems to be interested in defending them by the same means that it uses to defend itself. As in ages of equality no man is compelled to lend his assistance to his fellow men, and none has any right to expect much support from them, everyone is at once independent and powerless. These two conditions, which must never be either separately considered or confounded together, inspire the citizen of a democratic country with very contrary propensities. His independence fills him with self-reliance and pride amongst his equals; his debility makes him feel from time to time the want of some outward assistance, which he cannot expect from any of them, because they are all impotent and unsympathizing. In this predicament he naturally turns his eyes to that imposing power which alone rises above the level of universal depression. Of that power his wants and especially his desires continually remind him, until he ultimately views it as the sole and necessary support of his own weakness.[1] This may more completely explain what frequently takes place in democratic

1. In democratic communities nothing but the central power has any stability in its position or any permanence in its undertakings. All the members of society are in ceaseless stir and transformation. Now it is in the nature of all governments to seek constantly to enlarge their sphere of action; hence it is almost impossible that such a government should not ultimately succeed, because it acts with a fixed principle and a constant will upon men, whose position, whose notions, and whose desires are in continual vacillation. It frequently happens that the members of the community promote the influence of the central power without intending it. Democratic ages are periods of experiment, innovation, and adventure. At such times there are always a multitude of men engaged in difficult or novel undertakings, which they follow alone, without caring for their fellow men. Such persons may be ready to admit, as a general principle, that the public authority ought not to interfere in private concerns; but, by an exception to that rule, each of them craves for its assistance in the particular concern on which he is engaged, and seeks to draw upon the influence of the government for his own benefit, though he would restrict it on all other occasions. If a large number of men apply this particular exception to a great variety of different purposes, the sphere of the central power extends insensibly in all directions, although each of them wishes it to be circumscribed. Thus a democratic government increases its power simply by the fact of its permanence. Time is on its side; every incident befriends it; the passions of individuals unconsciously promote it; and it may be asserted, that the older a democratic community is, the more centralized will its government become.

countries, where the very men who are so impatient of superiors patiently submit to a master, exhibiting at once their pride and their servility.

The hatred which men bear to privilege increases in proportion as privileges become more scarce and less considerable, so that democratic passions would seem to burn most fiercely at the very time when they have least fuel. I have already given the reason of this phenomenon. When all conditions are unequal, no inequality is so great as to offend the eye; whereas the slightest dissimilarity is odious in the midst of general uniformity: the more complete is this uniformity, the more insupportable does the sight of such a difference become. Hence it is natural that the love of equality should constantly increase together with equality itself, and that it should grow by what it feeds upon. This never-dying, ever-kindling hatred, which sets a democratic people against the smallest privileges, is peculiarly favourable to the gradual concentration of all political rights in the hands of the representative of the state alone. The sovereign, being necessarily and incontestably above all the citizens, excites not their envy, and each of them thinks that he strips his equals of the prerogative which he concedes to the crown. The man of a democratic age is extremely reluctant to obey his neighbour who is his equal; he refuses to acknowledge in such a person ability superior to his own; he mistrusts his justice, and is jealous of his power; he fears and he contemns him; and he loves continually to remind him of the common dependence in which both of them stand to the same master. Every central power which follows its natural tendencies courts and encourages the principle of equality; for equality singularly facilitates, extends, and secures the influence of a central power.

In like manner it may be said that every central government worships uniformity: uniformity relieves it from inquiry into an infinite number of small details which must be attended to if rules were to be adapted to men, instead of indiscriminately subjecting men to rules; thus the government likes what the citizens like, and naturally hates what they hate. These common sentiments, which, in democratic nations, constantly unite the sovereign and every member of the community in one and the same conviction, establish a secret and lasting sympathy between them. The faults of the government are pardoned for the sake of its tastes; public confidence is only reluctantly withdrawn in the midst even of its excesses and its errors, and it is restored at the first call. Democratic nations often hate those in whose hands the central power is vested; but they always love that power itself.

Thus, by two separate paths, I have reached the same conclusion. I have shown that the principle of equality suggests to men the notion of a sole, uniform, and strong government: I have now shown that the principle of equality imparts to them a taste for it. To governments of this kind the nations of our age are therefore tending. They are drawn thither by the natural inclination of mind and heart; and in order to reach that result, it is enough that they do not check themselves in their course. I am of opinion, that, in the democratic ages which are opening upon us, individual independence and local liberties will ever be the produce of artificial contrivance; that centralization will be the natural form of government.

CHAPTER VI

WHAT SORT OF DESPOTISM DEMOCRATIC NATIONS HAVE TO FEAR

I had remarked during my stay in the United States that a democratic state of society, similar to that of the Americans, might offer singular facilities for the establishment of despotism; and I perceived, upon my return to Europe, how much use had already been made by most of our rulers of the notions, the sentiments, and the wants engendered by this same social condition for the purpose of extending the circle of their power. This led me to think that the nations of Christendom would perhaps eventually undergo some sort of oppression like that which hung over several of the nations of the ancient world. A more accurate examination of the subject, and five years of further meditations, have not diminished my apprehensions, but they have changed the object of them. No sovereign ever lived in former ages so absolute or so powerful as to undertake to administer by his own agency, and without the assistance of intermediate powers, all the parts of a great empire: none ever attempted to subject all his subjects indiscriminately to strict uniformity of regulation, and personally to tutor and direct every member of the community. The notion of such an undertaking never occurred to the human mind; and if any man had conceived it, the want of information, the imperfection of the administrative system, and above all, the natural obstacles caused by the inequality of conditions would speedily have checked the execution of so vast a design. When the Roman emperors were at the height of their power, the different nations of the empire still preserved manners and customs of great diversity; although they were subject to the same monarch, most of the provinces were separately administered; they abounded in powerful and active municipalities; and although the whole government of the empire was centred in the hands of the emperor alone, and he always remained, upon occasions, the supreme arbiter in all matters, yet the details of social life and private occupations lay for the most part beyond his control. The emperors possessed, it is true, an immense and unchecked power, which allowed them to gratify all their whimsical tastes, and to employ for that purpose the whole strength of the state. They frequently abused that power arbitrarily to deprive their subjects of property or of life: their tyranny was extremely onerous to the few, but it did not reach the greater number; it was fixed to some few main objects, and neglected the rest; it was violent, but its range was limited.

But it would seem that if despotism were to be established amongst the democratic nations of our days, it might assume a different character; it would be more extensive and more mild; it would degrade men without tormenting them. I do not question, that in an age of instruction and equality like our own, sovereigns might more easily succeed in collecting all political power into their own hands, and might interfere more habitually and decidedly within the circle of private interests, than any sovereign of antiquity could ever do. But this same principle of equality which facilitates despotism, tempers its rigour. We have seen how the manners of society become more humane and gentle in proportion as men become more equal and alike. When no member of the community has much power or much wealth, tyranny is, as it were, without opportunities and a field of action. As all fortunes are scanty, the passions of men are naturally circumscribed—their imagination limited, their pleasures simple. This universal moderation moderates the sovereign himself, and checks within certain limits the inordinate extent of his desires.

Independently of these reasons drawn from the nature of the state of society itself, I might add many others arising from causes beyond my subject; but I shall keep within the limits I have laid down to myself.

Democratic governments may become violent and even cruel at certain periods of extreme effervescence or of great danger; but these crises will be rare and brief. When I consider the petty passions of our contemporaries, the mildness of their manners, the extent of their education, the purity of their religion, the gentleness of their morality, their regular and industrious habits, and the restraint which they almost all observe in their vices no less than in their virtues, I have no fear that they will meet with tyrants in their rulers, but rather guardians. I think then that the species of oppression by which democratic nations are menaced is unlike anything which ever before existed in the world: our contemporaries will find no prototype of it in their memories. I am trying myself to choose an expression which will accurately convey the whole of the idea I have formed of it, but in vain; the old words 'despotism' and 'tyranny' are inappropriate: the thing itself is new; and since I cannot name it, I must attempt to define it.

I seek to trace the novel features under which despotism may appear in the world. The first thing that strikes the observation is an innumerable multitude of men all equal and alike, incessantly endeavouring to procure the petty and paltry pleasures with which they glut their lives. Each of them, living apart, is as a stranger to the fate of all the rest—his children and his private friends constitute to him the whole of mankind; as for the rest of his fellow citizens, he is close to them, but he sees them not—he touches them, but he feels them not; he exists but in himself and for himself alone; and if his kindred still remain to him, he may be said at any rate to have lost his country. Above this race of men stands an immense and tutelary power, which takes upon itself alone to secure their gratifications, and to watch over their fate. That power is absolute, minute, regular, provident, and mild. It would be like the authority of a parent, if, like that authority, its object was to prepare men for manhood; but it seeks on the contrary to keep them in perpetual childhood: it is well content that the people should rejoice, provided they think of nothing but rejoicing. For their happiness such a government willingly labours, but it chooses to be the sole agent and the only arbiter of that happiness: it provides for their security, foresees and supplies their necessities, facilitates their pleasures, manages their principal concerns, directs their industry, regulates the descent of property, and subdivides their inheritances—what remains, but to spare them all the care of thinking and all the trouble of living? Thus it every day renders the exercise of the free agency of man less useful and less frequent; it circumscribes the will within a narrower range, and gradually robs a man of all the uses of himself. The principle of equality has prepared men for these things: it has predisposed men to endure them, and oftentimes to look on them as benefits.

After having thus successively taken each member of the community in its powerful grasp, and fashioned them at will, the supreme power then extends its arm over the whole community. It covers the surface of society with a network of small complicated rules, minute and uniform, through which the most original minds and the most energetic characters cannot penetrate to rise above the crowd. The will of man is not shattered, but softened, bent, and guided: men are seldom forced by it to act, but they are constantly restrained from acting; such a power does not destroy, but it prevents existence; it does not tyrannize, but it compresses, enervates, extinguishes, and stupefies a people, till each nation is reduced to be nothing better than a flock of timid and industrious animals, of which the government is the shepherd. I have always thought that servitude of the regular, quiet, and gentle kind which I have just described might be combined more easily than is commonly believed with some of the outward forms of freedom; and that it might even establish itself under the wing of the sovereignty of the people. Our contemporaries are constantly excited by two conflicting passions; they want to be led, and they wish to remain free: as they cannot destroy either one or the other of these contrary propensities, they strive to satisfy them both at once. They devise a sole, tutelary, and all-powerful form of government, but elected by the people. They combine the principle of centralization and that of popular sovereignty; this gives them a respite; they console themselves for being in tutelage by the reflection that they have chosen their own guardians. Every man allows himself to be put in leading-strings, because he sees that it is not a person or a class of persons, but the people at large that holds the end of his chain. By this system the people shake off their state of dependence just long enough to select their master, and then relapse into it again. A great many persons at the present day are quite contented with this sort of compromise between administrative despotism and the sovereignty of the people; and they think they have done enough for the protection of individual freedom when they have surrendered it to the power of the nation at large. This does not satisfy me: the nature of him I am to obey signifies less to me than the fact of extorted obedience.

I do not however deny that a constitution of this kind appears to me to be infinitely preferable to one which, after having concentrated all the powers of government, should vest them in the hands of an irresponsible person or body of persons. Of all the forms which democratic despotism could assume, the latter would assuredly be the worst. When the sovereign is elective, or narrowly watched by a legislature which is really elective and independent, the oppression which he exercises over individuals is sometimes greater, but it is always less degrading; because every man, when he is oppressed and disarmed, may still imagine that whilst he yields obedience it is to himself he yields it, and that it is to one of his own inclinations that all the rest give way. In like manner I can understand that when the sovereign represents the nation, and is dependent upon the people, the rights and the power of which every citizen is deprived not only serve the head of the state, but the state itself; and that private persons derive some return from the sacrifice of their independence which they have made to the public. To create a representation of the people in every centralized country, is therefore, to diminish the evil which extreme centralization may produce, but not to get rid of it. I admit that by this means room is left for the intervention of individuals in the more important affairs; but it is not the less suppressed in the smaller and more private ones. It must not be forgotten that it is especially dangerous to enslave men in the minor details of life. For my own part, I should be inclined to think freedom less necessary in great things than in little ones, if it were possible to be secure of the one without possessing the other. Subjection in minor affairs breaks out every day, and is felt by the whole community indiscriminately. It does not drive men to resistance, but it crosses them at every turn, till they are led to surrender the exercise of their will. Thus their spirit is gradually broken and their character enervated; whereas that obedience, which is exacted on a few important but rare occasions only exhibits servitude at certain intervals, and throws the burden of it upon a small number of men. It is in vain to summon a people, which has been rendered so dependent on the central power, to choose from time to time the representatives of that power; this rare and brief exercise of their free choice, however important it may be, will not prevent them from gradually losing the faculties of thinking, feeling, and acting for themselves, and thus gradually falling below the level of humanity. I add that they will soon become incapable of exercising the great and only privilege which remains to them. The democratic nations which have introduced freedom into their political constitution at the very time when they were augmenting the despotism of their administrative constitution, have been led into strange paradoxes. To manage those minor affairs in which good sense is all that is wanted—the people are held to be unequal to the task, but when the government of the country is at stake, the people are invested with immense powers; they are alternately made the playthings of their ruler, and his masters—more than kings, and less than men. After having exhausted all the different modes of election, without finding one to suit their purpose, they are still amazed, and still bent on seeking further; as if the evil they remark did not originate in the constitution of the country far more than in that of the electoral body. It is, indeed, difficult to conceive how men who have entirely given up the habit of self-government should succeed in making a proper choice of those by whom they are to be governed; and no one will ever believe that a liberal, wise, and energetic government can spring from the suffrages of a subservient people. A constitution, which should be republican in its head and ultra-monarchical in all its other parts, has ever appeared to me to be a short-lived monster. The vices of rulers and the ineptitude of the people would speedily bring about its ruin; and the nation, weary of its representatives and of itself, would create freer institutions, or soon return to stretch itself at the feet of a single master.

CHAPTER VII

CONTINUATION OF THE PRECEDING CHAPTERS

I believe that it is easier to establish an absolute and despotic government amongst a people in which the conditions of society are equal, than amongst any other; and I think that if such a government were once established amongst such a people, it would not only oppress men, but would eventually strip each of them of several of the highest qualities of humanity. Despotism therefore appears to me peculiarly to be dreaded in democratic ages. I should have loved freedom, I believe, at all times, but in the time in which we live I am ready to worship it. On the other hand, I am persuaded that all who shall attempt, in the ages upon which we are entering, to base freedom upon aristocratic privilege, will fail—that all who shall attempt to draw and to retain authority within a single class, will fail. At the present day no ruler is skilful or strong enough to found a despotism by re-establishing permanent distinctions of rank amongst his subjects: no legislator is wise or powerful enough to preserve free institutions if he does not take equality for his first principle and his watchword. All those of our contemporaries who would establish or secure the independence and the dignity of their fellow men must show themselves the friends of equality; and the only worthy means of showing themselves as such is to be so: upon this depends the success of their holy enterprise. Thus the question is not how to reconstruct aristocratic society, but how to make liberty proceed out of that democratic state of society in which God has placed us.

These two truths appear to me simple, clear, and fertile in consequences; and they naturally lead me to consider what kind of free government can be established amongst a people in which social conditions are equal. It results from the very constitution of democratic nations and from their necessities that the power of government amongst them must be more uniform, more centralized, more extensive, more searching, and more efficient than in other countries. Society at large is naturally stronger and more active, individuals more subordinate and weak; the former does more, the latter less; and this is inevitably the case. It is not therefore to be expected that the range of private independence will ever be as extensive in democratic as in aristocratic countries—nor is this to be desired; for, amongst aristocratic nations, the mass is often sacrificed to the individual, and the prosperity of the greater number to the greatness of the few. It is both necessary and desirable that the government of a democratic people should be active and powerful; and our object should not be to render it weak or indolent, but solely to prevent it from abusing its aptitude and its strength.

The circumstance which most contributed to secure the independence of private persons in aristocratic ages was that the supreme power did not affect to take upon itself alone the government and administration of the community; those functions were necessarily partially left to the members of the aristocracy: so that as the supreme power was always divided, it never weighed with its whole weight and in the same manner on each individual. Not only did the government not perform everything by its immediate agency; but as most of the agents who discharged its duties derived their power not from the state, but from the circumstance of their birth, they were not perpetually under its control. The government could not make or unmake them in an instant, at pleasure, nor bend them in strict uniformity to its slightest caprice—this was an additional guarantee of private independence. I readily admit that recourse cannot be had to the same means at the present time; but I discover certain democratic expedients which may be substituted for them. Instead of vesting in the government alone all the administrative powers of which corporations and nobles have been deprived, a portion of them may be entrusted to secondary public bodies, temporarily composed of private citizens: thus the liberty of private persons will be more secure, and their equality will not be diminished.

The Americans, who care less for words than the French, still designate by the name of 'county' the largest of their administrative districts: but the duties of the count or lord lieutenant are in part performed by a provincial assembly. At a period of equality like our own it would be unjust and unreasonable to institute hereditary officers; but there is nothing to prevent us from substituting elective public officers to a certain extent. Election is a democratic expedient which insures the independence of the public officer in relation to the government as much and even more than hereditary rank can insure it amongst aristocratic nations. Aristocratic countries abound in wealthy and influential persons who are competent to provide for themselves, and who cannot be easily or secretly oppressed: such persons restrain a government within general habits of moderation and reserve. I am very well aware that democratic countries contain no such persons naturally; but something analogous to them may be created by artificial means. I firmly believe that an aristocracy cannot again be founded in the world; but I think that private citizens, by combining together, may constitute bodies of great wealth, influence, and strength, corresponding to the persons of an aristocracy. By this means many of the greatest political advantages of aristocracy would be obtained without its injustice or its dangers. An association for political, commercial, or manufacturing purposes, or even for those of science and literature, is a powerful and enlightened member of the community, which cannot be disposed of at pleasure, or oppressed without remonstrance; and which, by defending its own rights against the encroachments of the government, saves the common liberties of the country.

In periods of aristocracy every man is always bound so closely to many of his fellow citizens that he cannot be assailed without their coming to his assistance. In ages of equality every man naturally stands alone; he has no hereditary friends whose co-operation he may demand—no class upon whose sympathy he may rely: he is easily got rid of, and he is trampled on with impunity. At the present time, an oppressed member of the community has therefore only one method of self-defence—he may appeal to the whole nation; and if the whole nation is deaf to his complaint, he may appeal to mankind: the only means he has of making this appeal is by the press. Thus the liberty of the press is infinitely more valuable amongst democratic nations than amongst all others; it is the only cure for the evils which equality may produce. Equality sets men apart and weakens them; but the press places a powerful weapon within every man's reach, which the weakest and loneliest of them all may use. Equality deprives a man of the support of his connections; but the press enables him to summon all his fellow countrymen and all his fellow men to his assistance. Printing has accelerated the progress of equality, and it is also one of its best correctives.

I think that men living in aristocracies may, strictly speaking, do without the liberty of the press: but such is not the case with those who live in democratic countries. To protect their personal independence I trust not to great political assemblies, to parliamentary privilege, or to the assertion of popular sovereignty. All these things may, to a certain extent, be reconciled with personal servitude—but that servitude cannot be complete if the press is free: the press is the chiefest democratic instrument of freedom.

Something analogous may be said of the judicial power. It is a part of the essence of judicial power to attend to private interests, and to fix itself with predilection on minute objects submitted to its observation;

another essential quality of judicial power is never to volunteer its assistance to the oppressed, but always to be at the disposal of the humblest of those who solicit it; their complaint, however feeble they may themselves be, will force itself upon the ear of justice and claim redress, for this is inherent in the very constitution of the courts of justice. A power of this kind is therefore peculiarly adapted to the wants of freedom, at a time when the eye and finger of the government are constantly intruding into the minutest details of human actions, and when private persons are at once too weak to protect themselves, and too much isolated for them to reckon upon the assistance of their fellows. The strength of the courts of law has ever been the greatest security which can be offered to personal independence; but this is more especially the case in democratic ages: private rights and interests are in constant danger, if the judicial power does not grow more extensive and more strong to keep pace with the growing equality of conditions.

Equality awakens in men several propensities extremely dangerous to freedom, to which the attention of the legislator ought constantly to be directed. I shall only remind the reader of the most important amongst them. Men living in democratic ages do not readily comprehend the utility of forms: they feel an instinctive contempt for them—I have elsewhere shown for what reasons. Forms excite their contempt and often their hatred; as they commonly aspire to none but easy and present gratifications, they rush onwards to the object of their desires, and the slightest delay exasperates them. This same temper, carried with them into political life, renders them hostile to forms, which perpetually retard or arrest them in some of their projects. Yet this objection which the men of democracies make to forms is the very thing which renders forms so useful to freedom; for their chief merit is to serve as a barrier between the strong and the weak, the ruler and the people, to retard the one, and give the other time to look about him. Forms become more necessary in proportion as the government becomes more active and more powerful, whilst private persons are becoming more indolent and more feeble. Thus democratic nations naturally stand more in need of forms than other nations, and they naturally respect them less. This deserves most serious attention. Nothing is more pitiful than the arrogant disdain of most of our contemporaries for questions of form; for the smallest questions of form have acquired in our time an importance which they never had before: many of the greatest interests of mankind depend upon them. I think that if the statesmen of aristocratic ages could sometimes contemn forms with impunity, and frequently rise above them, the statesmen to whom the government of nations is now confided ought to treat the very least among them with respect, and not neglect them without imperious necessity. In aristocracies the observance of forms was superstitious; amongst us they ought to be kept with a deliberate and enlightened deference.

Another tendency, which is extremely natural to democratic nations and extremely dangerous, is that which leads them to despise and undervalue the rights of private persons. The attachment which men feel to a right, and the respect which they display for it, is generally proportioned to its importance, or to the length of time during which they have enjoyed it. The rights of private persons amongst democratic nations are commonly of small importance, of recent growth, and extremely precarious—the consequence is that they are often sacrificed without regret, and almost always violated without remorse. But it happens that at the same period and amongst the same nations in which men conceive a natural contempt for the rights of private persons, the rights of society at large are naturally extended and consolidated: in other words, men become less attached to private rights at the very time at which it would be most necessary to retain and to defend what little remains of them. It is therefore most especially in the present democratic ages that the true friends of the liberty and the greatness of man ought constantly to be on the alert to prevent the power of government from lightly sacrificing the private rights of individuals to the general execution of its designs. At such times no citizen is so obscure that it is not very dangerous to allow him to be oppressed—no private rights are so unimportant that they can be surrendered with impunity to the caprices of a government. The reason is plain: if the private right of an individual is violated at a time when the human mind is fully impressed with the importance and the sanctity of such rights, the injury done is confined to the individual whose right is infringed; but to violate such a right, at the present day, is deeply to corrupt the manners of the nation and to put the whole community in jeopardy, because the very notion of this kind of right constantly tends amongst us to be impaired and lost.

There are certain habits, certain notions, and certain vices which are peculiar to a state of revolution, and which a protracted revolution cannot fail to engender and to propagate, whatever be, in other respects, its character, its purpose, and the scene on which it takes place. When any nation has, within a short space of time, repeatedly varied its rulers, its opinions, and its laws, the men of whom it is composed eventually contract a taste for change, and grow accustomed to see all changes effected by sudden violence. Thus they naturally conceive a contempt for forms which daily prove ineffectual; and they do not support without impatience the dominion of rules which they have so often seen infringed. As the ordinary notions of equity and morality no longer suffice to explain and justify all the innovations daily begotten by a revolution, the principle of public utility is called in, the doctrine of political necessity is conjured up, and men accustom themselves to sacrifice private interests without scruple, and to trample on the rights of individuals in order more speedily to accomplish any public purpose.

These habits and notions, which I shall call revolutionary, because all revolutions produce them, occur in aristocracies just as much as amongst democratic nations; but amongst the former they are often less powerful and always less lasting, because there they meet with habits, notions, defects, and impediments, which counteract them: they consequently disappear as soon as the revolution is terminated, and the nation reverts to its former political courses. This is not always the case in democratic countries, in which it is ever to be feared that revolutionary tendencies, becoming more gentle and more regular, without entirely disappearing from society, will be gradually transformed into habits of subjection to the administrative authority of the government. I know of no countries in which revolutions are more dangerous than in democratic countries; because, independently of the accidental and transient evils which must always attend them, they may always create some evils which are permanent and unending. I believe that there are such things as justifiable resistance and legitimate rebellion: I do not therefore assert, as an absolute proposition, that the men of democratic ages ought never to make revolutions; but I think that they have especial reason to hesitate before they embark in them, and that it is far better to endure many grievances in their present condition than to have recourse to so perilous a remedy.

I shall conclude by one general idea, which comprises not only all the particular ideas which have been expressed in the present chapter, but also most of those which it is the object of this book to treat of. In the ages of aristocracy which preceded our own, there were private persons of great power, and a social authority of extreme weakness. The outline of society itself was not easily discernible, and constantly confounded with the different powers by which the community was ruled. The principal efforts of the men of those times were required to strengthen, aggrandize, and secure the supreme power; and on the other hand, to circumscribe individual independence within narrower limits, and to subject private interests to the interests of the public. Other perils and other cares await the men of our age. Amongst the greater part of modern nations, the government, whatever may be its origin, its constitution, or its name, has become almost omnipotent, and private persons are falling, more and more, into the lowest stage of weakness and dependence. In olden society everything was different; unity and uniformity were nowhere to be met with. In modern society everything threatens to become so much alike, that the peculiar characteristics of each individual will soon be entirely lost in the general aspect of the world. Our forefathers were ever prone to make an improper use of the notion that private rights ought to be respected; and we are naturally prone on the other hand to exaggerate the idea that the interest of a private individual ought always to bend to the interest of the many. The political world is metamorphosed: new remedies must henceforth be sought for new disorders. To lay down extensive, but distinct and settled limits, to the action of the government; to confer certain rights on private persons, and to secure to them the undisputed enjoyment of those rights; to enable individual man to maintain whatever independence, strength, and original power he still possesses; to raise him by the side of society at large, and uphold him in that position—these appear to me the main objects of legislators in the ages upon which we are now entering. It would seem as if the rulers of our time sought only to use men in order to make things great; I wish that they would try a little more to make great men; that they would set less value on the work, and more upon the workman; that they would never forget that a nation cannot long remain strong when every man belonging to it is individually weak, and that no form or combination of social polity has yet been devised to make an energetic people out of a community of pusillanimous and enfeebled citizens.

I trace amongst our contemporaries two contrary notions which are equally injurious. One set of men can perceive nothing in the principle of equality but the anarchical tendencies which it engenders: they dread their own free agency—they fear themselves. Other thinkers, less numerous but more enlightened, take a different view: besides that track which starts from the principle of equality to terminate in anarchy, they have at last discovered the road which seems to lead men to inevitable servitude. They shape their souls beforehand to this necessary condition; and, despairing of remaining free, they already do obeisance in their hearts to the master who is soon to appear. The former abandon freedom, because they think it dangerous; the latter, because they hold it to be impossible. If I had entertained the latter conviction, I should not have written this book, but I should have confined myself to deploring in secret the destiny of mankind. I have sought to point out the dangers to which the principle of equality exposes the independence of man, because I firmly believe that these dangers are the most formidable, as well as the least foreseen, of all those which futurity holds in store: but I do not think that they are insurmountable. The men who live in the democratic ages upon which we are entering have naturally a taste for independence: they are naturally impatient of regulation, and they are wearied by the permanence even of the condition they themselves prefer. They are fond of power; but they are prone to despise and hate those who wield it, and they easily elude its grasp by their own mobility and insignificance. These propensities will always manifest themselves, because they originate in the groundwork of society, which will undergo no change: for a long time they will prevent the establishment of any despotism, and they will furnish fresh weapons to each succeeding generation which shall struggle in favour of the liberty of mankind. Let us then look forward to the future with that salutary fear which makes men keep watch and ward for freedom, not with that faint and idle terror which depresses and enervates the heart.

CHAPTER VIII

GENERAL SURVEY OF THE SUBJECT

Before I close forever the theme that has detained me so long, I would fain take a parting survey of all the various characteristics of modern society, and appreciate at last the general influence to be exercised by the principle of equality upon the fate of mankind; but I am stopped by the difficulty of the task, and in presence of so great an object my sight is troubled, and my reason fails. The society of the modern world which I have sought to delineate, and which I seek to judge, has but just come into existence. Time has not yet shaped it into perfect form: the great revolution by which it has been created is not yet over; and amidst the occurrences of our time, it is almost impossible to discern what will pass away with the revolution itself, and what will survive its close. The world which is rising into existence is still half encumbered by the remains of the world which is waning into decay; and amidst the vast perplexity of human affairs, none can say how much of ancient institutions and former manners will remain, or how much will completely disappear. Although the revolution which is taking place in the social condition, the laws, the opinions, and the feelings of men, is still very far from being terminated, yet its results already admit of no comparison with anything that the world has ever before witnessed. I go back from age to age up to the remotest antiquity; but I find no parallel to what is occurring before my eyes: as the past has ceased to throw its light upon the future, the mind of man wanders in obscurity. Nevertheless, in the midst of a prospect so wide, so novel and so confused, some of the more prominent characteristics may already be discerned and pointed out. The good things and the evils of life are more equally distributed in the world: great wealth tends to disappear, the number of small fortunes to increase; desires and gratifications are multiplied, but extraordinary prosperity and irremediable penury are alike unknown. The sentiment of ambition is universal, but the scope of ambition is seldom vast. Each individual stands apart in solitary weakness; but society at large is active, provident, and powerful: the performances of private persons are insignificant, those of the state immense. There is little energy of character; but manners are mild, and laws humane. If there be few instances of exalted heroism or of virtues of the highest, brightest, and purest temper, men's habits are regular, violence is rare, and cruelty almost unknown. Human existence becomes longer, and property more secure: life is not adorned with brilliant trophies, but it is extremely easy and tranquil. Few pleasures are either very refined or very coarse; and highly polished manners are as uncommon as great brutality of tastes. Neither men of great learning, nor extremely ignorant communities, are to be met with; genius becomes more rare, information more diffused. The human mind is impelled by the small efforts of all mankind combined together, not by the strenuous activity of certain men. There is less perfection, but more abundance, in all the productions of the arts. The ties of race, of rank, and of country are relaxed; the great bond of humanity is strengthened. If I endeavour to find out the most general and the most prominent of all these different characteristics, I shall have occasion to perceive that what is taking place in men's fortunes manifests itself under a thousand other forms. Almost all extremes are softened or blunted: all that was most prominent is superseded by some mean term, at once less lofty and less low, less brilliant and less obscure, than what before existed in the world.

When I survey this countless multitude of beings shaped in each other's likeness, amidst whom nothing rises and nothing falls, the sight of such universal uniformity saddens and chills me, and I am tempted to regret that state of society which has ceased to be. When the world was full of men of great importance and extreme insignificance, of great wealth and extreme poverty, of great learning and extreme ignorance, I turned aside from the latter to fix my observation on the former alone, who gratified my sympathies. But I admit that this gratification arose from my own weakness: it is because I am unable to see at once all that is around me that I am allowed thus to select and separate the objects of my predilection from among so many others. Such is not the case with that almighty and eternal Being whose gaze necessarily includes the whole of created things, and who surveys distinctly, though at once, mankind and man. We may naturally believe that it is not the singular prosperity of the few, but the greater well-being of all, which is most pleasing in the sight of the Creator and Preserver of men. What appears to me to be man's decline, is to His eye advancement; what afflicts me is acceptable to Him. A state of equality is perhaps less elevated, but it is more just; and its justice constitutes its greatness and its beauty. I would strive then to raise myself to this point of the divine contemplation, and thence to view and to judge the concerns of men.

No man, upon the earth, can as yet affirm absolutely and generally that the new state of the world is better than its former one; but it is already easy to perceive that this state is different. Some vices and some virtues were so inherent in the constitution of an aristocratic nation, and are so opposite to the character of a modern people, that they can never be infused into it; some good tendencies and some bad propensities which were unknown to the former are natural to the latter; some ideas suggest themselves spontaneously to the imagination of the one which are utterly repugnant to the mind of the other. They are like two distinct orders of human beings, each of which has its own merits and defects, its own advantages and its own evils. Care must therefore be taken not to judge the state of society, which is now coming into existence, by notions derived from a state of society which no longer exists; for as these states of society are exceedingly different in their structure, they cannot be submitted to a just or fair comparison. It would be scarcely more reasonable to require of our own contemporaries the peculiar virtues which originated in the social condition of their forefathers, since that social condition is itself fallen, and has drawn into one promiscuous ruin the good and evil which belonged to it.

But as yet these things are imperfectly understood. I find that a great number of my contemporaries undertake to make a certain selection from amongst the institutions, the opinions, and the ideas which originated in the aristocratic constitution of society as it was: a portion of these elements they would willingly relinquish, but they would keep the remainder and transplant them into their new world. I apprehend that such men are wasting their time and their strength in virtuous but unprofitable efforts. The object is not to retain the peculiar advantages which the inequality of conditions bestows upon mankind, but to secure the new benefits which equality may supply. We have not to seek to make ourselves like our progenitors, but to strive to work out that species of greatness and happiness which is our own. For myself, who now look back from this extreme limit of my task, and discover from afar, but at once, the various objects which have attracted my more attentive investigation upon my way, I am full of apprehensions and of hopes. I perceive mighty dangers which it is possible to ward off—mighty evils which may be avoided or alleviated; and I cling with a firmer hold to the belief that for democratic nations to be virtuous and prosperous they require but to will it. I am aware that many of my contemporaries maintain that nations are never their own masters here below, and that they necessarily obey some insurmountable and unintelligent power, arising from anterior events, from their race, or from the soil and climate of their country. Such principles are false and cowardly; such principles can never produce aught but feeble men and pusillanimous nations. Providence has not created mankind entirely independent or entirely free. It is true that around every man a fatal circle is traced, beyond which he cannot pass; but within the wide verge of that circle he is powerful and free: as it is with man, so with communities. The nations of our time cannot prevent the conditions of men from becoming equal; but it depends upon themselves whether the principle of equality is to lead them to servitude or freedom, to knowledge or barbarism, to prosperity or to wretchedness.

10

FRÉDÉRIC BASTIAT, THE LAW

INTRODUCTION

The concept of 'legal plunder'—the seizing and appropriating by the state or its proxies of the goods and property of others using the very laws and legal system that should have protected them—is an essential one to grasp in the era of the all-encompassing state. It is, admittedly, an idea that lawmakers and those holding positions of political power will tend to find uncongenial, for the self-evident reason that it is lawmakers and those in power who make the laws that make the plunder possible. The general public, relatedly, is likely to find the notion unfamiliar, for the reason that it is rarely made much of in schools and colleges or in state-owned or controlled media—these being also, on the whole, beneficiaries of plunder. However, for those who are willing to retain an open mind, it can be the first step towards understanding how the existing way of organizing our societies may not necessarily be the best—and that things can be different, fairer, and better.

Frédéric Bastiat (1801-1850) was born in Bayonne, a port town in the south of France, the son of a prominent businessman. His father and mother both died when he was young, leaving him an orphan in the care of his paternal grandfather and aunt. Upon the death of his grandfather, which occurred while he was still in his mid-twenties, Bastiat inherited the family estate in the town of Mugron further inland. The inheritance provided him with the means to live the life of a gentleman farmer and independent scholar, and he read voraciously for the following two decades before rising to prominence in 1845 with his *Economic Sophisms*, a spirited attack on statist policies and the various forms of false consciousness that underpin them. Bastiat was elected to the French national legislative assembly after the 1848 Revolution, but shortly thereafter he contracted tuberculosis, and he died the same year that he published his greatest work, *The Law* (1850). It is said that on his deathbed he called those attending him to come close and murmured the words 'the truth' twice before he died.

Bastiat was clear in *The Law* as to how things should be. He started from the basics: we are endowed firstly with existence, secondly with faculties that we may apply to existence, and thirdly with the fruits of assimilating and appropriating, through the application of our faculties, the external elements with which we work—in short, life, liberty, and property. The right to defend these, said Bastiat, is anterior and superior to all human legislation. Law is the organization of this right in collective form; it cannot, therefore, properly be used for purposes other than to secure and give effect to it.

What tends to happen, however, is that the legislative power falls into the hands of a single man or group of men who proceed to employ it—whether openly or (more likely) under the guise of public welfare or philanthropy—for their own purposes. Law through this process becomes not an instrument for security against plunder but an agent of plunder itself; worse, it treats the plundered party, when he defends himself, as a criminal. While those in control of the law continue to seek to profit by means of this 'lawful plunder', the victimized masses will be inclined to assert their own political rights in response. Once the masses seize the legislative power they will have a choice: either to end plunder, or take part in it themselves. They will inevitably take the latter course and seek to organize a system of reprisals against their former oppressors. The outcome of this process is what Bastiat calls 'universal plunder'—the wholesale co-option of the law for the purposes of appropriating the goods and property of those it was meant to protect.

In the sense employed by Bastiat, legal plunder is everywhere. The test for it is simple: ask yourself whether the law performs what a citizen cannot so perform without committing a crime; if so, this is plunder. In practice, legal plunder may be carried out in an infinite number of ways and there will be an infinite number of plans for organizing it: tariffs, protection, benefits, subsidies, encouragements, progressive taxation, guaranteed jobs, guaranteed profits, minimum wages, a right to relief, free credit, and so on. Taken as a whole, these plans for legal plunder constitute what is more widely known as 'socialism'. Admittedly, there are forms of plunder other than socialism; notably, Bastiat includes slavery as a form of plunder too. But socialism is the quintessentially modern form that legal plunder has deigned to take. As Bastiat observes: 'It can only be an instrument of equalization as far as it takes from one party to give to another, and then it is an instrument of plunder.'

The socialist has, Bastiat explains, a particular kind of worldview. Socialists divide mankind into two parts: for the one part there is the politician—the organizer, discoverer, legislator, instructor, founder—whose sublime mission it is to gather together into society, and thereafter work upon and 'improve', that scattered material known as man; for the other part there remains the rest of mankind, considered by the politician to be a kind of 'inert matter', devoid of any principle of action or means of discernment, lacking initiative, and indifferent towards its own mode of existence. The socialist looks upon mankind as a subject for social experiments intended to remedy what he perceives to be its various incompetencies, prejudices, and other deficiencies. That the very deficiencies in mankind that the socialist seeks to remedy are liable also to affect himself—being but a man too—does not, however, appear to cross his mind.

The solution to the problem of plunder, says Bastiat, is liberty—law not as fraternity but as justice. When you make law a vehicle for the realization of social dreams and utopias, you open the door to a multitude of troubles and revolutions, for whose dream and whose utopia (and we all have dreams and utopias) is the law to bring into being—and whose life, liberty, and property are to be plundered in order to pay for it? No doubt you can point to inequality—we all can—and no doubt inequality is, in general, unattractive and unjustifiable. Remember, though, that inequality is likely to have proceeded from previous acts of plunder (whether legal or otherwise), and there is no reason to believe that further plundering is going to effect a final solution to the problem. Too many people place themselves above the world to rule and patronize it. Give men, instead, their liberty and security, and allow them to unfold the qualities that they have been blessed with, and we will all be better off.

THE LAW

The law perverted! The law—and, in its wake, all the collective forces of the nation—the law, I say, not only diverted from its proper direction, but made to pursue one entirely contrary! The law become the tool of every kind of avarice, instead of being its check! The law guilty of that very iniquity which it was its mission to punish! Truly, this is a serious fact, if it exists, and one to which I feel bound to call the attention of my fellow citizens.

We hold from God the gift that, as far as we are concerned, contains all others, Life—physical, intellectual, and moral life.

But life cannot support itself. He who has bestowed it, has entrusted us with the care of supporting it, of developing it, and of perfecting it. To that end, He has provided us with a collection of wonderful faculties; He has plunged us into the midst of a variety of elements. It is by the application of our faculties to these elements that the phenomena of assimilation and of appropriation, by which life pursues the circle that has been assigned to it, are realized.

Existence, faculties, assimilation—in other words, personality, liberty, property—this is man.

It is of these three things that it may be said, apart from all demagogic subtlety, that they are anterior and superior to all human legislation.

It is not because men have made laws that personality, liberty, and property exist. On the contrary, it is because personality, liberty, and property exist beforehand that men make laws. What, then, is law? As I have said elsewhere, it is the collective organization of the individual right to lawful defence.

Nature, or rather God, has bestowed upon every one of us the right to defend his person, his liberty, and his property, since these are the three constituent or preserving elements of life; elements, each of which is rendered complete by the others, and that cannot be understood without them. For what are our faculties, but the extension of our personality? And what is property, but an extension of our faculties?

If every man has the right of defending, even by force, his person, his liberty, and his property, a number of men have the right to combine together to extend, to organize a common force to provide regularly for this defence.

Collective right, then, has its principle, its reason for existing, its lawfulness, in individual right; and the common force cannot rationally have any other end, or any other mission, than that of the isolated forces for which it is substituted. Thus, as the force of an individual cannot lawfully touch the person, the liberty, or the property of another individual—for the same reason, the common force cannot lawfully be used to destroy the person, the liberty, or the property of individuals or of classes.

For this perversion of force would be, in one case as in the other, in contradiction to our premises. For who will dare to say that force has been given to us, not to defend our rights, but to annihilate the equal rights of our brethren? And if this be not true of every individual force, acting independently, how can it be true of the collective force, which is only the organized union of isolated forces?

Nothing, therefore, can be more evident than this: The law is the organization of the natural right of lawful defence; it is the substitution of collective for individual forces, for the purpose of acting in the sphere in which they have a right to act, of doing what they have a right to do, to secure persons, liberties, and properties, and to maintain each in its right, so as to cause justice to reign over all.

And if a people established upon this basis were to exist, it seems to me that order would prevail among them in their acts as well as in their ideas. It seems to me that such a people would have the most simple, the most economical, the least oppressive, the least to be felt, the most restrained, the most just, and, consequently, the most stable government that could be imagined, whatever its political form might be.

For under such an administration, everyone would feel that he possessed all the fullness, as well as all the responsibility, of his existence. So long as personal safety was ensured, so long as labour was free, and the fruits of labour secured against all unjust attacks, no one would have any difficulties to contend with in the state. When prosperous, we should not, it is true, have to thank the state for our success; but when unfortunate, we should no more think of taxing it with our disasters than our peasants think of attributing to it the arrival of hail or of frost. We should know it only by the inestimable blessing of safety.

It may further be affirmed, that, thanks to the nonintervention of the state in private affairs, our wants and their satisfactions would develop themselves in their natural order. We should not see poor families seeking for literary instruction before they were supplied with bread. We should not see towns peopled at the expense of rural districts, nor rural districts at the expense of towns. We should not see those great displacements of capital, of labour, and of population, that legislative measures occasion; displacements that render so uncertain and precarious the very sources of existence, and thus enlarge to such an extent the responsibility of governments.

Unhappily, law is by no means confined to its own sphere. Nor is it merely in some ambiguous and debatable views that it has left its proper sphere. It has done more than this. It has acted in direct opposition to its proper end; it has destroyed its own object; it has been employed in annihilating that justice which it ought to have established, in effacing amongst rights that limit which it was its true mission to respect; it has placed the collective force in the service of those who wish to traffic, without risk and without scruple, in the persons, the liberty, and the property of others; it has converted plunder into a right, that it may protect it, and lawful defence into a crime, that it may punish it.

How has this perversion of law been accomplished? And what has resulted from it?

The law has been perverted through the influence of two very different causes—naked greed and misconceived philanthropy.

Let us speak of the former. Self-preservation and development is the common aspiration of all men, in such a way that if everyone enjoyed the free exercise of his faculties and the free disposition of their fruits, social progress would be incessant, uninterrupted, inevitable.

But there is also another disposition which is common to them. This is to live and to develop, when they can, at the expense of one another. This is no rash imputation, emanating from a gloomy, uncharitable spirit. History bears witness to the truth of it, by the incessant wars, the migrations of races, sectarian oppressions, the universality of slavery, the frauds in trade, and the monopolies with which its annals abound. This fatal disposition has its origin in the very constitution of man—in that primitive, and universal, and invincible sentiment that urges it towards its well-being, and makes it seek to escape pain.

Man can only derive life and enjoyment from a perpetual search and appropriation; that is, from a perpetual application of his faculties to objects, or from labour. This is the origin of property.

But also he may live and enjoy by seizing and appropriating the productions of the faculties of his fellow men. This is the origin of plunder.

Now, labour being in itself a pain, and man being naturally inclined to avoid pain, it follows, and history proves it, that wherever plunder is less burdensome than labour, it prevails; and neither religion nor morality can, in this case, prevent it from prevailing.

When does plunder cease, then? When it becomes more burdensome and more dangerous than labour. It is very evident that the proper aim of law is to oppose the fatal tendency to plunder with the powerful obstacle of collective force; that all its measures should be in favour of property, and against plunder.

But the law is made, generally, by one man, or by one class of men. And as law cannot exist without the sanction and the support of a preponderant force, it must finally place this force in the hands of those who legislate.

This inevitable phenomenon, combined with the fatal tendency that, we have said, exists in the heart of man, explains the almost universal perversion of law. It is easy to conceive that, instead of being a check upon injustice, it becomes its most invincible instrument.

It is easy to conceive that, according to the power of the legislator, it destroys for its own profit, and in different degrees amongst the rest of the community, personal independence by slavery, liberty by oppression, and property by plunder.

It is in the nature of men to rise against the injustice of which they are the victims. When, therefore, plunder is organized by law, for the profit of those who perpetrate it, all the plundered classes tend, either by peaceful or revolutionary means, to enter in some way into the manufacturing of laws. These classes, according to the degree of enlightenment at which they have arrived, may propose to themselves two very different ends, when they thus attempt the attainment of their political rights; either they may wish to put an end to lawful plunder, or they may desire to take part in it.

Woe to the nation where this latter thought prevails amongst the masses at the moment when they, in their turn, seize upon the legislative power!

Up to that time, lawful plunder has been exercised by the few upon the many, as is the case in countries where the right of legislating is confined to a few hands. But now it has become universal, and the equilibrium is sought in universal plunder. The injustice that society contains, instead of being rooted out of it, is generalized. As soon as the injured classes have recovered their political rights, their first thought is not to abolish plunder (this would suppose them to possess enlightenment, which they cannot have), but to organize against the other classes, and to their own detriment, a system of reprisals—as if it was necessary, before the reign of justice arrives, that all should undergo a cruel retribution—some for their iniquity and some for their ignorance.

It would be impossible, therefore, to introduce into society a greater change and a greater evil than this—the conversion of the law into an instrument of plunder.

What would be the consequences of such a perversion? It would require volumes to describe them all. We must content ourselves with pointing out the most striking.

In the first place, it would efface from everybody's conscience the distinction between justice and injustice. No society can exist unless the laws are respected to a certain degree, but the safest way to make them respected is to make them respectable. When law and morality are in contradiction to each other, the citizen finds himself in the cruel alternative of either losing his moral sense, or of losing his respect for the law—two evils of equal magnitude, between which it would be difficult to choose.

It is so much in the nature of law to support justice that in the minds of the masses they are one and the same. There is in all of us a strong disposition to regard what is lawful as legitimate, so much so that many falsely derive all justice from law. It is sufficient, then, for the law to order and sanction plunder, that it may appear to many consciences just and sacred. Slavery, protection, and monopoly find defenders, not only in those who profit by them, but in those who suffer by them. If you suggest a doubt as to the morality of these institutions, it is said directly: 'You are a dangerous experimenter, a utopian, a theorist, a despiser of the laws; you would shake the basis upon which society rests.'

If you lecture upon morality, or political economy, official bodies will be found to make this request to the government:

That henceforth science be taught not only with sole reference to free exchange (to liberty, property, and justice), as has been the case up to the present time, but also, and especially, with reference to the facts and legislation (contrary to liberty, property, and justice) that regulate French industry. That, in public lecterns salaried by the treasury, the professor abstain rigorously from endangering in the slightest degree the respect due to the laws now in force.[1]

So that if a law exists that sanctions slavery or monopoly, oppression or plunder, in any form whatever, it must not even be mentioned—for how can it be mentioned without damaging the respect that it inspires? Still further, morality and political economy must be taught in connection with this law—that is, under the supposition that it must be just, only because it is law.

Another effect of this deplorable perversion of the law is that it gives to human passions and to political struggles, and, in general, to politics, properly so called, an exaggerated importance.

I could prove this assertion in a thousand ways. But I shall confine myself, by way of an illustration, to bringing it to bear upon a subject which has of late occupied everybody's mind: universal suffrage.

Whatever may be thought of it by the adepts of the school of Rousseau, which professes to be very far advanced, but which I consider twenty centuries behind, universal suffrage (taking the word in its strictest sense) is not one of those sacred dogmas with respect to which examination and doubt are crimes.

Serious objections may be made to it.

In the first place, the word universal conceals a gross sophism. There are, in France, thirty-six million inhabitants. To make the right of suffrage universal, thirty-six million electors should be reckoned. The

1. General Council of Manufactures, Agriculture, and Commerce, 6th of May, 1850.

CLASSIC POLITICAL PHILOSOPHY FOR THE MODERN MAN

most extended system reckons only nine million. Three persons out of four, then, are excluded; and more than this, they are excluded by the fourth. Upon what principle is this exclusion founded? Upon the principle of incapacity. Universal suffrage, then, means: universal suffrage of those who are capable. In point of fact, who are the capable? Are age, sex, and judicial condemnations the only conditions to which incapacity is to be attached?

On taking a nearer view of the subject, we may soon perceive the reason why the right of suffrage depends upon the presumption of incapacity; the most extended system differing from the most restricted in the conditions on which this incapacity depends, and which constitutes not a difference in principle, but in degree.

This motive is that the elector does not stipulate for himself, but for everybody.

If, as the republicans of the Greek and Roman tone pretend, the right of suffrage had fallen to the lot of everyone at his birth, it would be an injustice to adults to prevent women and children from voting. Why are they prevented? Because they are presumed to be incapable. And why is incapacity a reason for exclusion? Because the elector does not reap alone the responsibility of his vote; because every vote engages and affects the community at large; because the community has a right to demand some assurances as regards the acts upon which its well-being and its existence depend.

I know what might be said in answer to this. I know what might be objected. But this is not the place to settle a controversy of this kind. What I wish to observe is this, that this same controversy (in common with the greater part of political questions) that agitates, excites, and unsettles the nations, would lose almost all its importance if the law had always been what it ought to be.

In fact, if law were confined to causing all persons, all liberties, and all properties to be respected—if it were merely the organization of individual right and individual defence—if it were the obstacle, the check, the chastisement opposed to all oppression, to all plunder—is it likely that we should dispute much, as citizens, on the subject of the greater or lesser universality of suffrage? Is it likely that it would compromise that greatest of advantages, the public peace? Is it likely that the excluded classes would not quietly wait for their turn? Is it likely that the enfranchised classes would be very jealous of their privilege? And is it not clear, that the interest of all being one and the same, some would act without much inconvenience to the others?

But if the fatal principle should come to be introduced that, under pretense of organization, regulation, protection, or encouragement, the law may take from one party in order to give to another, help itself to the wealth acquired by all the classes that it may increase that of one class, whether that of the agriculturists, the manufacturers, the ship owners, or artists and comedians; then certainly, in this case, there is no class which may not try, and with reason, to place its hand upon the law, that would not demand with fury its right of election and eligibility, and that would overturn society rather than not obtain it. Even beggars and vagabonds will prove to you that they have an incontestable title to it. They will say:

> We never buy wine, tobacco, or salt, without paying the tax, and a part of this tax is given by law in perquisites and gratuities to men who are richer than we are. Others make use of the law to create an artificial rise in the price of bread, meat, iron, or cloth. Since everybody traffics in law for his own profit, we should like to do the same. We should like to make it produce the right to assistance, which is the poor man's plunder. To effect this, we ought to be electors and legislators, that we may organize, on a large scale, alms for our own class, as you have organized, on a large scale, protection for yours.

Don't tell us that you will take our cause upon yourselves, and throw to us six hundred thousand francs to keep us quiet, like giving us a bone to pick. We have other claims, and, at any rate, we wish to stipulate for ourselves, as other classes have stipulated for themselves!

How is this argument to be answered? Yes, as long as it is admitted that the law may be diverted from its true mission, that it may violate property instead of securing it, everybody will be wanting to manufacture law, either to defend himself against plunder, or to organize it for his own profit. The political question will always be prejudicial, predominant, and absorbing; in a word, there will be fighting around the door of the Legislative Palace. The struggle will be no less furious within it. To be convinced of this, it is hardly necessary to look at what passes in the Chambers in France and in England; it is enough to know how the question stands.

Is there any need to prove that this odious perversion of law is a perpetual source of hatred and discord, that it even tends to social disorganization? Look at the United States. There is no country in the world where the law is kept more within its proper domain—which is, to secure to everyone his liberty and his property. Therefore, there is no country in the world where social order appears to rest upon a more solid basis. Nevertheless, even in the United States, there are two questions, and only two, that from the beginning have endangered political order. And what are these two questions? That of slavery and that of tariffs; that is, precisely the only two questions in which, contrary to the general spirit of this republic, law has taken the character of a plunderer. Slavery is a violation, sanctioned by law, of the rights of the person. Protection is a violation perpetrated by the law upon the rights of property; and certainly it is very remarkable that, in the midst of so many other debates, this double legal scourge, the sorrowful inheritance of the Old World, should be the only one which can, and perhaps will, cause the rupture of the Union. Indeed, a more astounding fact, in the heart of society, cannot be conceived than this: That law should have become an instrument of injustice. And if this fact occasions consequences so formidable to the United States, where there is but one exception, what must it be with us in Europe, where it is a principle—a system?

Mr Montalembert, adopting the thought of a famous proclamation of Mr Carlier, said, 'We must make war against socialism.' And by socialism, according to the definition of Mr Charles Dupin, he meant plunder. But what plunder did he mean? For there are two sorts: extralegal and legal plunder.

As to extralegal plunder, such as theft, or swindling, which is defined, foreseen, and punished by the penal code, I do not think it can be adorned by the name of socialism. It is not this that systematically threatens the foundations of society. Besides, the war against this kind of plunder has not waited for the signal of Mr Montalembert or Mr Carlier. It has gone on since the beginning of the world; France was carrying it on long before the revolution of February—long before the appearance of socialism—with all the ceremonies of magistracy, police, gendarmerie, prisons, dungeons, and scaffolds. It is the law itself that is conducting this war, and it is to be wished, in my opinion, that the law should always maintain this attitude with respect to plunder.

But this is not the case. The law sometimes takes its own part.

Sometimes it accomplishes it with its own hands, in order to save the parties benefited the shame, the danger, and the scruple. Sometimes it places all this ceremony of magistracy, police, gendarmerie, and prisons, at the service of the plunderer, and treats the plundered party, when he defends himself, as the criminal. In a word, there is a legal plunder, and it is, no doubt, this that is meant by Mr Montalembert.

This plunder may be only an exceptional blemish in the legislation of a people, and in this case, the best thing that can be done is, without so many speeches and lamentations, to do away with it as soon as possible, notwithstanding the clamors of interested parties. But how is it to be distinguished? Very easily. See whether the law takes from some persons that which belongs to them, to give to others what does not belong to them. See whether the law performs, for the profit of one citizen, and, to the injury of others, an act that this citizen cannot perform without committing a crime. Abolish this law without delay; it is not merely an iniquity—it is a fertile source of iniquities, for it invites reprisals; and if you do not take care, the exceptional case will extend, multiply, and become systematic. No doubt the party benefited will exclaim loudly; he will assert his acquired rights. He will say that the state is bound to protect and encourage his industry; he will plead that it is a good thing for the state to be enriched, that it may spend the more, and thus shower down salaries upon the poor workmen. Take care not to listen to this sophistry, for it is just by the systematizing of these arguments that legal plunder becomes systematized.

And this is what has taken place. The delusion of the day is to enrich all classes at the expense of each other; it is to generalize plunder under pretense of organizing it. Now, legal plunder may be exercised in an infinite multitude of ways. Hence come an infinite multitude of plans for organization; tariffs, protection, perquisites, gratuities, encouragements, progressive taxation, free public education, right to work, right to profit, right to wages, right to assistance, right to instruments of labor, gratuity of credit, etc., etc. And it is all these plans, taken as a whole, with what they have in common, legal plunder, that takes the name of socialism.

Now socialism, thus defined, and forming a doctrinal body, what other war would you make against it than a war of doctrine? You find this doctrine false, absurd, abominable. Refute it. This will be all the easier, the more false, absurd, and abominable it is. Above all, if you wish to be strong, begin by rooting out of your legislation every particle of socialism which may have crept into it—and this will be no light work.

Mr Montalembert has been reproached with wishing to turn brute force against socialism. He ought to be exonerated from this reproach, for he has plainly said: 'The war that we must make against socialism must be one that is compatible with the law, honour, and justice.'

But how is it that Mr Montalembert does not see that he is placing himself in a vicious circle? You would oppose law to socialism. But it is the law that socialism invokes. It aspires to legal, not extralegal plunder. It is of the law itself, like monopolists of all kinds, that it wants to make an instrument; and when once it has the law on its side, how will you be able to turn the law against it? How will you place it under the power of your tribunals, your gendarmes, and of your prisons? What will you do then? You wish to prevent it from taking any part in the making of laws. You would keep it outside the Legislative Palace. In this you will not succeed, I venture to prophesy, so long as legal plunder is the basis of the legislation within.

It is absolutely necessary that this question of legal plunder should be determined, and there are only three solutions of it:

1. When the few plunder the many.
2. When everybody plunders everybody else.
3. When nobody plunders anybody.

Partial plunder, universal plunder, absence of plunder, amongst these we have to make our choice. The law can only produce one of these results.

Partial plunder. This is the system that prevailed so long as the elective privilege was partial; a system that is resorted to to avoid the invasion of socialism.

Universal plunder. We have been threatened by this system when the elective privilege has become universal; the masses having conceived the idea of making law on the principle of legislators who had preceded them.

Absence of plunder. This is the principle of justice, peace, order, stability, conciliation, and of good sense, which I shall proclaim with all the force of my lungs (which is very inadequate, alas!) till the day of my death.

And, in all sincerity, can anything more be required at the hands of the law? Can the law, whose necessary sanction is force, be reasonably employed upon anything beyond securing to every one his right? I defy anyone to remove it from this circle without perverting it, and consequently turning force against right. And as this is the most fatal, the most illogical social perversion that can possibly be imagined, it must be admitted that the true solution, so much sought after, of the social problem, is contained in these simple words—LAW IS ORGANIZED JUSTICE.

Now it is important to remark, that to organize justice by law, that is to say by force, excludes the idea of organizing by law, or by force any manifestation whatever of human activity—labor, charity, agriculture, commerce, industry, instruction, the fine arts, or religion; for any one of these organizings would inevitably destroy the essential organization. How, in fact, can we imagine force encroaching upon the liberty of citizens without infringing upon justice, and so acting against its proper aim?

Here I am taking on the most popular prejudice of our time. It is not considered enough that law should be just, it must be philanthropic. It is not sufficient that it should guarantee to every citizen the free and inoffensive exercise of his faculties, applied to his physical, intellectual, and moral development; it is required to extend well-being, instruction, and morality directly over the nation. This is the fascinating side of socialism.

But, I repeat it, these two missions of the law contradict each other. We have to choose between them. A citizen cannot at the same time be free and not free. Mr de Lamartine wrote to me one day thus: 'Your doctrine is only the half of my program; you have stopped at liberty, I go on to fraternity.' I answered him: 'The second part of your program will destroy the first.' And in fact it is impossible for me to separate the word fraternity from the word voluntary. I cannot possibly conceive fraternity legally enforced, without liberty being legally destroyed, and justice legally trampled underfoot. Legal plunder has two roots: one of them, as we have already seen, is in human greed; the other is in misconceived philanthropy.

Before I proceed, I think I ought to explain myself upon the word plunder.

I do not take it, as it often is taken, in a vague, undefined, relative, or metaphorical sense. I use it in its scientific acceptation, and as expressing the opposite idea to property. When a portion of wealth passes out of the hands of him who has acquired it, without his consent, and without compensation, to him who has not created it, whether by force or by artifice, I say that property is violated, that plunder is perpetrated. I say that this is exactly what the law ought to repress always and everywhere. If the law itself performs the action it ought to repress, I say that plunder is still perpetrated, and even, in a social point of view, under aggravated circumstances. In this case, however, he who profits from the plunder is not responsible for it; it is the law, the lawgiver, society itself, and this is where the political danger lies.

It is to be regretted that there is something offensive in the word. I have sought in vain for another, for I would not wish at any time, and especially just now, to add an irritating word to our disagreements; therefore, whether I am believed or not, I declare that I do not mean to impugn the intentions nor the morality of anybody. I am attacking an idea that I believe to be false—a system that appears to me to be unjust; and this is so independent of intentions that each of us profits by it without wishing it, and suffers from it without being aware of the cause.

Any person must write under the influence of party spirit or of fear who would call into question the sincerity of protectionism, of socialism, and even of communism, which are one and the same plant, in three different periods of its growth. All that can be said is that plunder is more visible by its partiality in protectionism,[2] and by its universality in communism; whence it follows that, of the three systems, socialism is still the most vague, the most undefined, and consequently the most sincere.

Be that as it may, to conclude that legal plunder has one of its roots in misconceived philanthropy is evidently to put intentions out of the question.

With this understanding, let us examine the value, the origin, and the tendency of this popular aspiration, which pretends to realize the general good by general plunder.

---

2. If protection were only granted in France to a single class, to the engineers, for instance, it would be so absurdly plundering, as to be unable to maintain itself. Thus we see all the protected trades combine, make common cause, and even recruit themselves in such a way as to appear to embrace the mass of the national labour. They feel instinctively that plunder is slurred over by being generalized.

The socialists say, since the law organizes justice, why should it not organize labour, instruction, and religion?

Why? Because it could not organize labour, instruction, and religion, without disorganizing justice.

For remember, that law is force, and that consequently the domain of the law cannot properly extend beyond the domain of force.

When law and force keep a man within the bounds of justice, they impose nothing upon him but a mere negation. They only oblige him to abstain from doing harm. They violate neither his personality, his liberty, nor his property. They only guard the personality, the liberty, the property of others. They hold themselves on the defensive; they defend the equal right of all. They fulfil a mission whose harmlessness is evident, whose utility is palpable, and whose legitimacy is not to be disputed. This is so true that, as a friend of mine once remarked to me, to say that the aim of the law is to cause justice to reign is to use an expression that is not rigorously exact. It ought to be said, the aim of the law is to prevent injustice from reigning. In fact, it is not justice that has an existence of its own, it is injustice. The one results from the absence of the other.

But when the law, through the medium of its necessary agent—force—imposes a form of labour, a method or a subject of instruction, a creed, or a worship, it is no longer negative; it acts positively upon men. It substitutes the will of the legislator for their own will, the initiative of the legislator for their own initiative. They have no need to consult, to compare, or to foresee; the law does all that for them. The intellect is for them a useless encumbrance; they cease to be men; they lose their personality, their liberty, their property.

Try to imagine a form of labour imposed by force that is not a violation of liberty; a transmission of wealth imposed by force, that is not a violation of property. If you cannot succeed in reconciling this, you are bound to conclude that the law cannot organize labour and industry without organizing injustice.

When, from the seclusion of his office, a politician takes a view of society, he is struck with the spectacle of inequality that presents itself. He mourns over the sufferings that are the lot of so many of our brethren, sufferings whose aspect is rendered yet more sorrowful by the contrast of luxury and wealth.

He ought, perhaps, to ask himself whether such a social state has not been caused by the plunder of ancient times, exercised in the way of conquests; and by plunder of more recent times, effected through the medium of the laws? He ought to ask himself whether, granting the aspiration of all men to well-being and improvement, the reign of justice would not suffice to realize the greatest activity of progress, and the greatest amount of equality compatible with that individual responsibility that God has awarded as a just retribution of virtue and vice?

He never gives this a thought. His mind turns towards combinations, arrangements, legal or factitious organizations. He seeks the remedy in perpetuating and exaggerating what has produced the evil.

For, justice apart, which we have seen is only a negation, is there any one of these legal arrangements that does not contain the principle of plunder?

You say, 'There are men who have no money,' and you apply to the law. But the law is not a self-supplied fountain, whence every stream may obtain supplies independently of society. Nothing can enter the public treasury, in favour of one citizen or one class, but what other citizens and other classes have been forced to send to it. If everyone draws from it only the equivalent of what he has contributed to it, your law, it is true, is no plunderer, but it does nothing for men who want money—it does not promote equality. It can only be an instrument of equalization as far as it takes from one party to give to another, and then it is an instrument of plunder. Examine, in this light, the protection of tariffs, subsidies, right to profit, right to labour, right to assistance, free public education, progressive taxation, gratuitousness of credit, social workshops, and you will always find at the bottom legal plunder, organized injustice.

You say, 'There are men who want knowledge,' and you apply to the law. But the law is not a torch that sheds light that originates within itself. It extends over a society where there are men who have knowledge, and others who have not; citizens who want to learn, and others who are disposed to teach. It can only do one of two things: either allow a free operation to this kind of transaction, i.e., let this kind of want satisfy itself freely; or else preempt the will of the people in the matter, and take from some of them sufficient to pay professors commissioned to instruct others for free. But, in this second case there cannot fail to be a violation of liberty and property—legal plunder.

You say, 'Here are men who are wanting in morality or religion,' and you apply to the law; but law is force, and need I say how far it is a violent and absurd enterprise to introduce force in these matters?

As the result of its systems and of its efforts, it would seem that socialism, notwithstanding all its self-complacency, can scarcely help perceiving the monster of legal plunder. But what does it do? It disguises it cleverly from others, and even from itself, under the seductive names of fraternity, solidarity, organization, association. And because we do not ask so much at the hands of the law, because we only ask it for justice, it alleges that we reject fraternity, solidarity, organization, and association; and they brand us with the name of individualists.

We can assure them that what we repudiate is not natural organization, but forced organization.

It is not free association, but the forms of association that they would impose upon us.

It is not spontaneous fraternity, but legal fraternity.

It is not providential solidarity, but artificial solidarity, which is only an unjust displacement of responsibility.

Socialism, like the old policy from which it emanates, confounds government and society. And so, every time we object to a thing being done by government, it concludes that we object to its being done at all. We disapprove of education by the state—then we are against education altogether. We object to a state religion—then we would have no religion at all. We object to an equality which is brought about by the state then we are against equality, etc., etc. They might as well accuse us of wishing men not to eat, because we object to the cultivation of corn by the state.

How is it that the strange idea of making the law produce what it does not contain—prosperity, in a positive sense, wealth, science, religion—should ever have gained ground in the political world? The modern politicians, particularly those of the socialist school, found their different theories upon one common hypothesis; and surely a more strange, a more presumptuous notion, could never have entered a human brain.

They divide mankind into two parts. Men in general, except one, form the first; the politician himself forms the second, which is by far the most important.

In fact, they begin by supposing that men are devoid of any principle of action, and of any means of discernment in themselves; that they have no initiative; that they are inert matter, passive particles, atoms without impulse; at best a vegetation indifferent to its own mode of existence, susceptible of assuming, from an exterior will and hand an infinite number of forms, more or less symmetrical, artistic, and perfected.

Moreover, every one of these politicians does not hesitate to assume that he himself is, under the names of organizer, discoverer, legislator, institutor or founder, this will and hand, this universal initiative, this creative power, whose sublime mission it is to gather together these scattered materials, that is, men, into society.

Starting from these data, as a gardener according to his caprice shapes his trees into pyramids, parasols, cubes, cones, vases, espaliers, distaffs, or fans; so the socialist, following his chimera, shapes poor humanity into groups, series, circles, subcircles, honeycombs, or social workshops, with all kinds of variations. And as the gardener, to bring his trees into shape, needs hatchets, pruning hooks, saws, and shears, so the politician, to bring society into shape, needs the forces which he can only find in the laws; the law of tariffs, the law of taxation, the law of assistance, and the law of education.

It is so true that the socialists look upon mankind as a subject for social experiments that if, by chance, they are not quite certain of the success of these experiments, they will request a portion of mankind as a subject to experiment upon. It is well known how popular the idea of trying all systems is, and one of their chiefs has been known seriously to demand of the Constituent Assembly a parish, with all its inhabitants, upon which to make his experiments.

It is thus that an inventor will make a small machine before he makes one of the regular size. Thus the chemist sacrifices some substances, the agriculturist some seed and a corner of his field, to make trial of an idea.

But think of the difference between the gardener and his trees, between the inventor and his machine, between the chemist and his substances, between the agriculturist and his seed! The socialist thinks, in all sincerity, that there is the same difference between himself and mankind.

No wonder the politicians of the nineteenth century look upon society as an artificial production of the legislator's genius. This idea, the result of a classical education, has taken possession of all the thinkers and great writers of our country.

To all these persons, the relations between mankind and the legislator appear to be the same as those that exist between the clay and the potter.

Moreover, if they have consented to recognize in the heart of man a capability of action, and in his intellect a faculty of discernment, they have looked upon this gift of God as a fatal one, and thought that mankind, under these two impulses, tended fatally towards ruin. They have taken it for granted that if abandoned to their own inclinations, men would only occupy themselves with religion to arrive at atheism, with instruction to come to ignorance, and with labour and exchange to be extinguished in misery.

Happily, according to these writers, there are some men, termed governors and legislators, upon whom Heaven has bestowed opposite tendencies, not for their own sake only, but for the sake of the rest of the world.

Whilst mankind tends to evil, they incline to good; whilst mankind is advancing towards darkness, they are aspiring to enlightenment; whilst mankind is drawn towards vice, they are attracted by virtue. And, this granted, they demand the assistance of force, by means of which they are to substitute their own tendencies for those of the human race.

...

I shall now resume the subject by remarking that immediately after the economical part[3] of the question, and before the political part, a leading question presents itself. It is the following:

What is law? What ought it to be? What is its domain? What are its limits? Where, in fact, does the prerogative of the legislator stop?

I have no hesitation in answering, law is common force organized to prevent injustice—in short, law is justice.

It is not true that the legislator has absolute power over our persons and property, since they pre-exist, and his work is only to secure them from injury.

It is not true that the mission of the law is to regulate our

---

3. Political economy precedes politics: the former has to discover whether human interests are harmonious or antagonistic, a fact which must be settled before the latter can determine the prerogatives of government.

consciences, our ideas, our will, our education, our sentiments, our works, our exchanges, our gifts, our enjoyments. Its mission is to prevent the rights of one from interfering with those of another, in any one of these things.

Law, because it has force for its necessary sanction, can only have the domain of force, which is justice.

And as every individual has a right to have recourse to force only in cases of lawful defence, so collective force, which is only the union of individual forces, cannot be rationally used for any other end.

The law, then, is solely the organization of individual rights that existed before law.

Law is justice.

So far from being able to oppress the people, or to plunder their property, even for a philanthropic end, its mission is to protect the people, and to secure to them the possession of their property.

It must not be said, either, that it may be philanthropic, so long as it abstains from all oppression; for this is a contradiction. The law cannot avoid acting upon our persons and property; if it does not secure them, then it violates them if it touches them.

The law is justice.

Nothing can be more clear and simple, more perfectly defined and bounded, or more visible to every eye; for justice is a given quantity, immutable and unchangeable, and which admits of neither increase or diminution.

Depart from this point, make the law religious, fraternal, equalizing, industrial, literary, or artistic, and you will be lost in vagueness and uncertainty; you will be upon unknown ground, in a forced utopia, or, what is worse, in the midst of a multitude of contending utopias, each striving to gain possession of the law, and to impose it upon you; for fraternity and philanthropy have no fixed limits, as justice has. Where will you stop? Where is the law to stop? One person, Mr de Saint Cricq, will only extend his philanthropy to some of the industrial classes, and will require the law to slight the consumers in favor of the producers. Another, like Mr Considérant, will take up the cause of the working classes, and claim for them by means of the law, at a fixed rate, clothing, lodging, food, and everything necessary for the support of life. A third, Mr Louis Blanc, will say, and with reason, that this would be an incomplete fraternity, and that the law ought to provide them with tools of labor and education. A fourth will observe that such an arrangement still leaves room for inequality, and that the law ought to introduce into the most remote hamlets luxury, literature, and the arts. This is the high road to communism; in other words, legislation will be—as it now is—the battlefield for everybody's dreams and everybody's covetousness.

Law is justice.

In this proposition we represent to ourselves a simple, immovable government. And I defy anyone to tell me whence the thought of a revolution, an insurrection, or a simple disturbance could arise against a public force confined to the repression of injustice. Under such a system, there would be more well-being, and this well-being would be more equally distributed; and as to the sufferings inseparable from humanity, no one would think of accusing the government of them, for it would be as innocent of them as it is of the variations of the temperature. Have the people ever been known to rise against the court of appeals, or assail the justices of the peace, for the sake of claiming the rate of wages, free credit, tools of labor, the advantages of the tariff, or the social workshop? They know perfectly well that these matters are beyond the jurisdiction of the justices of the peace, and they would soon learn that they are not within the jurisdiction of the law quite as much.

But if the law were to be made upon the principle of fraternity, if it were to be proclaimed that from it proceed all benefits and all evils—that it is responsible for every individual grievance and for every social inequality—then you open the door to an endless succession of complaints, irritations, troubles, and revolutions.

Law is justice.

And it would be very strange if it could properly be anything else! Is not justice right? Are not rights equal? With what show of right can the law interfere to subject me to the social plans of Messrs Mimerel, de Melun, Thiers, or Louis Blanc, rather than to subject these gentlemen to my plans? Is it to be supposed that nature has not bestowed upon me sufficient imagination to invent a utopia too? Is it for the law to make choice of one amongst so many fancies, and to make use of the public force in its service?

Law is justice.

And let it not be said, as it continually is, that the law, in this sense, would be atheistic, individual, and heartless, and that it would mold mankind in its own image. This is an absurd conclusion, quite worthy of the governmental infatuation which sees mankind in the law.

What then? Does it follow that if we are free, we shall cease to act? Does it follow that if we do not receive an impulse from the law, we shall receive no impulse at all? Does it follow that if the law confines itself to securing to us the free exercise of our faculties, our faculties will be paralyzed? Does it follow that if the law does not impose upon us forms of religion, modes of association, methods of education, rules for labour, directions for exchange, and plans for charity, we shall plunge headlong into atheism, isolation, ignorance, misery, and greed? Does it follow that we shall no longer recognize the power and goodness of God; that we shall cease to associate together, to help each other, to love and assist our unfortunate brethren, to study the secrets of nature, and to aspire after perfection in our existence?

Law is justice.

And it is under the law of justice, under the reign of right, under the influence of liberty, security, stability, and responsibility, that every man will attain to the fullness of his worth, to all the dignity of his being, and that mankind will accomplish with order and with calmness—slowly, it is true, but with certainty—the progress ordained for it.

I believe that my theory is correct; for whatever be the question upon which I am arguing, whether it be religious, philosophical, political, or economical; whether it affects well-being, morality, equality, right, justice, progress, responsibility, property, labour, exchange, capital, wages, taxes, population, credit, or government; at whatever point of the scientific horizon I start from, I invariably come to the same thing—the solution of the social problem is in liberty.

And have I not experience on my side? Cast your eye over the globe. Which are the happiest, the most moral, and the most peaceable nations? Those where the law interferes the least with private activity; where the government is the least felt; where individuality has the most scope, and public opinion the most influence; where the machinery of the administration is the least important and the least complicated; where taxation is lightest and least unequal, popular discontent the least excited and the least justifiable; where the responsibility of individuals and classes is the most active, and where, consequently, if morals are not in a perfect state, at any rate they tend incessantly to correct themselves; where transactions, meetings, and associations are the least fettered; where labour, capital, and production suffer the least from artificial displacements; where mankind follows most completely its own natural course; where the thought of God prevails the most over the inventions of men; those, in short, who realize the most nearly this idea that within the limits of right, all should flow from the free, perfectible, and voluntary action of man; nothing be attempted by the law or by force, except the administration of universal justice.

I cannot avoid coming to this conclusion—that there are too many great men in the world; there are too many legislators, organizers, institutors of society, conductors of the people, fathers of nations, etc., etc. Too many persons place themselves above mankind, to rule and patronize it; too many persons make a trade of looking after it. It will be answered: 'You yourself are occupied upon it all this time.' Very true. But it must be admitted that it is in another sense entirely that I am speaking; and if I join the reformers it is solely for the purpose of inducing them to relax their hold.

I am not doing as Vaucauson[4] did with his automaton, but as a physiologist does with the human frame; I would study and admire it.

I am acting with regard to it in the spirit that animated a celebrated traveller. He found himself in the midst of a savage tribe. A child had just been born, and a crowd of soothsayers, magicians, and quacks were around it, armed with rings, hooks, and bandages. One said: 'This child will never smell the perfume of a calumet, unless I stretch his nostrils.' Another said: 'He will be without the sense of hearing, unless I draw his ears down to his shoulders.' A third said: 'He will never see the light of the sun, unless I give his eyes an oblique direction.' A fourth said: 'He will never be upright, unless I bend his legs.' A fifth said: 'He will not be able to think, unless I press his brain.' 'Stop!' said the traveller. 'Whatever God does, is well done; do not pretend to know more than He; and as He has given organs to this frail creature, allow those organs to develop themselves, to strengthen themselves by exercise, use, experience, and liberty.'

God has implanted in mankind also all that is necessary to enable it to accomplish its destinies. There is a providential social physiology,

4. Jacques de Vaucanson (1709-1782): French inventor of robotic devices and automata.

as well as a providential human physiology. The social organs are constituted so as to enable them to develop harmoniously in the grand air of liberty. Away, then, with quacks and organizers! Away with their rings, and their chains, and their hooks, and their pincers! Away with their artificial methods! Away with their social laboratories, their governmental whims, their centralization, their tariffs, their universities, their state religions, their inflationary or monopolizing banks, their limitations, their restrictions, their moralizations, and their equalization by taxation! And now, after having vainly inflicted upon the social body so many systems, let them end where they ought to have begun—reject all systems, and try liberty—liberty, which is an act of faith in God and in His work.

11

JOHN STUART MILL, ON LIBERTY

INTRODUCTION

Why does freedom matter?

That is the central question addressed in John Stuart Mill's essay, 'On Liberty'. The work is a milestone in the history of classical liberalism and the most spirited defence of free speech and free action ever written. At its heart is the basic insight that the individual is sovereign over his own body and mind, and the only purpose for which power can be exercised over any member of a civilised community against his will is to prevent harm to others.

John Stuart Mill (1806-1883) was born in London around the turn of the nineteenth century. His was an unusual upbringing: his father set out with the intention of cultivating in his son a genius intellect to carry forward the cause of utilitarianism, which was to be effected by teaching him Greek at three and Latin at eight, encouraging him to ask questions about everything he read, and shielding him from association with children his own age other than siblings. When Mill's father took up a post as a senior administrator with the East India Company, the younger Mill followed him into the company's employment, where he would remain until the Company was abolished around a quarter of a century later. A turning point for Mill came, however, when he was hit by a mental crisis upon arriving at a realisation that even the creation of a just society, his life's goal, would not make him happy; he concluded from this episode that education must cultivate the emotions as well as the intellect, and that there are important values existing outside the scope of utilitarian philosophy, such as autonomy and dignity. Mill published his major work on political democracy, *Considerations on Representative Government*, in 1862, in which he advocated for a 'democratic elitism' whereby the franchise would be extended to those who possessed basic educational competencies and who were not reliant upon public support, while the more competent would be given greater say in government, through plural voting and a Second Chamber composed of those who had already held high employment. In his later years, Mill was elected Liberal MP for the City of Westminster. He died in Avignon, France, where he was buried next to his wife.

Freedom for Mill meant, in the first place, freedom of thought and freedom of speech. There are, he says, three kinds of belief: those wholly true, those partly true, and those wholly false. If an opinion is condemned to silence, it may be one that is wholly true—to deny this possibility would be to assume our own infallibility. The silenced opinion may, on the other hand, be an error containing a portion of truth—in which case the only chance of the full truth being obtained would be through the 'collision of adverse opinions'. The condemned doctrine may, of course, be entirely false. Even this, though, would not justify censorship, as it is only when vigorously and earnestly contested that true beliefs become more than mere convention and prejudice.

Freedom for Mill also meant optimal cultivation of individuality: a man should be free not only to think and speak as he pleases, but also to act as he pleases, subject only to the condition that he cause no harm to others. Individuality is the basis for improvement of society: it is as a result of citizens expressing the full scope of their individuality that society becomes aware of new and better practices. Individuality is, just as importantly, the basis for the growth of each human being according to his own particular needs. This is a good in itself. The end of man is not to act as a cog in a societal machine; the end of man is 'the highest and most harmonious development of his powers'.

These principles are profound and have stood the test of time. They are well known and, nominally at least, widely accepted. And yet some of Mill's most penetrating observations remain overlooked despite their enduring—and indeed increasing—significance for modern man.

In the first place, Mill has much of importance to say about the opponents of free speech, their motivations, and the gravity of their error. He rightly establishes that underlying the belief that one person or group has the right to silence another person or group is the assumption of infallibility. He accepts, admittedly, that men acknowledge, in theory at least, their own fallibility; but very few of them think it necessary to guard against this fallibility, or indeed recognise the possibility that they could be fallible in matters of which they feel certain. Men place this unbounded confidence not in every idea they have, but in those ideas that are shared by all around them, or by those to whom they habitually defer. In short, they tend to repose trust in the infallibility of 'the world'. But—and here is where Mill displays his characteristic perspicacity—what this means in practice is the part of the world with which each particular man comes in contact: 'his party, his sect, his church, his class of society'. Few, unfortunately, care to reflect that other ages, countries, sects, churches, classes, and parties have thought, and still do think, the exact opposite. In fact, it is precisely where a man is at the same time most un-self-reflective and most parochial that he is likely to be the most convinced of the infallibility of his belief.

In an insight that has the greatest of implications for contemporary man, Mill explained that the main tool by which 'mental freedom' is impaired is social stigma; neither actual persecution nor legal restrictions, as such, are strictly necessary. Indeed, Mill observed that in England, at least, the profession of opinions under the 'ban of society' is much less common than those that incur the risk of actual judicial punishment in other nations. The only people in a position to effectively resist the use of social stigma to shut down dissent are persons of independent means; those dependent upon 'earning their bread' are at constant risk of having their social reputations, and livelihoods, destroyed. The attraction to the oppressor of working through the method of social stigma, rather than legal punishment, is obvious: it maintains the dominance of the permitted opinions, and the exclusion of dissenting viewpoints and contradicting facts, without 'the unpleasant business of fining or imprisoning anybody'. The cost to individuals as well as to society at large, however, is immense. It goes without saying that those who profess the 'heretical' views will be deprived of a fair opportunity of putting their case to the world. Beyond this obvious result lie two other serious consequences. On the one hand, the general level of society is brought down, for the sort of men who prosper in such an environment will tend to be mere conformers, those 'time-servers for truth' who are willing to say whatever is necessary to get along, rather than the 'open, fearless characters and logical, consistent intellects who once adorned the thinking world'. On the other hand, the 'multitude of promising intellects combined with timid characters', who might in freer circumstances have made valuable contributions to society, will find their whole mental development cramped and distorted through self-censorship, and their resources exhausted in attempting to reconcile their reasoning faculty with the demands of orthodoxy.

Mill deprecates, in particular, the idea that any part of education should be in the hands of the state. His position is that state education is 'a mere contrivance for moulding people to be exactly like one another' and 'as the mould in which it casts them is that which pleases the predominant power in the government, whether this be a monarch, a priesthood, an aristocracy, or the majority of the existing generation in proportion as it is efficient and successful, it establishes a despotism over the mind, leading by natural tendency to one over the body'. The state's role in public examinations or certifications is also, Mill argues, pernicious, and to prevent it from exercising, through these arrangements, any improper influence over opinion, the knowledge required for such examinations should be confined to facts and 'positive science' exclusively. Even then, examinations should be entirely voluntary and no one should be excluded from any profession on the basis of alleged deficiency of qualifications.

In a troublingly prescient section of the essay, Mill turns his guns upon the argument that opinions ought to be silenced insofar as they cause offence to others. It is here that he is at his indomitable best. He states the obvious objection to this position—namely, the difficulty of identifying where the supposed bounds are to be placed—and that experience shows that offence tends to be given whenever the person or persons who claim to be offended perceive that the attack against their ideas has been, or is about to become, 'telling and powerful'. He points out the hypocrisy that while great efforts are made to disallow the giving of offence by those who challenge the prevailing dogma, offence is routinely allowed against such freethinkers. Such 'offence' (if any) that we ought to object to is the tendency 'to stigmatise those who hold the contrary opinion as bad and immoral men'—a calumny to which those who hold any unpopular opinion are peculiarly exposed.

There has arisen to prominence another tradition, alien to that of John Stuart Mill and classical liberalism, deriving in spirit and in substance from Marxism and its modern variants, the primary tenets of which, insofar as they relate to questions of freedom of thought and speech, are contained in Herbert Marcuse's essay, 'Repressive Tolerance'.[1] While paying lip service to Mill, Marcuse's starting point is that free speech cannot be granted equally and cannot protect what he calls 'false words'; nor is free speech, he says, appropriate for the mass of men who have been 'manipulated and indoctrinated' to parrot the views of their masters. Withdrawal of toleration of free speech and assembly is, therefore, necessary for those who 'promote aggressive policies, armament, chauvinism, discrimination on the grounds of race and religion,' and even for those who 'oppose the extension of public services, social security, medical care, etc.'; there would also need to be, he said, 'new and rigid restrictions on teachings and practices in the educational institutions', although he expected—not unreasonably it turns out—that this aspect could be enforced by students and teachers themselves. In startlingly Orwellian terms, Marcuse indicated that this approach would bring about the 'restoration of freedom' from 'false tolerance'. 'Liberating tolerance,' he explained, 'would mean intolerance against movements from the Right and toleration of movements from the Left.' It is palpably clear that free speech, in this view, is to be reserved for those who belong to preferred groups and who espouse a 'correct view'. The question of which groups are to be privileged and which viewpoints are correct is, presumably, to be determined by Marcuse and others like him.

The battle for free speech today is fought in substance between these two viewpoints. Admittedly, it is difficult, based upon the respective philosophical merits, to imagine how classical liberalism could have lost so much ground to its challenger. Indeed, reading Mill's essay alongside that of Marcuse reveals the quality of the former's thinking to be far superior to that of the latter: where Mill builds his argument step by step with impeccable logic and consistency, Marcuse's effort

---

1. First published in 1965 and republished in 1969 with a '1968 Postscript' appended.

is clumsy, unsophisticated, and at times outright self-contradictory. Indeed, it seems that Marcuse misunderstands, or misrepresents, and therefore fails to answer Mill's fundamental point: that to arrogate to oneself the right to restrict another's thought or speech presupposes one's own infallibility, and that it is only through allowing men generally the right to have and to express opinions that we approach the truth. Nevertheless, there is no denying that free speech is under threat not only in Mill's homeland but also across the Western world, and not only in the media but also in the universities, corporations, government, and across the public and even private spheres. This resurgence of opposition to free thought and free speech can be explained to a considerable degree by its age-old emotional appeal: to censor, or deplatform, or mob, or prosecute, or otherwise harm the fundamental economic interests of one's opponents confers, presumably, pleasant feelings of power, superiority, and self-righteousness. It is also in the interests of those currently holding power to quash dissent almost before it has formed, and that is done by ensuring the human mind is not exposed, in the first place, to the materials out of which dissenting viewpoints could arise.

John Stuart Mill's great essay constitutes a standing—and monumental—rebuke to this tendency, and a reminder of our capacity arrive at, or to return to, a more civilised mode of being.

CHAPTER 2

OF THE LIBERTY OF THOUGHT AND DISCUSSION

The time, it is to be hoped, is gone by, when any defence would be necessary of the 'liberty of the press' as one of the securities against corrupt or tyrannical government. No argument, we may suppose, can now be needed against permitting a legislature or an executive, not identified in interest with the people, to prescribe opinions to them, and determine what doctrines or what arguments they shall be allowed to hear. This aspect of the question, besides, has been so often and so triumphantly enforced by preceding writers, that it needs not be specially insisted on in this place. Though the law of England, on the subject of the press, is as servile to this day as it was in the time of the Tudors, there is little danger of its being actually put in force against political discussion, except during some temporary panic, when fear of insurrection drives ministers and judges from their propriety;[2] and, speaking generally, it is not, in constitutional countries, to be apprehended that the government, whether completely responsible to the people or not, will often attempt to control the expression of opinion, except when in doing so it makes itself the organ of the general intolerance of the public. Let us suppose, therefore, that the government is entirely at one with the people, and never thinks of exerting any power of coercion unless in agreement with what it conceives to be their voice. But I deny the right of the people to exercise such coercion, either by themselves or by their government. The power itself is illegitimate. The best government has no more title to it than the worst. It is as noxious, or more noxious, when exerted in accordance with public opinion, than when in opposition to it. If all mankind minus one, were of one opinion, and only one person were of the contrary opinion, mankind would be no more justified in silencing that one person, than he, if he had the power, would be justified in silencing mankind. Were an opinion a personal possession of no value except to the owner; if to be obstructed in the enjoyment of it were simply a private injury, it would make some difference whether the injury was inflicted only on a few persons or on many. But the peculiar

2. These words had scarcely been written, when, as if to give them an emphatic contradiction, occurred the Government Press Prosecutions of 1858. That ill-judged interference with the liberty of public discussion has not, however, induced me to alter a single word in the text, nor has it at all weakened my conviction that, moments of panic excepted, the era of pains and penalties for political discussion has, in our own country, passed away. For, in the first place, the prosecutions were not persisted in; and, in the second, they were never, properly speaking, political prosecutions. The offence charged was not that of criticising institutions, or the acts or persons of rulers, but of circulating what was deemed an immoral doctrine, the lawfulness of tyrannicide. If the arguments of the present chapter are of any validity, there ought to exist the fullest liberty of professing and discussing, as a matter of ethical conviction, any doctrine, however immoral it may be considered. It would, therefore, be irrelevant and out of place to examine here whether the doctrine of tyrannicide deserves that title. I shall content myself with saying that the subject has been at all times one of the open questions of morals; that the act of a private citizen in striking down a criminal, who, by raising himself above the law, has placed himself beyond the reach of legal punishment or control, has been accounted by whole nations, and by some of the best and wisest of men, not a crime, but an act of exalted virtue; and that, right or wrong, it is not of the nature of assassination, but of civil war. As such, I hold that the instigation to it, in a specific case, may be a proper subject of punishment, but only if an overt act has followed, and at least a probable connexion can be established between the act and the instigation. Even then, it is not a foreign government, but the very government assailed, which alone, in the exercise of self-defence, can legitimately punish attacks directed against its own existence.

evil of silencing the expression of an opinion is that it is robbing the human race; posterity as well as the existing generation; those who dissent from the opinion, still more than those who hold it. If the opinion is right, they are deprived of the opportunity of exchanging error for truth: if wrong, they lose, what is almost as great a benefit, the clearer perception and livelier impression of truth, produced by its collision with error.

It is necessary to consider separately these two hypotheses, each of which has a distinct branch of the argument corresponding to it. We can never be sure that the opinion we are endeavouring to stifle is a false opinion; and if we were sure, stifling it would be an evil still.

First: the opinion which it is attempted to suppress by authority may possibly be true. Those who desire to suppress it, of course, deny its truth; but they are not infallible. They have no authority to decide the question for all mankind, and exclude every other person from the means of judging. To refuse a hearing to an opinion, because they are sure that it is false, is to assume that *their* certainty is the same thing as *absolute* certainty. All silencing of discussion is an assumption of infallibility. Its condemnation may be allowed to rest on this common argument, not the worse for being common.

Unfortunately for the good sense of mankind, the fact of their fallibility is far from carrying the weight in their practical judgment which is always allowed to it in theory; for while everyone well knows himself to be fallible, few think it necessary to take any precautions against their own fallibility, or admit the supposition that any opinion, of which they feel very certain, may be one of the examples of the error to which they acknowledge themselves to be liable. Absolute princes, or others who are accustomed to unlimited deference, usually feel this complete confidence in their own opinions on nearly all subjects. People more happily situated, who sometimes hear their opinions disputed, and are not wholly unused to be set right when they are wrong, place the same unbounded reliance only on such of their opinions as are shared by all who surround them, or to whom they habitually defer: for in proportion to a man's want of confidence in his own solitary judgment does he usually repose, with implicit trust, on the infallibility of 'the world' in general. And the world, to each individual, means the part of it with which he comes in contact; his party, his sect, his church, his class of society: the man may be called, by comparison, almost liberal and large-minded to whom it means anything so comprehensive as his own country or his own age. Nor is his faith in this collective authority at all shaken by his being aware that other ages, countries, sects, churches, classes, and parties have thought, and even now think, the exact reverse. He devolves upon his own world the responsibility of being in the right against the dissentient worlds of other people; and it never troubles him that mere accident has decided which of these numerous worlds is the object of his reliance, and that the same causes which make him a Churchman in London, would have made him a Buddhist or a Confucian in Peking. Yet it is as evident in itself, as any amount of argument can make it, that ages are no more infallible than individuals; every age having held many opinions which subsequent ages have deemed not only false but absurd; and it is as certain that many opinions, now general, will be rejected by future ages, as it is that many, once general, are rejected by the present.

The objection likely to be made to this argument would probably take some such form as the following. There is no greater assumption of infallibility in forbidding the propagation of error than in any other thing which is done by public authority on its own judgment and responsibility. Judgment is given to men that they may use it. Because it may be used erroneously, are men to be told that they ought not to use it at all? To prohibit what they think pernicious is not claiming exemption from error, but fulfilling the duty incumbent on them, although fallible, of acting on their conscientious conviction. If we were never to act on our opinions, because those opinions may be wrong, we should leave all our interests uncared for, and all our duties unperformed. An objection which applies to all conduct can be no valid objection to any conduct in particular. It is the duty of governments, and of individuals, to form the truest opinions they can; to form them carefully, and never impose them upon others unless they are quite sure of being right. But when they are sure (such reasoners may say), it is not conscientiousness but cowardice to shrink from acting on their opinions, and allow doctrines which they honestly think dangerous to the welfare of mankind, either in this life or in another, to be scattered abroad without restraint, because other people, in less enlightened times, have persecuted opinions now believed to be true. Let us take care, it may be said, not to make the same mistake: but governments and nations have made mistakes in other things, which are not denied to be fit subjects for the exercise of authority: they have laid on bad taxes, made unjust wars. Ought we therefore to lay on no taxes, and, under whatever provocation, make no wars? Men, and governments, must act to the best of their ability. There is no such thing as absolute certainty, but there is assurance sufficient for the purposes of human life. We may, and must, assume our opinion to be true for the guidance of our own conduct: and it is assuming no more when we forbid bad men to pervert society by the propagation of opinions which we regard as false and pernicious.

I answer, that it is assuming very much more. There is the greatest difference between presuming an opinion to be true because, with every opportunity for contesting it, it has not been refuted, and assuming its truth for the purpose of not permitting its refutation. Complete liberty of contradicting and disproving our opinion is the very condition which justifies us in assuming its truth for purposes of action; and on no other terms can a being with human faculties have any rational assurance of being right.

When we consider either the history of opinion, or the ordinary conduct of human life, to what is it to be ascribed that the one and the other are no worse than they are? Not certainly to the inherent force of the human understanding; for, on any matter not self-evident, there are ninety-nine persons totally incapable of judging of it, for one who is capable; and the capacity of the hundredth person is only comparative; for the majority of the eminent men of every past generation held many opinions now known to be erroneous, and did or approved numerous things which no one will now justify. Why is it, then, that there is on the whole a preponderance among mankind of rational opinions and rational conduct? If there really is this preponderance—which there must be unless human affairs are, and have always been, in an almost desperate state—it is owing to a quality of the human mind, the source of everything respectable in man, either as an intellectual or as a moral being, namely, that his errors are corrigible. He is capable of rectifying his mistakes by discussion and experience. Not by experience alone. There must be discussion to show how experience is to be interpreted. Wrong opinions and practices gradually yield to fact and argument: but facts and arguments, to produce any effect on the mind, must be brought before it. Very few facts are able to tell their own story without comments to bring out their meaning. The whole strength and value, then, of human judgment, depending on the one property, that it can be set right when it is wrong, reliance can be placed on it only when the means of setting it right are kept constantly at hand. In the case of any person whose judgment is really deserving of confidence, how has it become so? Because he has kept his mind open to criticism of his opinions and conduct. Because it has been his practice to listen to all that could be said against him; to profit by as much of it as was just, and expound to himself, and upon occasion to others, the fallacy of what was fallacious. Because he has felt that the only way in which a human being can make some approach to knowing the whole of a subject is by hearing what can be said about it by persons of every variety of opinion, and studying all modes in which it can be looked at by every character of mind. No wise man ever acquired his wisdom in any mode but this; nor is it in the nature of human intellect to become wise in any other manner. The steady habit of correcting and completing his own opinion by collating it with those of others, so far from causing doubt and hesitation in carrying it into practice, is the only stable foundation for a just reliance on it: for, being cognisant of all that can, at least obviously, be said against him, and having taken up his position against all gainsayers—knowing that he has sought for objections and difficulties, instead of avoiding them, and has shut out no light which can be thrown upon the subject from any quarter—he has a right to think his judgment better than that of any person, or any multitude, who have not gone through a similar process.

It is not too much to require that what the wisest of mankind, those who are best entitled to trust their own judgment, find necessary to warrant their relying on it, should be submitted to by that miscellaneous collection of a few wise and many foolish individuals, called the public. The most intolerant of churches, the Roman Catholic Church, even at the canonization of a saint, admits, and listens patiently to, a 'devil's advocate'. The holiest of men, it appears, cannot be admitted to posthumous honours until all that the devil could say against him is known and weighed. If even the Newtonian philosophy were not permitted to be questioned, mankind could not feel as complete assurance of its truth as they now do. The beliefs which we have most warrant for have no safeguard to rest on, but a standing invitation to the whole world to prove them unfounded. If the challenge is not accepted, or is accepted and the attempt fails, we are far enough from certainty still; but we have done the best that the existing state of human reason admits of; we have neglected nothing that could give the truth a chance of reaching us: if the lists are kept open, we may hope that if there be a better truth, it will be found when the human mind is capable of receiving it; and in the meantime we may rely on having attained such approach to truth as is possible in our own day. This is the amount of certainty attainable by a fallible being, and this the sole way of attaining it.

Strange it is that men should admit the validity of the arguments for free discussion, but object to their being 'pushed to an extreme'; not seeing that unless the reasons are good for an extreme case, they are not good for any case. Strange that they should imagine that they are not assuming infallibility when they acknowledge that there should be free discussion on all subjects which can possibly be *doubtful*, but think that some particular principle or doctrine should be forbidden to be questioned because it is so *certain*, that is, because *they are certain* that it is certain. To call any proposition certain, while there is anyone who would deny its certainty if permitted, but who is not permitted, is to assume that we ourselves, and those who agree with us, are the judges of certainty, and judges without hearing the other side.

In the present age—which has been described as 'destitute of faith, but terrified at scepticism'—in which people feel sure, not so much that their opinions are true, as that they should not know what to do without them—the claims of an opinion to be protected from public attack are rested not so much on its truth as on its importance to society. There are, it is alleged, certain beliefs so useful, not to say indispensable to well-being, that it is as much the duty of governments to uphold those beliefs as to protect any other of the interests of society. In a case of such necessity, and so directly in the line of their duty, something less than infallibility may, it is maintained, warrant, and even bind, governments to act on their own opinion, confirmed by the general opinion of mankind. It is also often argued, and still oftener thought, that none but bad men would desire to weaken these salutary beliefs; and there can be nothing wrong, it is thought, in restraining bad men, and prohibiting what only such men would wish to practise. This mode of thinking makes the justification of restraints on discussion not a question of the truth of doctrines, but of their usefulness; and flatters itself by that means to escape the responsibility of claiming to be an infallible judge of opinions. But those who thus satisfy themselves do not perceive that the assumption of infallibility is merely shifted from one point to another. The usefulness of an opinion is itself matter of opinion: as disputable, as open to discussion, and requiring discussion as much, as the opinion itself. There is the same need of an infallible judge of opinions to decide an opinion to be noxious, as to decide it to be false, unless the opinion condemned has full opportunity of defending itself. And it will not do to say that the heretic may be allowed to maintain the utility or harmlessness of his opinion, though forbidden to maintain its truth. The truth of an opinion is part of its utility. If we would know whether or not it is desirable that a proposition should be believed, is it possible to exclude the consideration of whether or not it is true? In the opinion, not of bad men, but of the best men, no belief which is contrary to truth can be really useful: and can you prevent such men from urging that plea, when they are charged with culpability for denying some doctrine which they are told is useful, but which they believe to be false? Those who are on the side of received opinions never fail to take all possible advantage of this plea; you do not find *them* handling the question of utility as if it could be completely abstracted from that of truth: on the contrary, it is, above all, because their doctrine is 'the truth,' that the knowledge or the belief of it is held to be so indispensable. There can be no fair discussion of the question of usefulness, when an argument so vital may be employed on one side, but not on the other. And in point of fact, when law or public feeling do not permit the truth of an opinion to be disputed, they are just as little tolerant of a denial of its usefulness. The utmost they allow is an extenuation of its absolute necessity, or of the positive guilt of rejecting it.

...

For a long time past, the chief mischief of the legal penalties is that they strengthen the social stigma. It is that stigma which is really effective, and so effective is it, that the profession of opinions which are under the ban of society is much less common in England than is, in many other countries, the avowal of those which incur risk of judicial punishment. In respect to all persons but those whose pecuniary circumstances make them independent of the good will of other people, opinion, on this subject, is as efficacious as law; men might as well be imprisoned, as excluded from the means of earning their bread. Those whose bread is already secured, and who desire no favours from men in power, or from bodies of men, or from the public, have nothing to fear from the open avowal of any opinions, but to be ill-thought of and ill-spoken of, and this it ought not to require a very heroic mould to enable them to bear. There is no room for any appeal *ad misericordiam* in behalf of such persons. But though we do not now inflict so much evil on those who think differently from us as it was formerly our custom to do, it may be that we do ourselves as much evil as ever by our treatment of them. Socrates was put to death, but the Socratic philosophy rose like the sun in heaven, and spread its illumination over the whole intellectual firmament. Christians were cast to the lions, but the Christian church grew up a stately and spreading tree, overtopping the older and less vigorous growths, and stifling them by its shade. Our merely social intolerance kills no one, roots out no opinions, but induces men to disguise them, or to abstain from any active effort for their diffusion. With us, heretical opinions do not perceptibly gain, or even lose, ground in each decade or generation; they never blaze out far and wide, but continue to smoulder in the narrow circles of thinking and studious persons among whom they originate, without ever lighting up the general affairs of mankind with either a true or a deceptive light. And thus is kept up a state of things very satisfactory to some minds, because, without the unpleasant process of fining or imprisoning anybody, it maintains all prevailing opinions outwardly undisturbed, while it does not absolutely interdict the exercise of reason by dissentients afflicted with the malady of thought. A convenient plan for having peace in the intellectual world, and keeping all things going on therein very much as they do already. But the price paid for this sort of intellectual pacification is the sacrifice of the entire moral courage of the human mind. A state of things in which a large portion of the most active and inquiring intellects find it advisable to keep the general principles and grounds of their convictions within their own breasts, and attempt, in what they address to the public, to fit as much as they can of their own conclusions to premises which they have internally renounced, cannot send forth the open, fearless characters, and logical, consistent intellects who once adorned the thinking world. The sort of men who can be looked for under it are either mere conformers to commonplace, or time-servers for truth, whose arguments on all great subjects are meant for their hearers, and are not those which have convinced themselves. Those who avoid this alternative do so by narrowing their thoughts and interest to things which can be spoken of without venturing within the region of principles, that is, to small practical matters, which would come right of themselves, if but the minds of mankind were strengthened and enlarged, and which will never be made effectually right until then: while that which would strengthen and enlarge men's minds, free and daring speculation on the highest subjects, is abandoned.

Those in whose eyes this reticence on the part of heretics is no evil should consider, in the first place, that in consequence of it there is never any fair and thorough discussion of heretical opinions; and that such of them as could not stand such a discussion, though they may be prevented from spreading, do not disappear. But it is not the minds of heretics that are deteriorated most by the ban placed on all inquiry which does not end in the orthodox conclusions. The greatest harm done is to those who are not heretics, and whose whole mental development is cramped, and their reason cowed, by the fear of heresy. Who can compute what the world loses in the multitude of promising intellects combined with timid characters, who dare not follow out any bold, vigorous, independent train of thought, lest it should land them in something which would admit of being considered irreligious or immoral? Among them we may occasionally see some man of deep conscientiousness, and subtle and refined understanding, who spends a life in sophisticating with an intellect which he cannot silence, and exhausts the resources of ingenuity in attempting to reconcile the promptings of his conscience and reason with orthodoxy, which yet he does not, perhaps, to the end succeed in doing. No one can be a great thinker who does not recognise that as a thinker it is his first duty to follow his intellect to whatever conclusions it may lead. Truth gains more even by the errors of one who, with due study and preparation, thinks for himself, than by the true opinions of those who only hold them because they do not suffer themselves to think. Not that it is solely, or chiefly, to form great thinkers that freedom of thinking is required. On the contrary, it is as much and even more indispensable to enable average human beings to attain the mental stature which they are capable of. There have been, and may again be, great individual thinkers, in a general atmosphere of mental slavery. But there never has been, nor ever will be, in that atmosphere, an intellectually active people. When any people has made a temporary approach to such a character, it has been because the dread of heterodox speculation was for a time suspended. Where there is a tacit convention that principles are not to be disputed; where the discussion of the greatest questions which can occupy humanity is considered to be closed, we cannot hope to find that generally high scale of mental activity which has made some periods of history so remarkable. Never when controversy avoided the subjects which are large and important enough to kindle enthusiasm was the mind of a people stirred up from its foundations, and the impulse given which raised even persons of the most ordinary intellect to something of the dignity of thinking beings. Of such we have had an example in the condition of Europe during the times immediately following the Reformation; another, though limited to the Continent and to a more cultivated class, in the speculative movement of the latter half of the eighteenth century; and a third, of still briefer duration, in the intellectual fermentation of Germany during the Goethian and Fichtean period. These periods differed widely in the particular opinions which they developed; but were alike in this, that during all three the yoke of authority was broken. In each, an old mental despotism had been thrown off, and no new one had yet taken its place. The impulse given at these three periods has made Europe what it now is. Every single improvement which has taken place either in the human mind or in institutions may be traced distinctly to one or other of them. Appearances have for some time indicated that all three impulses are well nigh spent; and we can expect no fresh start until we again assert our mental freedom.

Let us now pass to the second division of the argument, and, dismissing the supposition that any of the received opinions may be false, let us assume them to be true, and examine into the worth of the manner in which they are likely to be held when their truth is not freely and openly canvassed. However unwillingly a person who has a strong opinion may admit the possibility that his opinion may be false, he ought to be moved by the consideration that however true it may be, if it is not fully, frequently, and fearlessly discussed, it will be held as a dead dogma, not a living truth.

There is a class of persons (happily not quite so numerous as formerly) who think it enough if a person assents undoubtingly to what they think true, though he has no knowledge whatever of the grounds of the opinion, and could not make a tenable defence of it against the most superficial objections. Such persons, if they can once get their creed taught from authority, naturally think that no good, and some harm, comes of its being allowed to be questioned. Where their influence prevails, they make it nearly impossible for the received opinion to be rejected wisely and considerately, though it may still be rejected rashly and ignorantly; for to shut out discussion entirely is seldom possible, and when it once gets in, beliefs not grounded on conviction are apt to give way before the slightest semblance of an argument. Waiving, however, this possibility—assuming that the true opinion abides in the mind, but abides as a prejudice, a belief independent of, and proof against, argument—this is not the way in which truth ought to be held by a rational being. This is not knowing the truth. Truth, thus held, is but one superstition the more, accidentally clinging to the words which enunciate a truth.

If the intellect and judgment of mankind ought to be cultivated, a thing which Protestants at least do not deny, on what can these faculties be more appropriately exercised by anyone than on the things which concern him so much that it is considered necessary for him to hold opinions on them? If the cultivation of the understanding consists in one thing more than in another, it is surely in learning the grounds of one's own opinions. Whatever people believe, on subjects on which it is of the first importance to believe rightly, they ought to be able to defend against at least the common objections. But, someone may say, 'Let them be *taught* the grounds of their opinions. It does not follow that opinions must be merely parroted because they are never heard controverted. Persons who learn geometry do not simply commit the theorems to memory, but understand and learn likewise the demonstrations; and it would be absurd to say that they remain ignorant of the grounds of geometrical truths because they never hear anyone deny and attempt to disprove them.' Undoubtedly; and such teaching suffices on a subject like mathematics, where there is nothing at all to be said on the wrong side of the question. The peculiarity of the evidence of mathematical truths is that all the argument is on one side. There are no objections, and no answers to objections. But on every subject on which difference of opinion is possible, the truth depends on a balance to be struck between two sets of conflicting reasons. Even in natural philosophy, there is always some other explanation possible of the same facts; some geocentric theory instead of heliocentric, some phlogiston instead of oxygen; and it has to be shown why that other theory cannot be the true one; and until this is shown, and until we know how it is shown, we do not understand the grounds of our opinion. But when we turn to subjects infinitely more complicated, to morals, religion, politics, social relations, and the business of life, three-fourths of the arguments for every disputed opinion consist in dispelling the appearances which favour some opinion different from it. The greatest orator, save one, of antiquity, has left it on record that he always studied his adversary's case with as great, if not with still greater, intensity than even his own. What Cicero practised as the means of forensic success requires to be imitated by all who study any subject in order to arrive at the truth. He who knows only his own side of the case knows little of that. His reasons may be good, and no one may have been able to refute them. But if he is equally unable to refute the reasons on the opposite side; if he does not so much as know what they are, he has no ground for preferring either opinion. The rational position for him would be suspension of judgment, and unless he contents himself with that, he is either led by authority, or adopts, like the generality of the world, the side to which he feels most inclination. Nor is it enough that he should hear the arguments of adversaries from his own teachers, presented as they state them, and accompanied by what they offer as refutations. That is not the way to do justice to the arguments, or bring them into real contact with his own mind. He must be able to hear them from persons who actually believe them; who defend them in earnest, and do their very utmost for them. He must know them in their most plausible and persuasive form; he must feel the whole force of the difficulty which the true view of the subject has to encounter and dispose of; else he will never really possess himself of the portion of truth which meets and removes that difficulty. Ninety-nine in a hundred of what are called educated men are in this condition; even of those who can argue fluently for their opinions. Their conclusion may be true, but it might be false for anything they know: they have never thrown themselves into the mental position of those who think differently from them, and considered what such persons may have to say; and consequently they do not, in any proper sense of the word, know the doctrine which they themselves profess. They do not know those parts of it which explain and justify the remainder; the considerations which show that a fact which seemingly conflicts with another is reconcilable with it, or that, of two apparently strong reasons, one and not the other ought to be preferred. All that part of the truth which turns the scale, and decides the judgment of a completely informed mind, they are strangers to; nor is it ever really known but to those who have attended equally and impartially to both sides, and endeavoured to see the reasons of both in the strongest light. So essential is this discipline to a real understanding of moral and human subjects, that if opponents of all important truths do not exist, it is indispensable to imagine them, and supply them with the strongest arguments which the most skilful devil's advocate can conjure up.

To abate the force of these considerations, an enemy of free discussion may be supposed to say that there is no necessity for mankind in general to know and understand all that can be said against or for their opinions by philosophers and theologians. That it is not needful for common men to be able to expose all the misstatements or fallacies of an ingenious opponent. That it is enough if there is always somebody capable of answering them, so that nothing likely to mislead uninstructed persons remains unrefuted. That simple minds, having been taught the obvious grounds of the truths inculcated on them, may trust to authority for the rest, and being aware that they have neither knowledge nor talent to resolve every difficulty which can be raised, may repose in the assurance that all those which have been raised have been or can be answered by those who are specially trained to the task.

Conceding to this view of the subject the utmost that can be claimed for it by those most easily satisfied with the amount of understanding of truth which ought to accompany the belief of it; even so, the argument for free discussion is no way weakened. For even this doctrine acknowledges that mankind ought to have a rational assurance that all objections have been satisfactorily answered; and how are they to be answered if that which requires to be answered is not spoken? Or how can the answer be known to be satisfactory if the objectors have no opportunity of showing that it is unsatisfactory? If not the public, at least the philosophers and theologians who are to resolve the difficulties must make themselves familiar with those difficulties in their most puzzling form; and this cannot be accomplished unless they are freely stated, and placed in the most advantageous light which they admit of. The Catholic Church has its own way of dealing with this embarrassing problem. It makes a broad separation between those who can be permitted to receive its doctrines on conviction, and those who must accept them on trust. Neither, indeed, are allowed any choice as to what they will accept; but the clergy, such at least as can be fully confided in, may admissibly and meritoriously make themselves acquainted with the arguments of opponents, in order to answer them, and may, therefore, read heretical books; the laity, not unless by special permission, hard to be obtained. This discipline recognises a knowledge of the enemy's case as beneficial to the teachers, but finds means, consistent with this, of denying it to the rest of the world: thus giving to the elite more mental culture, though not more mental freedom, than it allows to the mass. By this device it succeeds in obtaining the kind of mental superiority which its purposes require; for though culture without freedom never made a large and liberal mind, it can make a clever *nisi prius* advocate of a cause. But in countries professing Protestantism, this resource is denied; since Protestants hold, at least in theory, that the responsibility for the choice of a religion must be borne by each for himself, and cannot be thrown off upon teachers. Besides, in the present state of the world, it is practically impossible that writings which are read by the instructed can be kept from the uninstructed. If the teachers of mankind are to be cognisant of all that they ought to know, everything must be free to be written and published without restraint.

If, however, the mischievous operation of the absence of free discussion, when the received opinions are true, were confined to leaving men ignorant of the grounds of those opinions, it might be thought that this, if an intellectual, is no moral evil, and does not affect the worth of the opinions, regarded in their influence on the character. The fact, however, is, that not only the grounds of the opinion are forgotten in the absence of discussion, but too often the meaning of the opinion itself. The words which convey it cease to suggest ideas, or suggest only a small portion of those they were originally employed to communicate. Instead of a vivid conception and a living belief, there remain only a few phrases retained by rote; or, if any part, the shell and husk only of the meaning is retained, the finer essence being lost. The great chapter in human history which this fact occupies and fills cannot be too earnestly studied and meditated on.

...

It still remains to speak of one of the principal causes which make diversity of opinion advantageous, and will continue to do so until mankind shall have entered a stage of intellectual advancement which at present seems at an incalculable distance. We have hitherto considered only two possibilities: that the received opinion may be false, and some other opinion, consequently, true; or that, the received opinion being true, a conflict with the opposite error is essential to a clear apprehension and deep feeling of its truth. But there is a commoner case than either of these; when the conflicting doctrines, instead of being one true and the other false, share the truth between them; and the nonconforming opinion is needed to supply the remainder of the truth, of which the received doctrine embodies only a part. Popular opinions, on subjects not palpable to sense, are often true, but seldom or never the whole truth. They are a part of the truth; sometimes a greater, sometimes a smaller part, but exaggerated, distorted, and disjoined from the truths by which they ought to be accompanied and limited. Heretical opinions, on the other hand, are generally some of these suppressed and neglected truths, bursting the bonds which kept them down, and either seeking reconciliation with the truth contained in the common opinion, or fronting it as enemies, and setting themselves up, with similar exclusiveness, as the whole truth. The latter case is hitherto the most frequent, as, in the human mind, one-sidedness has always been the rule, and many-sidedness the exception. Hence, even in revolutions of opinion, one part of the truth usually sets while another rises. Even progress, which ought to superadd, for the most part only substitutes, one partial and incomplete truth for another; improvement consisting chiefly in this, that the new fragment of truth is more wanted, more adapted to the needs of the time, than that which it displaces. Such being the partial character of prevailing opinions, even when resting on a true foundation, every opinion which embodies somewhat of the portion of truth which the common opinion omits ought to be considered precious, with whatever amount of error and confusion that truth may be blended. No sober judge of human affairs will feel bound to be indignant because those who force on our notice truths which we should otherwise have overlooked, overlook some of those which we see. Rather, he will think that so long as popular truth is one-sided, it is more desirable than otherwise that unpopular truth should have one-sided asserters too; such being usually the most energetic, and the most likely to compel reluctant attention to the fragment of wisdom which they proclaim as if it were the whole.

...

We have now recognised the necessity to the mental well-being of mankind (on which all their other well-being depends) of freedom of opinion, and freedom of the expression of opinion, on four distinct grounds; which we will now briefly recapitulate.

First, if any opinion is compelled to silence, that opinion may, for aught we can certainly know, be true. To deny this is to assume our own infallibility.

Secondly, though the silenced opinion be an error, it may, and very commonly does, contain a portion of truth; and since the general or prevailing opinion on any subject is rarely or never the whole truth, it is only by the collision of adverse opinions that the remainder of the truth has any chance of being supplied.

Thirdly, even if the received opinion be not only true, but the whole truth; unless it is suffered to be, and actually is, vigorously and earnestly contested, it will, by most of those who receive it, be held in the manner of a prejudice, with little comprehension or feeling of its rational grounds. And not only this, but, fourthly, the meaning of the doctrine itself will be in danger of being lost, or enfeebled, and deprived of its vital effect on the character and conduct: the dogma becoming a mere formal profession, inefficacious for good, but cumbering the ground, and preventing the growth of any real and heartfelt conviction, from reason or personal experience.

Before quitting the subject of freedom of opinion, it is fit to take some notice of those who say, that the free expression of all opinions should be permitted, on condition that the manner be temperate, and do not pass the bounds of fair discussion. Much might be said on the impossibility of fixing where these supposed bound are to be placed; for if the test be offence to those whose opinion is attacked, I think experience testifies that this offence is given whenever the attack is telling and powerful, and that every opponent who pushes them hard, and whom they find it difficult to answer, appears to them, if he shows any strong feeling on the subject, an intemperate opponent. But this, though an important consideration in a practical point of view, merges in a more fundamental objection. Undoubtedly the manner of asserting an opinion, even though it be a true one, may be very objectionable, and may justly incur severe censure. But the principal offences of the kind are such as it is mostly impossible, unless by accidental self-betrayal, to bring home to conviction. The gravest of them is to argue sophistically, to suppress facts or arguments, to misstate the elements of the case, or misrepresent the opposite opinion. But all this, even to the most aggravated degree, is so continually done in perfect good faith, by persons who are not considered, and in many other respects may not deserve to be considered, ignorant or incompetent, that it is rarely possible on adequate grounds conscientiously to stamp the misrepresentation as morally culpable; and still less could law presume to interfere with this kind of controversial misconduct. With regard to what is commonly meant by intemperate discussion, namely invective, sarcasm, personality, and the like, the denunciation of these weapons would deserve more sympathy if it were ever proposed to interdict them equally to both sides; but it is only desired to restrain the employment of them against the prevailing opinion: against the unprevailing they may not only be used without general disapproval, but will be likely to obtain for him who uses them the praise of honest zeal and righteous indignation. Yet whatever mischief arises from their use is greatest when they are employed against the comparatively defenceless; and whatever unfair advantage can be derived by any opinion from this mode of asserting it accrues almost exclusively to received opinions. The worst offence of this kind which can be committed by a polemic is to stigmatize those who hold the contrary opinion as bad and immoral men. To calumny of this sort, those who hold any unpopular opinion are peculiarly exposed, because they are in general few and uninfluential, and nobody but themselves feels much interested in seeing justice done them; but this weapon is, from the nature of the case, denied to those who attack a prevailing opinion: they can neither use it with safety to themselves, nor, if they could, would it do anything but recoil on their own cause. In general, opinions contrary to those commonly received can only obtain a hearing by studied moderation of language, and the most cautious avoidance of unnecessary offence, from which they hardly ever deviate even in a slight degree without losing ground: while unmeasured vituperation employed on the side of the prevailing opinion really does deter people from professing contrary opinions, and from listening to those who profess them. For the interest, therefore, of truth and justice, it is far more important to restrain this employment of vituperative language than the other; and, for example, if it were necessary to choose, there would be much more need to discourage offensive attacks on infidelity, than on religion. It is, however, obvious that law and authority have no business with restraining either, while opinion ought, in every instance, to determine its verdict by the circumstances of the individual case; condemning everyone, on whichever side of the argument he places himself, in whose mode of advocacy either want of candour, or malignity, bigotry, or intolerance of feeling manifest themselves; but not inferring these vices from the side which a person takes, though it be the contrary side of the question to our own; and giving merited honour to every one, whatever opinion he may hold, who has calmness to see and honesty to state what his opponents and their opinions really are, exaggerating nothing to their discredit, keeping nothing back which tells, or can be supposed to tell, in their favour. This is the real morality of public discussion; and if often violated, I am happy to think that there are many controversialists who to a great extent observe it, and a still greater number who conscientiously strive towards it.

CHAPTER 5

APPLICATIONS

...I have already observed that, owing to the absence of any recognised general principles, liberty is often granted where it should be withheld, as well as withheld where it should be granted; and one of the cases in which, in the modern European world, the sentiment of liberty is the strongest, is a case where, in my view, it is altogether misplaced. A person should be free to do as he likes in his own concerns; but he ought not to be free to do as he likes in acting for another, under the pretext that the affairs of the other are his own affairs. The state, while it respects the liberty of each in what specially regards himself, is bound to maintain a vigilant control over his exercise of any power which it allows him to possess over others. This obligation is almost entirely disregarded in the case of the family relations, a case, in its direct influence on human happiness, more important than all others taken together. The almost despotic power of husbands over wives needs not be enlarged upon here, because nothing more is needed for the complete removal of the evil, than that wives should have the same rights, and should receive the protection of law in the same manner, as all other persons; and because, on this subject, the defenders of established injustice do not avail themselves of the plea of liberty, but stand forth openly as the champions of power. It is in the case of children that misapplied notions of liberty are a real obstacle to the fulfilment by the state of its duties. One would almost think that a man's children were supposed to be literally, and not metaphorically, a part of himself, so jealous is opinion of the smallest interference of law with his absolute and exclusive control over them; more jealous than of almost any interference with his own freedom of action: so much less do the generality of mankind value liberty than power. Consider, for example, the case of education. Is it not almost a self-evident axiom, that the state should require and compel the education, up to a certain standard, of every human being who is born its citizen? Yet who is there that is not afraid to recognise and assert this truth? Hardly anyone indeed will deny that it is one of the most sacred duties of the parents (or, as law and usage now stand, the father), after summoning a human being into the world, to give to that being an education fitting him to perform his part well in life towards others and towards himself. But while this is unanimously declared to be the father's duty, scarcely anybody, in this country, will bear to hear of obliging him to perform it. Instead of his being required to make any exertion or sacrifice for securing education to the child, it is left to his choice to accept it or not when it is provided gratis! It still remains unrecognised that to bring a child into existence without a fair prospect of being able, not only to provide food for its body, but instruction and training for its mind, is a moral crime, both against the unfortunate offspring and against society; and that if the parent does not fulfil this obligation, the state ought to see it fulfilled, at the charge, as far as possible, of the parent.

Were the duty of enforcing universal education once admitted, there would be an end to the difficulties about what the state should teach, and how it should teach, which now convert the subject into a mere battlefield for sects and parties, causing the time and labour which should have been spent in educating, to be wasted in quarrelling about education. If the government would make up its mind to *require* for every child a good education, it might save itself the trouble of *providing* one. It might leave to parents to obtain the education where and how they pleased, and content itself with helping to pay the school fees of the poorer classes of children, and defraying the entire school expenses of those who have no one else to pay for them. The objections which are urged with reason against state education do not apply to the enforcement of education by the state, but to the state's taking upon itself to direct that education: which is a totally different thing. That the whole or any large part of the education of the people should be in state hands, I go as far as any one in deprecating. All that has been said of the importance of individuality of character, and diversity in opinions and modes of conduct, involves, as of the same unspeakable importance, diversity of education. A general state education is a mere contrivance for moulding people to be exactly like one another; and as the mould in which it casts them is that which pleases the predominant power in the government, whether this be a monarch, a priesthood, an aristocracy, or the majority of the existing generation in proportion as it is efficient and successful, it establishes a despotism over the mind, leading by natural tendency to one over the body. An education established and controlled by the state should only exist, if it exist at all, as one among many competing experiments, carried on for the purpose of example and stimulus, to keep the others up to a certain standard of excellence. Unless, indeed, when society in general is in so backward a state that it could not or would not provide for itself any proper institutions of education, unless the government undertook the task: then, indeed, the government may, as the less of two great evils, take upon itself the business of schools and universities, as it may that of joint stock companies, when private enterprise, in a shape fitted for undertaking great works of industry, does not exist in the country. But in general, if the country contains a sufficient number of persons qualified to provide education under government auspices, the same persons would be able and willing to give an equally good education on the voluntary principle, under the assurance of remuneration afforded by a law rendering education compulsory, combined with state aid to those unable to defray the expense.

The instrument for enforcing the law could be no other than public examinations, extending to all children, and beginning at an early age. An age might be fixed at which every child must be examined, to ascertain if he (or she) is able to read. If a child proves unable, the father, unless he has some sufficient ground of excuse, might be subjected to a moderate fine, to be worked out, if necessary, by his labour, and the child might be put to school at his expense. Once in every year the examination should be renewed, with a gradually extending range of subjects, so as to make the universal acquisition, and what is more, retention, of a certain minimum of general knowledge, virtually compulsory. Beyond that minimum, there should be voluntary examinations on all subjects, at which all who come up to a certain standard of proficiency might claim a certificate. To prevent the state from exercising, through these arrangements, an improper influence over opinion, the knowledge required for passing an examination (beyond the merely instrumental parts of knowledge, such as languages and their use) should, even in the higher classes of examinations, be confined to facts and positive science exclusively. The examinations on religion, politics, or other disputed topics should not turn on the truth or falsehood of opinions, but on the matter of fact that such and such an opinion is held, on such grounds, by such authors, or schools, or churches. Under this system, the rising generation would be no worse off in regard to all disputed truths than they are at present; they would be brought up either churchmen or dissenters as they now are, the state merely taking care that they should be instructed churchmen, or instructed dissenters. There would be nothing to hinder them from being taught religion, if their parents chose, at the same schools where they were taught other things. All attempts by the state to bias the conclusions of its citizens on disputed subjects are evil; but it may very properly offer to ascertain and certify that a person possesses the knowledge requisite to make his conclusions, on any given subject, worth attending to. A student of philosophy would be the better for being able to stand an examination both in Locke and in Kant, whichever of the two he takes up with, or even if with neither; and there is no reasonable objection to examining an atheist in the evidences of Christianity, provided he is not required to profess a

251

belief in them. The examinations, however, in the higher branches of knowledge should, I conceive, be entirely voluntary. It would be giving too dangerous a power to governments were they allowed to exclude anyone from professions, even from the profession of teacher, for alleged deficiency of qualifications; and I think, with Wilhelm von Humboldt, that degrees, or other public certificates of scientific or professional acquirements, should be given to all who present themselves for examination, and stand the test; but that such certificates should confer no advantage over competitors, other than the weight which may be attached to their testimony by public opinion.

It is not in the matter of education only that misplaced notions of liberty prevent moral obligations on the part of parents from being recognised, and legal obligations from being imposed, where there are the strongest grounds for the former always, and in many cases for the latter also. The fact itself, of causing the existence of a human being, is one of the most responsible actions in the range of human life. To undertake this responsibility—to bestow a life which may be either a curse or a blessing—unless the being on whom it is to be bestowed will have at least the ordinary chances of a desirable existence, is a crime against that being. And in a country either over-peopled, or threatened with being so, to produce children, beyond a very small number, with the effect of reducing the reward of labour by their competition, is a serious offence against all who live by the remuneration of their labour. The laws which, in many countries on the Continent, forbid marriage unless the parties can show that they have the means of supporting a family, do not exceed the legitimate powers of the state; and whether such laws be expedient or not (a question mainly dependent on local circumstances and feelings), they are not objectionable as violations of liberty. Such laws are interferences of the state to prohibit a mischievous act—an act injurious to others, which ought to be a subject of reprobation, and social stigma, even when it is not deemed expedient to superadd legal punishment. Yet the current ideas of liberty, which bend so easily to real infringements of the freedom of the individual in things which concern only himself, would repel the attempt to put any restraint upon his inclinations when the consequence of their indulgence is a life or lives of wretchedness and depravity to the offspring, with manifold evils to those sufficiently within reach to be in any way affected by their actions. When we compare the strange respect of mankind for liberty, with their strange want of respect for it, we might imagine that a man had an indispensable right to do harm to others, and no right at all to please himself without giving pain to anyone.

I have reserved for the last place a large class of questions respecting the limits of government interference, which, though closely connected with the subject of this essay, do not, in strictness, belong to it. These are cases in which the reasons against interference do not turn upon the principle of liberty: the question is not about restraining the actions of individuals, but about helping them: it is asked whether the government should do, or cause to be done, something for their benefit, instead of leaving it to be done by themselves, individually, or in voluntary combination.

The objections to government interference, when it is not such as to involve infringement of liberty, may be of three kinds.

The first is, when the thing to be done is likely to be better done by individuals than by the government. Speaking generally, there is no one so fit to conduct any business, or to determine how or by whom it shall be conducted, as those who are personally interested in it. This principle condemns the interferences, once so common, of the legislature, or the officers of government, with the ordinary processes of industry. But this part of the subject has been sufficiently enlarged upon by political economists, and is not particularly related to the principles of this essay.

The second objection is more nearly allied to our subject. In many cases, though individuals may not do the particular thing so well, on the average, as the officers of government, it is nevertheless desirable that it should be done by them, rather than by the government, as a means to their own mental education—a mode of strengthening their active faculties, exercising their judgment, and giving them a familiar knowledge of the subjects with which they are thus left to deal. This is a principal, though not the sole, recommendation of jury trial (in cases not political); of free and popular local and municipal institutions; of the conduct of industrial and philanthropic enterprises by voluntary associations. These are not questions of liberty, and are connected with that subject only by remote tendencies; but they are questions of development. It belongs to a different occasion from the present to dwell on these things as parts of national education; as being, in truth, the peculiar training of a citizen, the practical part of the political education of a free people, taking them out of the narrow circle of personal and family selfishness, and accustoming them to the comprehension of joint interests, the management of joint concerns—habituating them to act from public or semi-public motives, and guide their conduct by aims which unite instead of isolating them from one another. Without these habits and powers, a free constitution can neither be worked nor preserved; as is exemplified by the too-often transitory nature of political freedom in countries where it does not rest upon a sufficient basis of local liberties. The management of purely local business by the localities, and of the great enterprises of industry by the union of those who voluntarily supply the pecuniary means, is further recommended by all the advantages which have been set forth in this essay as belonging to individuality of development, and diversity of modes of action. Government operations tend to be everywhere alike. With individuals and voluntary associations, on the contrary, there are varied experiments, and endless diversity of experience. What the state can usefully do is to make itself a central depository, and active circulator and diffuser, of the experience resulting from many trials. Its business is to enable each experimentalist to benefit by the experiments of others; instead of tolerating no experiments but its own.

The third and most cogent reason for restricting the interference of government is the great evil of adding unnecessarily to its power. Every function superadded to those already exercised by the government causes its influence over hopes and fears to be more widely diffused, and converts, more and more, the active and ambitious part of the public into hangers-on of the government, or of some party which aims at becoming the government. If the roads, the railways, the banks, the insurance offices, the great joint-stock companies, the universities, and the public charities, were all of them branches of the government; if, in addition, the municipal corporations and local boards, with all that now devolves on them, became departments of the central administration; if the employees of all these different enterprises were appointed and paid by the government, and looked to the government for every rise in life; not all the freedom of the press and popular constitution of the legislature would make this or any other country free otherwise than in name. And the evil would be greater, the more efficiently and scientifically the administrative machinery was constructed—the more skilful the arrangements for obtaining the best qualified hands and heads with which to work it. In England it has of late been proposed that all the members of the civil service of government should be selected by competitive examination to obtain for those employments the most intelligent and instructed persons procurable; and much has been said and written for and against this proposal. One of the arguments most insisted on by its opponents is that the occupation of a permanent official servant of the state does not hold out sufficient prospects of emolument and importance to attract the highest talents, which will always be able to find a more inviting career in the professions, or in the service of companies and other public bodies. One would not have been surprised if this argument had been used by the friends of the proposition as an answer to its principal difficulty. Coming from the opponents it is strange enough. What is urged as an objection is the safety-valve of the proposed system. If indeed all the high talent of the country *could* be drawn into the service of the government, a proposal tending to bring about that result might well inspire uneasiness. If every part of the business of society which required organized concert, or large and comprehensive views, were in the hands of the government, and if government offices were universally filled by the ablest men, all the enlarged culture and practised intelligence in the country, except the purely speculative, would be concentrated in a numerous bureaucracy, to whom alone the rest of the community would look for all things: the multitude for direction and dictation in all they had to do; the able and aspiring for personal advancement. To be admitted into the ranks of this bureaucracy, and when admitted, to rise therein, would be the sole objects of ambition. Under this régime, not only is the outside public ill-qualified, for want of practical experience, to criticize or check the mode of operation of the bureaucracy, but even if the accidents of despotic or the natural working of popular institutions occasionally raise to the summit a ruler or rulers of reforming inclinations, no reform can be effected which is contrary to the interest of the bureaucracy. Such is the melancholy condition of the Russian empire, as shown in the accounts of those who have had sufficient opportunity of observation. The Czar himself is powerless against the bureaucratic body; he can send any one of them to Siberia, but he cannot govern without them, or against their will. On every decree of his they have a tacit veto, by merely refraining from carrying it into effect. In countries of more advanced civilization and of a more insurrectionary spirit, the public, accustomed to expect everything to be done for them by the state, or at least to do nothing for themselves without asking from the state not only leave to do it, but even how it is to be done, naturally hold the state responsible for all evil which befalls them, and when the evil exceeds their amount of patience, they rise against the government and make what is called a revolution; whereupon somebody else, with or without legitimate authority from the nation, vaults into the seat, issues his orders to the bureaucracy, and everything goes on much as it did before; the bureaucracy being unchanged, and nobody else being capable of taking their place. ...

12

THEODORE ROOSEVELT, CITIZENSHIP IN A REPUBLIC

INTRODUCTION

'It is not the critic who counts; not the man who points out how the strong man stumbles, or where the doer of deeds could have done them better. The credit belongs to the man who is actually in the arena, whose face is marred by dust and sweat and blood; who strives valiantly; who errs, and comes short again and again, because there is no effort without error and shortcoming; but who does actually strive to do the deeds; who knows the great enthusiasms, the great devotions; who spends himself in a worthy cause; who at the best knows in the end the triumph of high achievement, and who at the worst, if he fails, at least fails while daring greatly, so that his place shall never be with those cold and timid souls who know neither victory nor defeat.'

The basic wisdom in these words rings out as loudly today as it did when they were first spoken by Theodore Roosevelt, former President of the United States, at the Sorbonne on 23 April 1910. Roosevelt speaks to us with a voice from another era: an era when intelligence, strength, erudition, and eloquence could be found together in a single man, and that single man could rise to the highest office in the land. His message is clear. Democratic republics are dependent on the quality of their average citizens. They require their citizens to be able to work, fight, reproduce, and provide for themselves and their families. Those citizens must have high ideals, but ideals that can be achieved in a practical fashion. Above all, they must act—and act with character. They must 'enter the arena'.

Roosevelt is strangely prescient in this speech that—delivered more than a century ago—speaks directly to certain of the ills affecting modern democracies today. The intellectual and social elites to whom he addressed his words were given advice and a warning. Intellectual aloofness that will not tolerate contact with life's realities, an attitude of sneering disbelief towards all that is great and lofty 'whether in achievement or in that noble effort which, even if it fails, comes to a second achievement', and a readiness to criticize work which the critic himself never tries to perform—these are marks not of superiority but of weakness. It is a cheap temptation to pose as one who has outgrown emotions and beliefs and to whom good and evil are as one. 'The poorest way to face life,' notes Roosevelt, 'is with a sneer.'

Roosevelt was also prescient in his focus on the nation and the forces that threaten it. The first aspect concerns the people of the land and the need to reproduce. This is a point so basic that it is often overlooked. Roosevelt, however, lays it out in no uncertain terms: the precondition of any civilization, he says, is for man and woman to be father and mother of healthy children, so that the nation will increase and not decrease; no material progress, wealth, or art can compensate for willful sterility; and it is idle to prattle of national achievements if the people that constitute the nation are not perpetuated. The second aspect concerns the balance between nationalism and globalism. Roosevelt had nothing but suspicion for advocates of no-borders globalism: 'the man who says that he does not care to be a citizen of any one country, because he is the citizen of the world, is in fact usually an exceedingly undesirable citizen of whatever corner of the world he happens at the moment to be in'. The correct course was a tempered nationalism awake, however, to the possibility of international cooperation.

And Roosevelt was prescient, above all, in his caution as to the doctrine of equality. The authors of the Declaration of Independence had intended to declare that all men are created equal in certain inalienable rights. They had not intended to declare that all men are equal in size, intellect, moral development, or social capacity. Equality of opportunity does not mean equality of outcome: the reward must go to those who do their work well—'for any other course is to create a new kind of privilege, the privilege of folly and weakness; and special privilege is injustice, whatever form it takes'. What really mattered was the effort not to bring all human beings to a single level but instead to 'turn the tool-user into a tool owner' and to prevent 'the inequality which is due to force or fraud'.

'Citizenship in a Republic' is directed towards the fundamental question of how man should live in society. The answers it gives may not be mainstream today. But, equally, the mainstream today does not appear to have all the answers. What is for sure is that we will not be able to find the right solutions when the parameters of debate are limited by the narrow prejudices of our era. Roosevelt's voice reminds us that we once spoke freely and openly about so many matters of real concern—of the arrogance of elites, of the duties owed by citizens, of the doctrine of equality, and of globalisation and loyalty to one's nation. And if we once knew how to speak freely and openly about these things, there's no reason why we can't relearn that skill and speak freely and openly once again.

CITIZENSHIP IN A REPUBLIC

Strange and impressive associations rise in the mind of a man from the New World who speaks before this august body in this ancient institution[1] of learning. Before his eyes pass the shadows of mighty kings and warlike nobles, of great masters of law and theology; through the shining dust of the dead centuries he sees crowded figures that tell of the power and learning and splendor of times gone by; and he sees also the innumerable host of humble students to whom clerkship meant emancipation, to whom it was well-nigh the only outlet from the dark thraldom of the Middle Ages.

This was the most famous university of medieval Europe at a time when no one dreamed that there was a New World to discover. Its services to the cause of human knowledge already stretched far back into the remote past at the time when my forefathers, three centuries ago, were among the sparse bands of traders, ploughmen, wood-

1. The Sorbonne.

choppers, and fisherfolk who, in hard struggle with the iron unfriendliness of the Indian-haunted land, were laying the foundations of what has now become the giant republic of the West. To conquer a continent, to tame the shaggy roughness of wild nature, means grim warfare; and the generations engaged in it cannot keep, still less add to, the stores of garnered wisdom which once were theirs, and which are still in the hands of their brethren who dwell in the old land. To conquer the wilderness means to wrest victory from the same hostile forces with which mankind struggled in the immemorial infancy of our race. The primeval conditions must be met by primeval qualities which are incompatible with the retention of much that has been painfully acquired by humanity as through the ages it has striven upward toward civilization. In conditions so primitive there can be but a primitive culture. At first only the rudest schools can be established, for no others would meet the needs of the hard-driven, sinewy folk who thrust forward the frontier in the teeth of savage man and savage nature; and many years elapse before any of these schools can develop into seats of higher learning and broader culture.

The pioneer days pass; the stump-dotted clearings expand into vast stretches of fertile farmland; the stockaded clusters of log cabins change into towns; the hunters of game, the fellers of trees, the rude frontier traders and tillers of the soil, the men who wander all their lives long through the wilderness as the heralds and harbingers of an oncoming civilization, themselves vanish before the civilization for which they have prepared the way. The children of their successors and supplanters, and then their children and children's children, change and develop with extraordinary rapidity. The conditions accentuate vices and virtues, energy and ruthlessness, all the good qualities and all the defects of an intense individualism, self-reliant, self-centred, far more conscious of its rights than of its duties, and blind to its own shortcomings. To the hard materialism of the frontier days succeeds the hard materialism of an industrialism even more intense and absorbing than that of the older nations; although these themselves have likewise already entered on the age of a complex and predominantly industrial civilisation.

As the country grows, its people, who have won success in so many lines, turn back to try to recover the possessions of the mind and the spirit, which perforce their fathers threw aside in order better to wage the first rough battles for the continent their children inherit. The leaders of thought and of action grope their way forward to a new life, realizing, sometimes dimly, sometimes clear-sightedly, that the life of material gain, whether for a nation or an individual, is of value only as a foundation, only as there is added to it the uplift that comes from devotion to loftier ideals. The new life thus sought can in part be developed afresh from what is round about in the New World; but it can be developed in full only by freely drawing upon the treasure-houses of the Old World, upon the treasures stored in the ancient abodes of wisdom and learning, such as this where I speak today. It is a mistake for any nation merely to copy another; but it is an even greater mistake, it is a proof of weakness in any nation, not to be anxious to learn from another, and willing and able to adapt that learning to the new national conditions and make it fruitful and productive therein. It is for us of the New World to sit at the feet of the Gamaliel of the Old; then, if we have the right stuff in us, we can show that Paul in his turn can become a teacher as well as a scholar.

Today I shall speak to you on the subject of individual citizenship, the one subject of vital importance to you, my hearers, and to me and my countrymen, because you and we are citizens of great democratic republics. A democratic republic such as each of ours—an effort to realise in its full sense government by, of, and for the people—represents the most gigantic of all possible social experiments, the one fraught with greatest possibilities alike for good and for evil. The success of republics like yours and like ours means the glory, and our failure the despair, of mankind; and for you and for us the question of the quality of the individual citizen is supreme. Under other forms of government, under the rule of one man or of a very few men, the quality of the rulers is all-important. If, under such governments, the quality of the rulers is high enough, then the nation may for generations lead a brilliant career, and add substantially to the sum of world achievement, no matter how low the quality of the average citizen; because the average citizen is an almost negligible quantity in working out the final results of that type of national greatness.

But with you and with us the case is different. With you here, and with us in my own home, in the long run, success or failure will be conditioned upon the way in which the average man, the average woman, does his or her duty, first in the ordinary, everyday affairs of life, and next in those great occasional crises which call for the heroic virtues. The average citizen must be a good citizen if our republics are to succeed. The stream will not permanently rise higher than the main source; and the main source of national power and national greatness is found in the average citizenship of the nation. Therefore it behooves us to do our best to see that the standard of the average citizen is kept high; and the average cannot be kept high unless the standard of the leaders is very much higher.

It is well if a large proportion of the leaders in any republic, in any democracy, are, as a matter of course, drawn from the classes represented in this audience today; but only provided that those classes possess the gifts of sympathy with plain people and of devotion to great ideals. You and those like you have received special advantages; you have all of you had the opportunity for mental training; many of you have had leisure; most of you have had a chance for the enjoyment of life far greater than comes to the majority of your fellows. To you and your kind much has been given, and from you much should be expected. Yet there are certain failings against which it is especially incumbent that both men of trained and cultivated intellect, and men of inherited wealth and position, should especially guard themselves, because to these failings they are especially liable; and if yielded to, their—your—chances of useful service are at an end.

Let the man of learning, the man of lettered leisure, beware of that queer and cheap temptation to pose to himself and to others as the cynic, as the man who has outgrown emotions and beliefs, the man to whom good and evil are as one. The poorest way to face life is to face it with a sneer. There are many men who feel a kind of twisted pride in cynicism; there are many who confine themselves to criticism of the way others do what they themselves dare not even attempt. There is no more unhealthy being, no man less worthy of respect, than he who either really holds, or feigns to hold, an attitude of sneering disbelief toward all that is great and lofty, whether in achievement or in that noble effort which, even if it fails, comes second to achievement. A cynical habit of thought and speech, a readiness to criticise work which the critic himself never tries to perform, an intellectual aloofness which will not accept contact with life's realities—all these are marks, not, as the possessor would fain think, of superiority, but of weakness. They mark the men unfit to bear their part manfully in the stern strife of living, who seek, in the affectation of contempt for the achievements of others, to hide from others and from themselves their own weakness. The role is easy; there is none easier, save only the role of the man who sneers alike at both criticism and performance.

It is not the critic who counts; not the man who points out how the strong man stumbles, or where the doer of deeds could have done them better. The credit belongs to the man who is actually in the arena, whose face is marred by dust and sweat and blood; who strives valiantly; who errs, and comes short again and again, because there is no effort without error and shortcoming; but who does actually strive to do the deeds; who knows the great enthusiasms, the great devotions; who spends himself in a worthy cause; who at the best knows in the end the triumph of high achievement, and who at the worst, if he fails, at least fails while daring greatly, so that his place shall never be with those cold and timid souls who know neither victory nor defeat. Shame on the man of cultivated taste who permits refinement to develop into a fastidiousness that unfits him for doing the rough work of a workaday world. Among the free peoples who govern themselves there is but a small field of usefulness open for the men of cloistered life who shrink from contact with their fellows. Still less room is there for those who deride or slight what is done by those who actually bear the brunt of the day; nor yet for those others who always profess that they would like to take action, if only the conditions of life were not what they actually are. The man who does nothing cuts the same sordid figure in the pages of history, whether he be cynic, or fop, or voluptuary. There is little use for the being whose tepid soul knows nothing of the great and generous emotion, of the high pride, the stern belief, the lofty enthusiasm, of the men who quell the storm and ride the thunder. Well for these men if they succeed; well also, though not so well, if they fail, given only that they have nobly ventured, and have put forth all their heart and strength. It is war-worn Hotspur, spent with hard fighting, he of the many errors and the valiant end, over whose memory we love to linger, not over the memory of the young lord who 'but for the vile guns would have been a soldier'.

France has taught many lessons to other nations: surely one of the most important is the lesson her whole history teaches, that a high artistic and literary development is compatible with notable leadership in arms and statecraft. The brilliant gallantry of the French soldier has for many centuries been proverbial; and during these same centuries at every court in Europe the 'freemasons of fashion' have treated the French tongue as their common speech; while every artist and man of letters, and every man of science able to appreciate that marvellous instrument of precision, French prose, has turned toward France for aid and inspiration. How long the leadership in arms and letters has lasted is curiously illustrated by the fact that the earliest masterpiece in a modern tongue is the splendid French epic which tells of Roland's doom and the vengeance of Charlemagne when the lords of the Frankish host were stricken at Roncesvalles.

Let those who have, keep, let those who have not, strive to attain, a high standard of cultivation and scholarship. Yet let us remember that these stand second to certain other things. There is need of a sound body, and even more need of a sound mind. But above mind and above body stands character—the sum of those qualities which we mean when we speak of a man's force and courage, of his good faith and sense of honor. I believe in exercise for the body, always provided that we keep in mind that physical development is a means and not an end. I believe, of course, in giving to all the people a good education. But the education must contain much besides book-learning in order to be really good. We must ever remember that no keenness and subtleness of intellect, no polish, no cleverness, in any way make up for the lack of the great solid qualities. Self-restraint, self-mastery, common sense, the power of accepting individual responsibility and yet of acting in conjunction with others, courage and resolution—these are the qualities which mark a masterful people. Without them no people can control itself, or save itself from being controlled from the outside. I speak to a brilliant assemblage; I speak in a great university which represents the flower of the highest intellectual development; I pay all homage to intellect, and to elaborate and specialized training of the intellect; and yet I know I shall have the assent of all of you present when I add that more important still are the commonplace, everyday qualities and virtues.

Such ordinary, everyday qualities include the will and the power to work, to fight at need, and to have plenty of healthy children. The need that the average man shall work is so obvious as hardly to warrant insistence. There are a few people in every country so born that they can lead lives of leisure. These fill a useful function if they make it evident that leisure does not mean idleness; for some of the most valuable work needed by civilisation is essentially non-remunerative in its character, and of course the people who do this work should in large part be drawn from those to whom remuneration is an object of indifference. But the average man must earn his own livelihood. He should be trained to do so, and he should be trained to feel that he occupies a contemptible position if he does not do so; that he is not an object of envy if he is idle, at whichever end of the social scale he stands, but an object of contempt, an object of derision.

In the next place, the good man should be both a strong and a brave man; that is, he should be able to fight, he should be able to serve his country as a soldier, if the need arises. There are well-meaning philosophers who declaim against the unrighteousness of war. They are right only if they lay all their emphasis upon the unrighteousness. War is a dreadful thing, and unjust war is a crime against humanity. But it is such a crime because it is unjust, not because it is war. The choice must ever be in favor of righteousness, and this whether the alternative be peace or whether the alternative be war. The question must not be merely, Is there to be peace or war? The question must be, Is the right to prevail? Are the great laws of righteousness once more to be fulfilled? And the answer from a strong and virile people must be, 'Yes', whatever the cost. Every honorable effort should always be made to avoid war, just as every honorable effort should always be made by the individual in private life to keep out of a brawl, to keep out of trouble; but no self-respecting individual, no self-respecting nation, can or ought to submit to wrong.

Finally, even more important than ability to work, even more important than ability to fight at need, is it to remember that the chief of blessings for any nation is that it shall leave its seed to inherit the land. It was the crown of blessings in Biblical times; and it is the crown of blessings now. The greatest of all curses is the curse of sterility, and the severest of all condemnations should be that visited upon wilful sterility. The first essential in any civilization is that the man and the woman shall be father and mother of healthy children, so that the race shall increase and not decrease. If this is not so, if through no fault of the society there is failure to increase, it is a great misfortune. If the failure is due to deliberate and wilful fault, then it is not merely a misfortune, it is one of those crimes of ease and self-indulgence, of shrinking from pain and effort and risk, which in the long run Nature punishes more heavily than any other. If we of the great republics, if we, the free people who claim to have emancipated ourselves from the thraldom of wrong and error, bring down on our heads the curse that comes upon the wilfully barren, then it will be an idle waste of breath to prattle of our achievements, to boast of all that we have done. No refinement of life, no delicacy of taste, no material progress, no sordid heaping up of riches, no sensuous development of art and literature, can in any way compensate for the loss of the great fundamental virtues; and of these great fundamental virtues the greatest is the race's power to perpetuate the race.

Character must show itself in the man's performance both of the duty he owes himself and of the duty he owes the state. The man's foremost duty is owed to himself and his family; and he can do this duty only by earning money, by providing what is essential to material well-being; it is only after this has been done that he can hope to build a higher superstructure on the solid material foundation; it is only after this has been done that he can help in movements for the general well-being. He must pull his own weight first, and only after this can his surplus strength be of use to the general public. It is not good to excite that bitter laughter which expresses contempt; and contempt is what we feel for the being whose enthusiasm to benefit mankind is such that he is a burden to those nearest him; who wishes to do great things for humanity in the abstract, but who can not keep his wife in comfort or educate his children.

Nevertheless, while laying all stress on this point, while not merely acknowledging but insisting upon the fact that there must be a basis of material well-being for the individual as for the nation, let us with equal emphasis insist that this material well-being represents nothing but the foundation, and that the foundation, though indispensable, is worthless unless upon it is raised the superstructure of a higher life. That is why I decline to recognize the mere multimillionaire, the man of mere wealth, as an asset of value to any country; and especially as not an asset to my own country. If he has earned or uses his wealth in a way that makes him of real benefit, of real use—and such is often the case—why, then he does become an asset of worth. But it is the way in which it has been earned or used, and not the mere fact of wealth, that entitles him to the credit. There is need in business, as in most other forms of human activity, of the great guiding intelligences. Their places can not be supplied by any number of lesser intelligences. It is a good thing that they should have ample recognition, ample reward. But we must not transfer our admiration to the reward instead of to the deed rewarded; and if what should be the reward exists without the service having been rendered, then admiration will come only from those who are mean of soul. The truth is that, after a certain measure of tangible material success or reward has been achieved, the question of increasing it becomes of constantly less importance compared to other things that can be done in life. It is a bad thing for a nation to raise and to admire a false standard of success; and there can be no falser standard than that set by the deification of material well-being in and for itself. The man who, for any cause for which he is himself accountable, has failed to support himself and those for whom he is responsible, ought to feel that he has fallen lamentably short in his prime duty. But the man who, having far surpassed the limit of providing for the wants, both of body and mind, of himself and of those depending upon him, then piles up a great fortune, for the acquisition or retention of which he returns no corresponding benefit to the nation as a whole, should himself be made to feel that, so far from being a desirable, he is an unworthy citizen of the community; that he is to be neither admired nor envied; that his right-thinking fellow countrymen put him low in the scale of citizenship, and leave him to be consoled by the admiration of those whose level of purpose is even lower than his own.

My position as regards the moneyed interests can be put in a few words. In every civilized society property rights must be carefully safeguarded; ordinarily, and in the great majority of cases, human rights and property rights are fundamentally and in the long run identical; but when it clearly appears that there is a real conflict between them, human rights must have the upper hand, for property belongs to man and not man to property.

In fact, it is essential to good citizenship clearly to understand that there are certain qualities which we in a democracy are prone to admire in and of themselves, which ought by rights to be judged admirable or the reverse solely from the standpoint of the use made of them. Foremost among these I should include two very distinct gifts—the gift of money-making and the gift of oratory. Money-making, the money touch, I have spoken of above. It is a quality which in a moderate degree is essential. It may be useful when developed to a very great degree, but only if accompanied and controlled by other qualities; and without such control the possessor tends to develop into one of the least attractive types produced by a modern industrial democracy. So it is with the orator. It is highly desirable that a leader of opinion in a democracy should be able to state his views clearly and convincingly. But all that the oratory can do of value to the community is to enable the man thus to explain himself; if it enables the orator to persuade his hearers to put false values on things, it merely makes him a power for mischief. Some excellent public servants have not the gift at all, and must rely upon their deeds to speak for them; and unless the oratory does represent genuine conviction based on good common sense and able to be translated into efficient performance, then the better the oratory the greater the damage to the public it deceives. Indeed, it is a sign of marked political weakness in any commonwealth if the people tend to be carried away by mere oratory, if they tend to value words in and for themselves, as divorced from the deeds for which they are supposed to stand. The phrase-maker, the phrase-monger, the ready talker, however great his power, whose speech does not make for courage, sobriety, and right understanding, is simply a noxious element in the body politic, and it speaks ill for the public if he has influence over them. To admire the gift of oratory without regard to the moral quality behind the gift is to do wrong to the republic.

Of course, all that I say of the orator applies with even greater force to the orator's latter-day and more influential brother, the journalist. The power of the journalist is great, but he is entitled neither to respect nor admiration because of that power unless it is used aright. He can do, and he often does, great good. He can do, and he often does, infinite mischief. All journalists, all writers, for the very reason that they appreciate the vast possibilities of their profession, should bear testimony against those who deeply discredit it. Offences against taste and morals, which are bad enough in a private citizen, are infinitely worse if made into instruments for debauching the community through a newspaper. Mendacity, slander, sensationalism, inanity, vapid triviality, all are potent factors for the debauchery of the public mind and conscience. The excuse advanced for vicious writing, that the public demands it and that the demand must be supplied, can no more be admitted than if it were advanced by the purveyors of food who sell poisonous adulterations.

In short, the good citizen in a republic must realise that he ought to possess two sets of qualities, and that neither avails without the other. He must have those qualities which make for efficiency; and he must also have those qualities which direct the efficiency into channels for the public good. He is useless if he is inefficient. There is nothing to be done with that type of citizen of whom all that can be said is that he is harmless. Virtue which is dependent upon a sluggish circulation is not impressive. There is little place in active life for the timid good man. The man who is saved by weakness from robust wickedness is likewise rendered immune from the robuster virtues. The good citizen in a republic must first of all be able to hold his own. He is no good citizen unless he has the ability which will make him work hard and which at need will make him fight hard. The good citizen is not a good citizen unless he is an efficient citizen.

But if a man's efficiency is not guided and regulated by a moral sense, then the more efficient he is the worse he is, the more dangerous to the body politic. Courage, intellect, all the masterful qualities, serve but to make a man more evil if they are used merely for that man's own advancement, with brutal indifference to the rights of others. It speaks ill for the community if the community worships these qualities and treats their possessors as heroes regardless of whether the qualities are used rightly or wrongly. It makes no difference as to the precise way in which this sinister efficiency is shown. It makes no difference whether such a man's force and ability betray themselves in the career of money-maker or politician, soldier or orator, journalist or popular leader. If the man works for evil, then the more successful he is the more he should be despised and condemned by all upright and far-seeing men. To judge a man merely by success is an abhorrent wrong; and if the people at large habitually so judge men, if they grow to condone wickedness because the wicked man triumphs, they show their inability to understand that in the last analysis free institutions rest upon the character of citizenship, and that by such admiration of evil they prove themselves unfit for liberty.

The homely virtues of the household, the ordinary workaday virtues which make the woman a good housewife and housemother, which make the man a hard worker, a good husband and father, a good soldier at need, stand at the bottom of character. But of course many others must be added thereto if a state is to be not only free but great. Good citizenship is not good citizenship if exhibited only in the home. There remain the duties of the individual in relation to the state, and these duties are none too easy under the conditions which exist where the effort is made to carry on free government in a complex, industrial civilization. Perhaps the most important thing the ordinary citizen, and, above all, the leader of ordinary citizens, has to remember in political life is that he must not be a sheer doctrinaire. The closet philosopher, the refined and cultured individual who from his library tells how men ought to be governed under ideal conditions, is of no use in actual governmental work; and the one-sided fanatic, and still more the mob leader, and the insincere man who to achieve power promises what by no possibility can be performed, are not merely useless but noxious.

The citizen must have high ideals, and yet he must be able to achieve them in practical fashion. No permanent good comes from aspirations so lofty that they have grown fantastic and have become impossible and indeed undesirable to realize. The impracticable visionary is far less often the guide and precursor than he is the embittered foe of the real reformer, of the man who, with stumblings and shortcomings, yet does in some shape, in practical fashion, give effect to the hopes and desires of those who strive for better things. Woe to the empty phrase-maker, to the empty idealist, who, instead of making ready the ground for the man of action, turns against him when he appears and hampers him as he does the work! Moreover, the preacher of ideals must remember how sorry and contemptible is the figure which he will cut, how great the damage that he will do, if he does not himself, in his own life, strive measurably to realize the ideals that he preaches for others. Let him remember also that the worth of the ideal must be largely determined by the success with which it can in practice be realized. We should abhor the so-called 'practical' men whose practicality assumes the shape of that peculiar baseness which finds its expression in disbelief in morality and decency, in disregard of high standards of living and conduct. Such a creature is the worst enemy of the body politic. But only less desirable as a citizen is his nominal opponent and real ally, the man of fantastic vision who makes the impossible better forever the enemy of the possible good.

We can just as little afford to follow the doctrinaires of an extreme individualism as the doctrinaires of an extreme socialism. Individual initiative, so far from being discouraged, should be stimulated; and yet we should remember that, as society develops and grows more complex, we continually find that things which once it was desirable to leave to individual initiative can, under the changed conditions, be performed with better results by common effort. It is quite impossible, and equally undesirable, to draw in theory a hard-and-fast line which shall always divide the two sets of cases. This every one who is not cursed with the pride of the closet philosopher will see, if he will only take the trouble to think about some of our commonest phenomena. For instance, when people live on isolated farms or in little hamlets, each house can be left to attend to its own drainage and water supply; but the mere multiplication of families in a given area produces new problems which, because they differ in size, are found to differ not only in degree but in kind from the old; and the questions of drainage and water supply have to be considered from the common standpoint. It is not a matter for abstract dogmatizing to decide when this point is reached; it is a matter to be tested by practical experiment. Much of the discussion about socialism and individualism is entirely pointless, because of failure to agree on terminology. It is not good to be the slave of names. I am a strong individualist by personal habit, inheritance, and conviction; but it is a mere matter of common sense to recognize that the state, the community, the citizens acting together, can do a number of things better than if they were left to individual action. The individualism which finds its expression in the abuse of physical force is checked very early in the growth of civilization, and we of today should in our turn strive to shackle or destroy that individualism which triumphs by greed and cunning, which exploits the weak by craft instead of ruling them by brutality. We ought to go with any man in the effort to bring about justice and the equality of opportunity, to turn the tool-user more and more into the tool-owner, to shift burdens so that they can be more equitably borne. The deadening effect on any race of the adoption of a logical and extreme socialistic system could not be overstated; it would spell sheer destruction; it would produce grosser wrong and outrage, fouler immorality, than any existing system. But this does not mean that we may not with great advantage adopt certain of the principles professed by some given set of men who happen to call themselves socialists; to be afraid to do so would be to make a mark of weakness on our part.

But we should not take part in acting a lie any more than in telling a lie. We should not say that men are equal where they are not equal, nor proceed upon the assumption that there is an equality where it does not exist; but we should strive to bring about a measurable equality, at least to the extent of preventing the inequality which is due to force or fraud. Abraham Lincoln, a man of the plain people, blood of their blood and bone of their bone, who all his life toiled and wrought and suffered for them, and at the end died for them, who always strove to represent them, who would never tell an untruth to or for them, spoke of the doctrine of equality with his usual mixture of idealism and sound common sense. He said (I omit what was of merely local significance):

'I think the authors of the Declaration of Independence intended to include all men, but that they did not mean to declare all men equal in all respects. They did not mean to say all men were equal in color, size, intellect, moral development, or social capacity. They defined with tolerable distinctness in what they did consider all men created equal—equal in certain inalienable rights, among which are life, liberty, and the pursuit of happiness. This they said, and this they meant. They did not mean to assert the obvious untruth that all were then actually enjoying that equality, or yet that they were about to confer it immediately upon them. They meant to set up a standard maxim for free society which should be familiar to all—constantly looked to, constantly labored for, and, even though never perfectly attained, constantly approximated, and thereby constantly spreading and deepening its influence, and augmenting the happiness and value of life to all people, everywhere.'

We are bound in honor to refuse to listen to those men who would make us desist from the effort to do away with the inequality which means injustice; the inequality of right, of opportunity, of privilege. We are bound in honor to strive to bring ever nearer the day when, as far as is humanly possible, we shall be able to realize the ideal that each man shall have an equal opportunity to show the stuff that is in him by the way in which he renders service. There should, so far as possible, be equality of opportunity to render service; but just so long as there is inequality of service there should and must be inequality of reward. We may be sorry for the general, the painter, the artist, the worker in any profession or of any kind, whose misfortune rather than whose fault it is that he does his work ill. But the reward must go to the man who does his work well; for any other course is to create a new kind of privilege, the privilege of folly and weakness; and special privilege is injustice, whatever form it takes.

To say that the thriftless, the lazy, the vicious, the incapable, ought to have the reward given to those who are far-sighted, capable, and upright, is to say what is not true and cannot be true. Let us try to level up, but let us beware of the evil of levelling down. If a man stumbles, it is a good thing to help him to his feet. Every one of us needs a helping hand now and then. But if a man lies down, it is a waste of time to try to carry him; and it is a very bad thing for every one if we make men feel that the same reward will come to those who shirk their work and to those who do it.

Let us, then, take into account the actual facts of life, and not be misled into following any proposal for achieving the millennium, for re-creating the golden age, until we have subjected it to hardheaded examination. On the other hand, it is foolish to reject a proposal merely because it is advanced by visionaries. If a given scheme is proposed, look at it on its merits, and, in considering it, disregard formulas. It does not matter in the least who proposes it, or why. If it seems good, try it. If it proves good, accept it; otherwise reject it. There are plenty of men calling themselves socialists with whom, up to a certain point, it is quite possible to work. If the next step is one which both we and they wish to take, why of course take it, without any regard to the fact that our views as to the tenth step may differ. But, on the other hand, keep clearly in mind that, though it has been worthwhile to take one step, this does not in the least mean that it may not be highly disadvantageous to take the next. It is just as foolish to refuse all progress because people demanding it desire at some points to go to absurd extremes, as it would be to go to these absurd extremes simply because some of the measures advocated by the extremists were wise.

The good citizen will demand liberty for himself, and as a matter of pride he will see to it that others receive the liberty which he thus claims as his own. Probably the best test of true love of liberty in any country is the way in which minorities are treated in that country. Not only should there be complete liberty in matters of religion and opinion, but complete liberty for each man to lead his life as he desires, provided only that in so doing he does not wrong his neighbor. Persecution is bad because it is persecution, and without reference to which side happens at the moment to be the persecutor and which the persecuted. Class hatred is bad in just the same way, and without any regard to the individual who, at a given time, substitutes loyalty to a class for loyalty to the nation, or substitutes hatred of men because they happen to come in a certain social category, for judgment awarded them according to their conduct. Remember always that the same measure of condemnation should be extended to the arrogance which would look down upon or crush any man because he is poor and to the envy and hatred which would destroy a man because he is wealthy. The overbearing brutality of the man of wealth or power, and the envious and hateful malice directed against wealth or power, are really at root merely different manifestations of the same quality, merely the two sides of the same shield. The man who, if born to wealth and power, exploits and ruins his less fortunate brethren is at heart the same as the greedy and violent demagogue who excites those who have not property to plunder those who have. The gravest wrong upon his country is inflicted by that man, whatever his station, who seeks to make his countrymen divide primarily on the line that separates class from class, occupation from occupation, men of more wealth from men of less wealth, instead of remembering that the only safe standard is that which judges each man on his worth as a man, whether he be rich or poor, without regard to his profession or to his station in life. Such is the only true democratic test, the only test that can with propriety be applied in a republic. There have been many republics in the past, both in what we call antiquity and in what we call the Middle Ages. They fell, and the prime factor in their fall was the fact that the parties tended to divide along the line that separates wealth from poverty. It made no difference which side was successful; it made no difference whether the republic fell under the rule of an oligarchy or the rule of a mob. In either case, when once loyalty to a class had been substituted for loyalty to the republic, the end of the republic was at hand. There is no greater need today than the need to keep ever in mind the fact that the cleavage between right and wrong, between good citizenship and bad citizenship, runs at right angles to, and not parallel with, the lines of cleavage between class and class, between occupation and occupation. Ruin looks us in the face if we judge a man by his position instead of judging him by his conduct in that position.

In a republic, to be successful we must learn to combine intensity of conviction with a broad tolerance of difference of conviction. Wide differences of opinion in matters of religious, political, and social belief must exist if conscience and intellect alike are not to be stunted, if there is to be room for healthy growth. Bitter internecine hatreds, based on such differences, are signs, not of earnestness of belief, but of that fanaticism which, whether religious or anti-religious, democratic or anti-democratic, is itself but a manifestation of the gloomy bigotry which has been the chief factor in the downfall of so many, many nations.

Of one man in especial, beyond any one else, the citizens of a republic should beware, and that is of the man who appeals to them to support him on the ground that he is hostile to other citizens of the republic, that he will secure for those who elect him, in one shape or another, profit at the expense of other citizens of the republic. It makes no difference whether he appeals to class hatred or class interest, to religious or anti-religious prejudice. The man who makes such an appeal should always be presumed to make it for the sake of furthering his own interest. The very last thing that an intelligent and self-respecting member of a democratic community should do is to reward any public man because that public man says he will get the private citizen something to which this private citizen is not entitled, or will gratify some emotion or animosity which this private citizen ought not to possess. Let me illustrate this by one anecdote from my own experience. A number of years ago I was engaged in cattle-ranching on the great plains of the western United States. There were no fences. The cattle wandered free, the ownership of each being determined by the brand; the calves were branded with the brand of the cows they followed. If on the round-up an animal was passed by, the following year it would appear as an unbranded yearling, and was then called a maverick. By the custom of the country these mavericks were branded with the brand of the man on whose range they were found. One day I was riding the range with a newly hired cowboy, and we came upon a maverick. We roped and threw it; then we built a little fire, took out a cinch-ring, heated it at the fire; and the cowboy started to put on the brand. I said to him, 'It is So-and-so's brand,' naming the man on whose range we happened to be. He answered: 'That's all right, boss; I know my business.' In another moment I said to him: 'Hold on, you are putting on my brand!' To which he answered: 'That's all right; I always put on the boss's brand.' I answered: 'Oh, very well. Now you go straight back to the ranch and get what is owing to you; I don't need you any longer.' He jumped up and said: 'Why, what's the matter? I was putting on your brand.' And I answered: 'Yes, my friend, and if you will steal for me you will steal from me.'

Now, the same principle which applies in private life applies also in public life. If a public man tries to get your vote by saying that he will do something wrong in your interest, you can be absolutely certain that if ever it becomes worth his while he will do something wrong against your interest.

So much for the citizenship of the individual in his relations to his family, to his neighbour, to the state. There remain duties of citizenship which the state, the aggregation of all the individuals, owes in connection with other states, with other nations. Let me say at once that I am no advocate of a foolish cosmopolitanism. I believe that a man must be a good patriot before he can be, and as the only possible way of being, a good citizen of the world. Experience teaches us that the average man who protests that his international feeling swamps his national feeling, that he does not care for his country because he cares so much for mankind, in actual practice proves himself the foe of mankind; that the man who says that he does not care to be a citizen of any one country, because he is a citizen of the world, is in very fact usually an exceedingly undesirable citizen of whatever corner of the world he happens at the moment to be in. In the dim future all moral needs and moral standards may change; but at present, if a man can view his own country and all other countries from the same level with tepid indifference, it is wise to distrust him, just as it is wise to distrust the man who can take the same dispassionate view of his wife and his mother. However broad and deep a man's sympathies, however intense his activities, he need have no fear that they will be cramped by love of his native land.

Now, this does not mean in the least that a man should not wish to do good outside of his native land. On the contrary, just as I think that the man who loves his family is more apt to be a good neighbour than the man who does not, so I think that the most useful member of the family of nations is normally a strongly patriotic nation. So far from patriotism being inconsistent with a proper regard for the rights of other nations, I hold that the true patriot, who is as jealous of the national honor as a gentleman is of his own honor, will be careful to see that the nation neither inflicts nor suffers wrong, just as a gentleman scorns equally to wrong others or to suffer others to wrong him. I do not for one moment admit that political morality is different from private morality, that a promise made on the stump differs from a promise made in private life. I do not for one moment admit that a man should act deceitfully as a public servant in his dealings with other nations, any more than that he should act deceitfully in his dealings as a private citizen with other private citizens. I do not for one moment admit that a nation should treat other nations in a different spirit from that in which an honorable man would treat other men.

In practically applying this principle to the two sets of cases there is, of course, a great practical difference to be taken into account. We speak of international law; but international law is something wholly different from private or municipal law, and the capital difference is that there is a sanction for the one and no sanction for the other; that there is an outside force which compels individuals to obey the one, while there is no such outside force to compel obedience as regards the other. International law will, I believe, as the generations pass, grow stronger and stronger until in some way or other there develops the power to make it respected. But as yet it is only in the first formative period. As yet, as a rule, each nation is of necessity obliged to judge for itself in matters of vital importance between it and its neighbors, and actions must of necessity, where this is the case, be different from what they are where, as among private citizens, there is an outside force whose action is all-powerful and must be invoked in any crisis of importance. It is the duty of wise statesmen, gifted with the power of looking ahead, to try to encourage and build up every movement which will substitute or tend to substitute some other agency for force in the settlement of international disputes. It is the duty of every honest statesman to try to guide the nation so that it shall not wrong any other nation. But as yet the great civilized peoples, if they are to be true to themselves and to the cause of humanity and civilization, must keep ever in mind that in the last resort they must possess both the will and the power to resent wrongdoing from others. The men who sanely believe in a lofty morality preach righteousness; but they do not preach weakness, whether among private citizens or among nations. We believe that our ideals should be high, but not so high as to make it impossible measurably to realize them. We sincerely and earnestly believe in peace; but if peace and justice conflict, we scorn the man who would not stand for justice though the whole world came in arms against him.

And now, my hosts, a word in parting. You and I belong to the only two republics among the great powers of the world. The ancient friendship between France and the United States has been, on the whole, a sincere and disinterested friendship. A calamity to you would be a sorrow to us. But it would be more than that. In the seething turmoil of the history of humanity certain nations stand out as possessing a peculiar power or charm, some special gift of beauty or wisdom or strength, which puts them among the immortals, which makes them rank forever with the leaders of mankind. France is one of these nations. For her to sink would be a loss to all the world. There are certain lessons of brilliance and of generous gallantry that she can teach better than any of her sister nations. When the French peasantry sang of Malbrook,[2] it was to tell how the soul of this warrior-foe took flight upward through the laurels he had won. Nearly seven centuries ago, Froissart, writing of a time of dire disaster, said that the realm of France was never so stricken that there were not left men who would valiantly fight for it. You have had a great past. I believe that you will have a great future. Long may you carry yourselves proudly as citizens of a nation which bears a leading part in the teaching and uplifting of mankind.

---

2. 'Malbrook s'en va-t-en guerre' ('Marlborough Has Left for the War') is a lament on the death of John Churchill, 1st Duke of Marlborough (1650–1722), written on a false rumour of that event after the Battle of Malplaquet in 1709, that tells how his wife, awaiting his return from battle, is given the news of her husband's death, how he was buried, and how a nightingale sang over his grave.

CONCLUSION

In 'The Country of the Blind', H.G. Wells tells a tale rich in implication for those who detect in the dominant political narratives of today at best a kind of smug complacency that 'all is for the best in the best of all possible worlds', and at worst a kind of deliberate closed-mindedness intent on shutting down dialogue on the most pressing issues of our day.

⸺⸺⸺⸺

The tale tells of a mountaineer, Nunez, who while climbing a mountain in the Ecuadorian Andes slips down a snow-slope into an isolated valley, cut off from the world by an earthquake that reshaped the surrounding mountains. All the inhabitants of the valley suffer from a hereditary disease rendering them blind at birth; they have adapted to life without sight and their other senses have sharpened. Nunez thinks that as the only sighted human being in the valley he will naturally be in a position to rule over them, but in fact they have no concept of sight and cannot understand his attempts to explain it to them. When he falls in love with and seeks to marry a local girl, the village elders refuse him, on the basis of his 'unstable' obsession with 'sight'; the village doctor, equally uncomprehending, advises that his eyes be removed because they are diseased and put his brain into 'a state of constant irritation and distraction'. Nunez consents, but at sunrise the next day he heads into the mountains, hoping to find a passage to the outside world. In Wells' revised 1939 version of the tale, Nunez sees from a distance that there is about to be a rock slide that will destroy the village. He attempts to warn the villagers, but they scoff at his 'imagined' sight and abuse him as a heretic. He leaves them to

279

their impending demise, taking with him the local girl with whom he has fallen in love.

⎯⎯⎯⎯⎯⎯⎯⎯⎯

Assume, if you will, that our philosophers could observe us from a distance, blind without knowing it—complacent and conventional in our own unacknowledged prejudices—while all around us the foundations of our civilizational order are beginning to fracture and come apart.

What would they be shouting from the mountaintops down into the valleys?

⎯⎯⎯⎯⎯⎯⎯⎯⎯

Entertain a more expansive notion of 'justice'. That's Plato's idea of justice as 'all-in rightness'. All-in rightness means cultivating a balanced and harmonious inner state while taking up one's proper place and proper function in society; true justice, for ourselves and others, comes from engaging in the work that is best for us in allowing us to exercise our faculties in the service of the community as a whole. Insofar as we can approximate the ideal state of being governed by a highly cultivated, self-disciplined, and responsible elite, we are right to have expectations of excellence of the individuals comprising it, and we are right to subject those persons to the very strictest of codes of conduct. Insofar as many of us now live under governments that are, on the other hand, at least notionally democratic, let us pay attention to the factors that tend to corrupt such regimes, not least when certain segments of the population seek to 'squeeze' other segments, paving the way for tyrannical regimes that take advantage of public discontent to everybody's detriment.

Remember that the proper end of political society is the cultivation of the excellence of its members. Political society exists for the sake of enabling and facilitating the full development and 'noble action' of its members, not merely for physical security or economic prosperity. It is absurd to insist that each man's achievements are his alone, owing nothing to his ancestors, his patrons, his associates, or his community. Strive for equality—but not abstract or indiscriminate equality: justice is

280

equality for equals. Furthermore, it is not necessarily the case that equality or inequality must prevail uniformly across all aspects of life. In a democracy, we can be equal in some respects without having to be equal in all respects, just as under an oligarchy we can be unequal in some respects without being unequal in all. Those who push unrealistically for absolutism in this respect bring instability to the state and society. This is Aristotle.

Accept that in the real world good men too need to master the dark arts of statecraft if they are to survive and prevail. If we want political change for the better we cannot be overly fastidious: we need our leaders to 'know how to do wrong'—judiciously, of course, and in the interests of the state—since no wholly virtuous politician would be likely to hold onto power long. We also need to disillusion ourselves as to the true nature of political activity: forget what politicians say about their motives; look instead at what they do, and ask *cui bono*—who benefits? This is Machiavelli.

Appreciate and take advantage of the benefits that political organization brings. Life in the state of nature is 'solitary, poor, nasty, brutish, and short'—that's Hobbes. Absolute authority is the price we may have to pay and it is not necessarily too high a price: there is a reason why monarchies have been one of the preferred forms of government, and that is, at least in part, because the identity between monarch and state means that the monarch will have every interest in enriching it and can have no interest in harming it. Harmful indeed, however, are factional and partisan pressure groups that are able to take advantage of a divided legislature to advance interests that enrich and empower certain group or tribal interests at the expense of the nation as a whole.

Liberty is not license—and liberalism is not licentiousness. Locke directs that while we may dispose of ourselves and our property without interference, we must not impair the life, liberty, health, or property of others. We ought to hold our governments to account to ensure that they carry out their proper function and go no further. And we ought to be tolerant—but not naively so. We must be on our guard against those who would abuse our toleration: the treacherous, the intolerant, and those who surreptitiously arrogate special privileges to themselves or their group.

Find your freedom and dignity through political engagement. This is Rousseau. It is our wants and our desires that subject us. Since we cannot return to our pre-civilizational simplicity in the state of nature, we are obliged to find our freedom and dignity through the state, so that through participation we are no longer merely subjects but also citizens.

Look with skepticism upon the harbingers of 'rights' and revolution. Conservative (Burke) and liberal (Bentham) agree on this. The English-speaking world, at least, has for centuries enjoyed ancient rights and liberties as the lifeblood of its tradition. Political progress is best made organically and incrementally: that way we can lock in advantages already obtained, while reaching forward for new ones. Those who assert universal rights arrogate to themselves the right to control mankind from now until the end of time; they employ 'terrorist language' of 'imprescriptible rights' to set up an overweening extra-legal order. This is 'nonsense on stilts'. In reality, statecraft is a matter not of asserting rights but of achieving balances between varieties of good, compromises between good and evil, and sometimes also balances and compromises between evil and evil.

Observe clearly and dispassionately the merits and demerits of democracy. Democratic eras display several tendencies that are not wholly for the good. There is a tendency to privilege equality over freedom. There is a tendency towards concentration of political power. And, with potentially the most devastating and far-reaching consequences, there is a tendency towards 'soft despotism': the state interferes continually in all aspects of life, with the result that men are condemned to perpetual childhood and their will is broken by subjection in minor affairs. This is Tocqueville.

Be on your guard against the state's plunder of its own citizens. Bastiat is the most clear on this: there is such a thing as 'lawful plunder', and it is carried out when the state seizes the goods and property of its own citizens using the legal system itself. Law doesn't have to be this way; it can be what it always should have been—namely, justice. But men having obtained the legislative power turn it into an instrument for domineering over and plundering their fellows.

We are entitled to the maximum freedom compatible with not harming others. It is through such freedom that we obtain true diversity and self-realization in and through our communities. We have to define harm restrictively and not find it where there is only offence or insult taken. But we also need to look at harm realistically and stamp out the conduct of those who would profit from real damage done to their fellow men. This is John Stuart Mill.

Finally—step into the arena. This is President Roosevelt. We have to maintain our national consciousness and we have to preserve our nations for the generations that come after. There is much to be done and this is no time to face life with a sneer.

'The Country of the Blind' is a commentary on the age-old adage: *In the land of the blind, the one-eyed man is king.* The saying encapsulates the belief that true understanding confers significant advantage when the great mass of men remain wholly blind to reality. H.G. Wells took a different view. *In the land of the blind*, he thought, *the fully sighted man is not king—but heretic.*

The reality is that twenty-first-century man undergoes such total immersion in the dominant narrative through mass education and mass media that it should be no surprise if philosophies outside that narrative are unbearably troubling to him. Of course, nobody is suggesting a return to the non-democratic regimes of the past. Equally, the historical record makes it plain that people have led happy and fulfilled lives under many types of political organization different from our own. It is not the type of political regime *per se* that has determined whether any particular polity has constituted a seedbed of human self-realization or blot on the face of human history: there have been cruel and repressive republics (Cromwellian England) and wholly fallible democracies (Weimar Germany) as there have been golden ages under traditional monarchies. The greatest of human self-realization, just like the greatest of human suffering and pain, can take place under any of the recognized political regimes. It is complacency of the highest order for a man to think that casting a ballot once every few years is sufficient to ensure the former and obviate the latter.

It is a telling aspect of 'The Country of the Blind' that the local girl who is rescued looks back on her former state with nostalgia: 'The loveliness of *your* world,' she explains, 'is a complicated and fearful loveliness and mine is simple and near.' But it was becoming aware of something of that complicated and fearful loveliness that allowed her to escape and survive. Of course, nobody knows if and when history

283

will move forward again, nor what disruptions it will bring when it begins to do so. What we do know and can say is that our blindness is a choice. There is a wealth of insight of which this book is merely the starting point. And there is no better or more urgent moment to open our eyes—liberating ourselves by drawing insight and inspiration from the great thinkers of the Western tradition—than right now.

Bibliography

Aristotle. *Politics of Aristotle*. Translated by Benjamin Jowett. Oxford: Clarendon Press, 1885.

Bastiat, Frédéric. *Essays on Political Economy*. Translated by Patrick James Stirling. 4th ed. London: Provost & Co, 1874.

Bentham, Jeremy.*The Works of Jeremy Bentham*. 11 vols. Edinburgh: William Tait, 1838-1843.

Burke, Edmund. *The Works of the Right Honourable Edmund Burke*. 12 vols. London: John C. Nimmo, 1887.

Hobbes, Thomas. *Leviathan*. 1651.

Locke, John. *Two Treatises of Government*. London: n.p., 1764.

Locke, John. *The Works of John Locke*. 9 vols. 12th ed. London: Rivington, 1824.

Machiavelli, Niccolò. *Machiavelli's Prince*. Translated by W.K. Marriott. London and Toronto: J.M. Dent & Sons and E.P.Dutton & Co, 1908.

Machiavelli, Niccolò. *Discourses on the First Decade of Titus Livius*. Translated by Ninian Hill Thomson. London: Kegan Paul, Trench & Co, 1883.

Mill, John Stuart. *On Liberty*. London: Longman, Green, Longman, Roberts & Green, 1864.

Plato. *The Republic of Plato*. Translated by Benjamin Jowett. 3rd ed. London: Oxford University Press, 1888.

Rousseau, Jean-Jacques. *The Social Contract & Discourses*. Translated by George Douglas Howard Cole. London and Toronto: J.M. Dent & Sons, 1910.

Tocqueville, Alexis de. *Democracy in America*. Translated by Henry Reeve. 7th ed. New York: Edward Walker, 1847.

Also Available

Classic Philosophy for the Modern Man

Andrew Lynn

'What you hold in your hands is a handbook for living: it is an account of how the greatest minds have spoken to us on how to grow and prosper as flesh-and-blood human beings.'

Classic Philosophy for the Modern Man is inspired by a single concept: that, to thrive in the world, we need ready access to the practical wisdom of our forebears. It answers that need by introducing for the general reader the most powerful and enduringly relevant works of great thinkers from around the world. Together these works teach us how to achieve excellence; how to obtain and exercise power, advance in the world, and live gracefully; how to cultivate nobility of soul; and – above all – how to be one's own man. There is no better primer in the art of living well.

CLASSIC SPIRITUALITY FOR THE MODERN MAN

ANDREW LYNN

'The basic premise of this book is that strength and weakness have a spiritual dimension.'

Classic Spirituality for the Modern Man brings the spiritual classics alive so that they can once again serve their original and true purpose: to guide and inspire us as we make our way through life. These works speak to us of the fundamental principles of spiritual wisdom, the mysterious primordial force of the 'Tao', the Buddhist art of maintaining mental and emotional equilibrium, and the essential features of Hindu and Sufi self-cultivation, as well as modern approaches to self-realization. There is no better primer in the art of awakened living.

SHAKESPEARE TALES

ANDREW LYNN

Shakespeare is widely considered to be the greatest playwright the world has known. But it has always been difficult and time-consuming to understand his works.

This series gives you classic prose retellings of the complete works, preserving as far as possible for the modern reader Shakespeare's original language and mood. In this totally new edition, the tales are collected by genre and arranged chronologically. Each genre and each tale is provided with a fresh and insightful introduction. The tales are presented in five volumes: Comedies; Tragedies; Tragicomedies; Roman Tales; and English Histories. They are sumptuously illustrated by Sir John Gilbert.

Perfect for the Shakespeare aficionado, the student, and the general reader. There is no better way to understand the Bard.

38320290R00180

Made in the USA
San Bernardino, CA
08 June 2019